Perl for C Programming

Contents at a Glance

D1605013

Perl for C Programmers

Steve Oualline

New Riders

www.newriders.com

201 West 103rd Street, Indianapolis, Indiana 46290
An Imprint of Pearson Education
Boston • Indianapolis • London • Munich • New York • San Francisco

Perl for C Programmers

Copyright © 2003 by New Riders Publishing

FIRST EDITION: August, 2002

All rights reserved. No part of this book may be reproduced or transmitted in any form or by any means, electronic or mechanical, including photocopying, recording, or by any information storage and retrieval system, without written permission from the publisher, except for the inclusion of brief quotations in a review.

International Standard Book Number: 0-7357-1228-X

Library of Congress Catalog Card Number: 2001096226

06 05 04 03 02   7 6 5 4 3 2 1

Interpretation of the printing code: The rightmost double-digit number is the year of the book's printing; the right-most single-digit number is the number of the book's printing. For example, the printing code 02-1 shows that the first printing of the book occurred in 2002.

Trademarks

All terms mentioned in this book that are known to be trademarks or service marks have been appropriately capitalized. New Riders Publishing cannot attest to the accuracy of this information. Use of a term in this book should not be regarded as affecting the validity of any trademark or service mark. ActiveState and ActivePerl are trademarks of ActiveState Corp.

Warning and Disclaimer

This book is designed to provide information about *Perl*. Every effort has been made to make this book as complete and as accurate as possible, but no warranty or fitness is implied.

The information is provided on an as-is basis. The authors and New Riders Publishing shall have neither liability nor responsibility to any person or entity with respect to any loss or damages arising from the information contained in this book or from the use of the discs or programs that may accompany it.

Publisher
David Dwyer

Associate Publisher
Stephanie Wall

Managing Editor
Kristy Knoop

Development Editor
Chris Zahn

Senior Marketing Manager
Tammy Detrich

Publicity Manager
Susan Nixon

Project Editors
Stacia Mellinger
Ben Lawson

Copy Editor
Geneil Breeze

Indexer
Lisa Stumpf

Manufacturing Coordinator
Jim Conway

Book Designer
Louisa Klucznik

Cover Designer
Brainstorm Design, Inc.

Cover Production
Aren Howell

Proofreader
Linda Seifert

Composition
Gloria Schurick

❖

I dedicate this book to Karen, my wonderful wife, who has endured eight months of watching television over the sound of my typing, and waiting until 3am for me to go to bed. And to my children, Daniel ("Yes, I have finished the book now!") and Zoe ("Yes, you can play a game on my computer now!").

❖

TABLE OF CONTENTS

About the Author

Steve Oualline is a professional software engineer who lives in San Diego with his wife and two dogs. When he's not programming, he can be found at the Poway Midland Railroad where he's a real engineer.

About the Technical Reviewers

These reviewers contributed their considerable hands-on expertise to the entire development process for *Perl for C Programmers*. As the book was being written, these dedicated professionals reviewed all the material for technical content, organization, and flow. Their feedback was critical to ensuring that *Perl for C Programmers* fits our readers' need for the highest-quality technical information.

Denis Scherbakov is a System Administrator at the Belarus National Academy of Science (BNAS). He has had nine years of progressively responsible experience in software development and management of corporate networks within Windows, Linux, UNIX, and IRIX. He has held positions ranging from Designer and Software Developer to Internet Security Specialist and System Administrator. In his projects, he mainly uses Java, C/C++, and Perl. He is presently working on a project for the NASA Goddard Space Flight Center and the Aerosol Robotic Network (AERONET) Group using MFC/C++, Perl, SOAP, and XML. Denis is a member of the European Aerosol Research Lidar Network (EARLINET) establishing aerosol climatology. He lives in Minsk, Belarus. Recently he bought a mountain bike and a new Volkswagen B5.

Jason A. Buss has been working in the IT field for about six years. He currently works for a leading general aviation manufacturer, designing and implementing applications for publishing service information, using a single-source SGML/XML publishing system, delivering hard copy, web, and CD-ROM publications. In his free time, he enjoys spending time with his wife and four children, playing guitar, watching cartoons, and working on his PCs (currently playing with XML and Python).

Acknowledgments

I would like to acknowledge all the efforts on the part of the people at New Riders who helped produce this book, particularly Stephanie Wall, Chris Zahn, and Stacia Mellinger.

Also, I need to say a big thanks to the technical reviewers, Denis Scherbakov and Jason Buss.

Tell Us What You Think

As the reader of this book, you are the most important critic and commentator. We value your opinion and want to know what we're doing right, what we could do better, what areas you'd like to see us publish in, and any other words of wisdom you're willing to pass our way.

As the Associate Publisher for New Riders Publishing, I welcome your comments. You can fax, email, or write me directly to let me know what you did or didn't like about this book—as well as what we can do to make our books stronger.

Please note that I cannot help you with technical problems related to the topic of this book, and that due to the high volume of mail I receive, I might not be able to reply to every message.

When you write, please be sure to include this book's title and author as well as your name and phone or fax number. I will carefully review your comments and share them with the author and editors who worked on the book.

Fax:	317-581-4663
Email:	stephanie.wall@newriders.com
Mail:	Stephanie Wall
	Associate Publisher
	New Riders Publishing
	201 West 103rd Street
	Indianapolis, IN 46290 USA

Introduction

This is the book I wish I'd had when I was learning Perl. The problem with most Perl books is that they are written by Perl programmers for Perl programmers. This makes things difficult for the C and C++ programmer coming to Perl.

This book explains Perl in a language you can understand. Good, simple programming style is stressed so that you can write not just Perl programs, but working, maintainable Perl programs.

You will find that this book is shorter, yet conveys more, than most other Perl books. That's because this book doesn't treat you like a dummy and doesn't reproduce a lot of online documentation. (I'll tell you how to find it online.) Because of this, you are getting all the information you need in a compact, well-formed package.

Perl is a language designed to process text. Some uses for Perl are

- **Report writing**—The basic business program is "read it, munch it, sort it, and write a report." Perl makes it simple and easy to write such programs.

- **System administration**—Most UNIX and Linux configuration files are text. With Perl, it is easy to manipulate these files.

- **Creation of dynamic web pages**—If you've ever filled in a web form and clicked Submit, you've probably used a Perl program. Perl's text-handling capabilities make it superb for generating forms and web pages. Add to this Perl's built-in database accessing capabilities, and you have a language that provides a complete solution for your web development needs.

Who Should Read This Book

As suggested previously, this book is written for the seasoned C or C++ programmer who wants to learn Perl. It does not teach programming per se but instead assumes that you already know how to program and that you know how to program in C or C++.

Overview

Each chapter in *Perl for C Programmers* is briefly described here.

Chapter 1, "Exploring Perl"

Perl is more than just a language. Perl's online documentation and a repository called CPAN hold thousands of Perl modules. This chapter describes how to exploit these features of the language.

In addition, the mechanics of writing, running, and debugging a Perl program are discussed.

In short, this chapter covers everything you need to know about programming Perl except the programming part.

Chapter 2, "Perl Basics"

C and Perl share many of the same basic operations and much of the same syntax. (They just use different words.) This chapter describes these simple operations and syntax.

Chapter 3, "Arrays"

Perl has a flexible array data type. This chapter teaches you about the various Perl array manipulation operations. These include merging two arrays, using the push/pop operators, manipulating array slices, filtering with the grep function, and other array manipulations.

Chapter 4, "Regular Expressions"

One of the most powerful features of Perl are regular expressions. They are used for text matching and manipulation. Regular expressions are a language unto themselves. This chapter examines them in detail.

Chapter 5, "Perl's New Syntax"

Perl has a number of new and unique syntax elements that have no equivalent in C or C++. This chapter explores things such as die, redo, foreach, and other Perl-specific operations.

Chapter 6, "Hashes, References, and Complex Data Structures"

Perl has a variable type that's not available in C; it is the hash. This chapter introduces you to hashes and shows you how to use them. Subjects covered include the basic hash, the key and values functions, iterating through hashes, erasing elements, and other hash-related operations.

Chapter 7, "Subroutines and Modules"

Writing a subroutine in Perl is not as simple as it is under C. This chapter describes how to write subroutines, pass parameters, and handle other special subroutine requirements.

The chapter then takes these subroutines and groups them together to form a package. Unfortunately, Perl's package logic is not as simple as the one that C uses, but this chapter makes it simple.

Chapter 8, "Object-Oriented Programming"

Perl has the capability to define your own classes. This chapter teaches you basic Perl object-oriented techniques and how to define your own object-oriented package.

Chapter 9, "Advanced I/O"

Perl has an I/O structure similar to C, but with many additional features. A number of tricks and surprises also lurk in the I/O system. This chapter covers them all.

Chapter 10, "POD"

POD is the Perl internal documentation format. This chapter shows you the basic POD syntax as well as gives you information on the standard format that should be used for program documentation.

This chapter takes you on a tour through a complete POD document to see how it is formatted and discusses each of the formatting operators.

Chapter 11, "Under the Hood"

C and C++ hide many details from you. Perl is no different. But sometimes it's a good idea to look under the hood and understand how the language operates. This chapter discusses many of the details skipped over in previous chapters.

Chapter 12, "CGI Programming"

Perl is the language of the web. This chapter covers the programming that runs web forms (CGI programming). Writing and debugging these types of programs brings its own unique set of challenges. Here's where you find out how to meet these challenges.

Chapter 13, "Creating GUIs with Tk"

Tk is the portable GUI module available for Perl. This chapter tells you how to create, debug, and run GUI-based Perl programs.

Chapter 14, "Combining C and Perl with Inline::C"

With the Inline module, you can embed a C or C++ program inside your Perl program. Thus you can have a Perl function call a C subroutine. You can even have a Perl function call a C subroutine that calls a Perl function.

Chapter 15, "Putting It All Together"

In this chapter, you take all your Perl know-how and make a real program. In this case, it's a program to organize your software. The program uses the Perl interface to manipulate a simple database (called DB_File).

Because Perl is so flexible, the program comes with three user interfaces: command-line tools, a Tk GUI version, and a web-based interface.

Chapter 16, "Cookbook"

Perl can do many different things. This chapter shows you how to design and implement a number of useful programs. This cookbook contains examples of many different types of programs. Hopefully, one will be similar to what you plan on doing in Perl.

Chapter 17, "Creating Modules"

Perl's real strength is in its extensive set of modules. There are some things you just can't find a module for, however, in which case you have to write your own. This chapter shows you how.

Conventions

This book follows a few typographical conventions:

- Commands, program text, functions, variables, and other "computer language" are set in a monospaced font—for example, `$size` or `use warnings;`.

- In computer code or syntax, placeholder items that are set or entered by the user are set in monospaced *italics*—for example, `$line =~ s/<old>/<new>/<flag>;`.

- In computer code or syntax, optional items are in brackets—for example, `cat [file]`.

I

Using Perl

Exploring Perl

EXPLORING A NEW PROGRAMMING LANGUAGE ALWAYS STARTS with understanding what it is and how it works. In the case of Perl, first there is a core language—called Perl—which is a Perl syntax and a set of basic functions. The Perl syntax lets you write very powerful and flexible programs. It is designed to take care of a lot of the bookkeeping and details for you.

At the beginning, Perl was a language for processing text, and because of its extensive built-in text-handling capabilities, it is an ideal language for creating business reports, doing system administration work, and handling HTML forms.

But now Perl is more than just a language for processing text. A large collection of modules comes with the system. The modules are like a programming library or DLL full of very useful features and functions.

However, the number of modules Perl comes with is nothing compared with the total number of modules available for the language on the Internet. In fact, so many modules are available that a group of people got together and created the web site Comprehensive Perl Archive Network (CPAN). The CPAN library now contains thousands of modules all ready for downloading and installation. Chances are there is a module that can significantly reduce your programming job.

Needless to say, all the modules and all the programs in the world won't do you any good if they don't have documentation explaining how to use them. That is why Perl was designed with a built-in documentation system. Even better, almost all Perl module writers use it to document their work.

So by exploiting the installed modules, CPAN, and the documentation to maximum effect, you can write your programs with minimal effort. To summarize, Perl is

- A core, extremely flexible language
- A set of installed modules
- CPAN, a repository containing thousands of useful modules
- Online module documentation

This chapter shows you how to discover the many different features of Perl and its modules and how to exploit them for maximum effect.

Have Perl Installed

This chapter assumes that you have Perl installed on your system. (If not, see Appendix A, "Installing Perl.") It is also a good idea to have access to your Perl system when reading this book.

Online Documentation

Perl comes with about 15,000 pages of online documentation. This book doesn't reproduce all this documentation, but instead tells you how to access it. (Sets of books are available for purchase that contain a paper copy of most of the online documentation, but they are expensive, out-of-date, and more difficult to access than the stuff that comes with Perl.) Why use your own money when there is a book 15,000 pages long right on your hard drive?

Perl's online documentation makes a reference manual unnecessary if you know how to tickle Perl in such a way that it gives you the information you want. In the next few sections, you learn how to do just that.

perldoc

The main way to access Perl's documentation is through the `perldoc` command. For example, to find out about Perl itself, use the following command:

```
$ perldoc perl
```

UNIX, Linux, and Windows
This command works for UNIX, Linux, and Microsoft Windows systems. (On Microsoft Windows, you need to create a command prompt window and then execute the command).

This example uses $ as the command prompt. That's the default UNIX/Linux prompt. If you are using Microsoft Windows, the prompt may look like `C:\WINDOWS>`.

The `perldoc perl` command prints the top-level Perl document. This document contains a list of the other documentation that gives details on the various parts of Perl. For example, the command `perldoc perlvar` discusses the built-in Perl variables, and `perldoc perlrun` tells you how to run Perl.

Suppose that while looking at a program you see that the code uses the operator `!~`. If you don't know what this operator does, you can use the online documentation to find out. First stop is the main Perl documentation page, which is obtained with the command

```
$ perldoc perl
```

Looking through the list of documentation, you see the lines

```
...
perlsyn        Perl syntax
perlop         Perl operators and precedence
perlre         Perl regular expressions
...
```

It looks like the `perlop` document might be of use, so you take a look at that with the command

```
$ perldoc perlop
```

Looking through this document, you find the definition of the operator `!~`. (It compares a string against a regular expression and returns true if the result is false—more on this in Chapter 4, "Regular Expressions.")

Function Definitions

Perl comes with many built-in functions. If you want to find out what a particular function does, you can read the `perlfunc` documentation—all 7,000 lines of it. Or you can ask `perldoc` to give you information on a specific function.

For example, if you want to find out what the function `join` does, use the following command:

```
$ perldoc -t -f join
```

The result looks like

```
join EXPR,LIST

Joins the separate strings of LIST into a single string with fields
separated by the value of EXPR, and returns that new string.
Example:

    $rec = join(':', $login,$passwd,$uid,$gid,$gcos,$home,$shell);

See split
```

From this, you can see that this function has something to do with joining together the items of a LIST. In this case, the documentation uses uppercase words such as LIST to indicate a variable. In this case, EXPR is a string expression such as ':', and LIST is a list of items such as $login, $password, and so on.

In this example, perldoc has two options. The -t option tells perldoc to use its internal formatter to format the text. If this option is not present, it tries to use the nroff command. The other option, -f, tells perldoc that you want information on a built-in function, in this case join.

–t Comes First
The perldoc command is picky when it comes to the order of its options on the command line. The –t must be first.

Module Documentation

Perl not only consists of a core language, but also many modules. To find out about a module, use the command

```
$ perldoc module-name
```

That's if you know the name of the module. If you don't, you can find out which modules are installed on your system by looking through the Perl library directory. The actual search commands are system-dependent.

Finding Modules (UNIX/Linux)

To search for modules on UNIX or Linux, use the command

```
$ find /usr/lib/perl5 -name "*.pm" -print
```

(If your Perl is installed in some other directory, say /usr/local, you'll need to adjust the directory used in the find command.)

For example, a typical run might look like

```
$ find /usr/lib/perl5 -name "*.pm" -print
/usr/lib/perl5/5.00503/AnyDBM_File.pm
/usr/lib/perl5/5.00503/AutoLoader.pm
/usr/lib/perl5/5.00503/AutoSplit.pm
/usr/lib/perl5/5.00503/Benchmark.pm
/usr/lib/perl5/5.00503/CPAN/FirstTime.pm
/usr/lib/perl5/5.00503/CPAN/Nox.pm
/usr/lib/perl5/5.00503/CPAN.pm
....
```

Version Number Difference
The version number you see (5.00503 in this case) may be different for your installation of Perl.

The Perl modules end in .pm. From the preceding code example, you can see that a module called AnyDBM_File is installed. To find out what this module does, use the command

```
$ perldoc AnyDBM_File
AnyDBM_File(3) User Contributed Perl Documentation AnyDBM_File(3)


NAME
        AnyDBM_File - provide framework for multiple DBMs

        NDBM_File, DB_File, GDBM_File, SDBM_File, ODBM_File -
        various DBM implementations

SYNOPSIS
            use AnyDBM_File;


DESCRIPTION
        This module is a "pure virtual base class"--it has nothing
```

In the directory listing, you can see that the directory CPAN holds a couple files (Nox.pm and FirstTime.pm). These are submodules. To find the documentation for these files, you need a slightly different perldoc command. For example, to find information on the Nox.pm module (in the CPAN directory), you need the following command:

```
$ perldoc CPAN::Nox
```

Directory Levels
There can be several levels of directories in the library. Use :: to separate each one when you use the perldoc command.

Searching for Modules (Microsoft Windows)

To search for module files under Microsoft Windows, open an MS-DOS command session. You'll need to know in which directory your Perl package is installed. (If you forget which directory it is, you can execute the command PATH to display your path settings. The Perl program should be in your path.) This example assumes that you installed it in the default directory C:\PERL. To find the modules, execute the command

```
C:\WINDOWS> dir/s/p C:\PERL\*.pm
```

All your Perl modules will be listed. Now you can use the perldoc command to extract the information from them as described in the previous section.

How to Print Nice-Looking Documentation

Perl keeps its documentation in a format called *POD* (Plain Old Documentation). It's easily converted into a wide variety of formats such as HTML, LaTeX, man, and text.

By default, the perldoc command turns POD into text for display on a terminal. You can turn it into HTML by using the command

```
$ perldoc -u subject ¦ pod2html >file.html
```

Next, you can use your web browser (Netscape, Internet Explorer, or other browser) to view and print the file.

For example, if you are on UNIX or Linux, you can view the results using the command

```
$ netscape file.html
```

On Microsoft Windows, you can double-click on the Internet Explorer icon and then use the File, Open command to open the file.

CPAN (The Module Archive)

The preceding commands tell you all about the installed modules; but what about the uninstalled ones? If you do any serious programming in Perl, you quickly learn that many modules are available to help you. Unfortunately, you have to download and install most of them.

The Perl people have set up a repository called CPAN (Comprehensive Perl Archive Network), which contains almost all the modules ever written for Perl.

You can access this archive through the web at http://cpan.perl.org. Figure 1.1 shows the top-level CPAN web page.

Figure 1.1   CPAN.

There are several different ways of searching this archive. This example uses the one connected to the Perl core and CPAN modules documentation link (the first link under "Searching"). When you click on this link, a search form appears as shown in Figure 1.2.

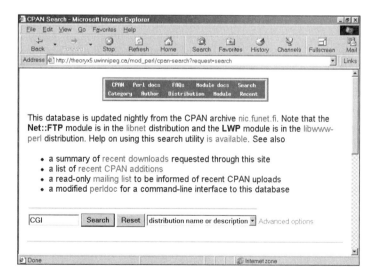

Figure 1.2   CPAN search.

This example searches for modules related to CGI programming. (CGI is the programming system used to handle web page forms.) So enter CGI in the blank and click Search. Figure 1.3 displays the results.

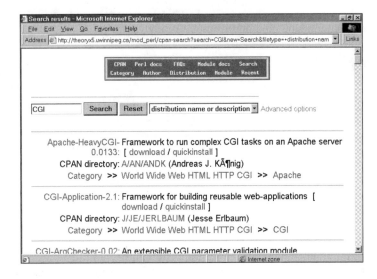

Figure 1.3   CPAN search results.

Clicking on the name of the modules (for example, CGI–Application-2.1) displays a page describing that application (see Figure 1.4).

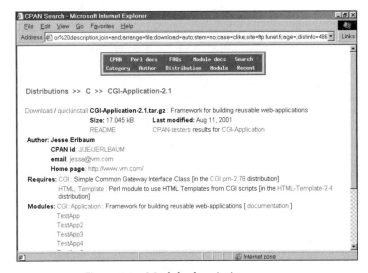

Figure 1.4   Module description page.

This page has several key links. The Download link downloads the module. (Downloading and installing modules is described later in this chapter.) The `quickinstall` link provides a way of downloading and installing all in one set.

The other links take you to documentation about the module, test results, or other module information.

Now that you know how to find modules, it's time to see how to install them.

Installing Modules

There are several different ways of installing modules, including the following:

- **Manual installation**—You download the modules and then manually execute the commands to compile and install it yourself. This method is generally only used if the other methods fail.
- **CPAN module**—A module called CPAN can download and install the modules for you. This method is primarily used on UNIX systems.
- **PPM (Perl Package Manager)**—This system automatically downloads and installs packages. The `ppm` command comes standard with ActiveState Perl for Microsoft Windows and is primarily used on that system.

Which method you need to use depends on your operating system and environment. For step-by-step instructions, see the "Cookbook" section later in this chapter.

To get through this chapter, you'll need to download and install two modules. These are

```
Tk      (Full name: Tk800.023)
ptkdb   (Full name: Devel-ptkdb-1.1074)
```

Later Versions
You may use later versions of these modules if ones are available.

Installing Manually (UNIX, Linux, and Microsoft Windows)

To install manually, you'll need the following programs:

- `gzip` and `tar` (UNIX systems)
- WinZip, WinRAR, or PowerArchiver (Microsoft Windows)
- `make` or `nmake`
- A C compiler

The C compiler is needed if you compile your files. If you are on UNIX or Linux, you'll probably need to do this. Almost all the modules for the Microsoft Windows version of Perl come precompiled.

Unpacking the Archive

Place your archive in a working directory. This is *not* the directory where you installed Perl. This is a temporary workspace that can be deleted after you install the module.

After downloading the module, you need to unpack the archive containing it. On UNIX and Linux, this is done with the `gzip` and `tar` commands. For example, if you want to install the `Tk` module, you need the command

```
$ gzip -d -c Tk800.023.tar.gz ¦ tar xf -
```

On Microsoft Windows, you can unpack the archive using the WinZip, WinRAR, or Powerarc utilities.

To unpack the archive using the free utility PowerArchiver (`http://www.sfsu.edu/ftp/win/utils`), first double-click on the PowerArchiver icon on your desktop or run the program using Start, PowerArchiver.

Figure 1.5 shows the initial screen.

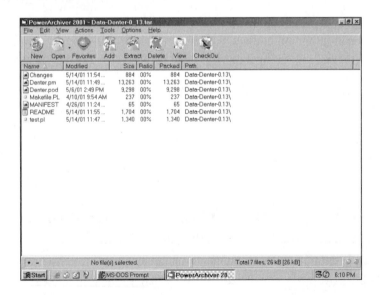

Figure 1.5   PowerArchiver.

Click the Open button to open an archive. (These usually have the `.gz` extension). To unpack it, click the Extract button.

Compiling the Program

The first step in compiling a Perl module is to create a Makefile. This is done by executing the Makefile.PL Perl script located in the directory where you just extracted archive contents using the command

```
$ perl Makefile.PL
```

(These commands work on both Microsoft Windows and UNIX.)

This command creates a file called Makefile, which controls the rest of the building and installation process. (By default, this file installs the module in the standard Perl library location. See the instructions in the upcoming section "Dealing with Permission Problems" if you don't have permission to write into this directory.)

Now you need to build sources into the modules using the command

```
$ make
```

(If you use Microsoft Visual C++, the make command is called nmake.)

If everything goes well, the module compiles without errors. (If there are errors, check for a README or INSTALL file. Also make sure that you have installed any modules that are a prerequisite to this one.)

Most modules come with a number of self-test modules. To run the self-tests, execute the command

```
$ make test
```

The tests should execute and report success. If there is a problem, check the documentation that comes with your module and try again.

X Windows Session

If you are testing the Tk module on UNIX or Linux, you'll need to have an X Windows session running. The testing system creates several windows during the testing process.

Finally, to install the modules, use the command

```
$ make install
```

Dealing with Permission Problems

The instructions just presented are designed to install the module in the standard location for the Perl library. But what if you are on a UNIX or Linux system and don't have permission to write into a system directory?

The Perl module system is flexible enough to let you install the module into any directory you want. This is done with the PREFIX option to the Makefile.PL command. For example, suppose that you want to install modules in /home/oualline/local. You would use the command

```
$ perl Makefile.PL PREFIX=/home/oualline/local
```

After the installation is complete, you need to tell Perl about the new, added library by setting the environment variable PERL5LIB. For example, if you are using the csh shell, you would execute the command

```
$ setenv PERL5LIB "/home/oualline/local/lib/perl5/5.00503:\
    /home/oualline/local/lib/perl5/site_perl/5.005/i386-linux/"
```

Note that this path variable includes both the version of Perl used (5.005) and the architecture of the machine it's running on (i386-linux). These may be different on your system. To find out what they are, execute the command

```
$ perl -V
```

Another way of locating the module directory is to use the find command to locate the .pm files:

```
$ find /home/oualline/local -name "*.pm" -print
```

For the sh, ksh, and bash shells, the commands are

```
$ PERL5LIB="/home/oualline/local/lib/perl5/5.00503:\
    /home/oualline/local/lib/perl5/site_perl/5.005/i386-linux/"
$ export PERL5LIB
```

You probably want to put commands to set PERL5LIB in your initialization files. These files are .cshrc for csh users and .profile for the other shells.

See "Cookbook" for More

The "Cookbook" section later in the chapter contains not only instructions for installing the modules needed by this chapter but also step-by-step instructions for setting the PERL5LIB variable.

Sample Run

This section presents a manual installation of the module Tk. (The full module name is: Tk800.023.tar.gz.)

First, you unpack the files. Note that a v option is added to the tar command, which causes a list of files to be printed as they are unpacked:

```
$ gzip -d -c Tk800.023.tar.gz ¦ tar xvf -
Tk800.023/Bitmap/Bitmap.pm
Tk800.023/Bitmap/Bitmap.xs
Tk800.023/Bitmap/Makefile.PL
Tk800.023/COPYING
Tk800.023/Canvas/Canvas.pm
... many more files
```

Now go into the directory and create the Makefile. Because you do not have access to the system files, you are going to install them in your local directory. This means that you need a PREFIX option:

```
$ cd Tk800.023
$ perl Makefile.PL PREFIX=/home/oualline/local
/usr/bin/perl is installed in /usr/lib/perl5/5.00503/i386-linux okay
PPM for perl5.00503
Test Compiling config/signedchar.c
Test Compiling config/Ksprintf.c
Test Compiling config/tod.c
Test Compiling -DTIMEOFDAY_TZ config/tod.c
.... lots of configuration chatter removed
Finding dependencies for tkWin32Dll.c
Writing Makefile for Tk
```

The next step is to build the module using the make command:

```
$ make
mkdir blib
mkdir blib/lib
mkdir blib/arch
...
cc -c -I.. -I/usr/X11R6/include -I. -Ibitmaps
    -I/usr/X11R6/include -Dbool=char
    -DHAS_BOOL -I/usr/local/include -O2
    -DVERSION=\"800.023\" -DXS_VERSION=\"800.0 23\" -fPIC
    -I/usr/lib/perl5/5.00503/i386-linux/CORE  -Wall
    -Wno-implicit-int -Wno-comment -Wno-unused
    -D__USE_FIXED_PROTOTYPES__ imgGIF.c
cc -c -I.. -I/usr/X11R6/include -I. -Ibitmaps
    -I/usr/X11R6/include -Dbool=char -DHAS_BOOL
    -I/usr/local/include -O2 -DVERSION=\"800.023\"
    -DXS_VERSION=\"800.0 23\" -fPIC
    -I/usr/lib/perl5/5.00503/i386-linux/CORE
    -Wall -Wno-implicit-int -Wno-comment
    -Wno-unused -D__USE_FIXED_PROTOTYPES__ imgInit.c
...
```

After the module is compiled, it needs to be tested:

```
$ make test
PERL_DL_NONLAZY=1 /usr/bin/perl -Iblib/arch -Iblib/lib
    -I/usr/lib/perl5/5.00503/ i386-linux
    -I/usr/lib/perl5/5.00503 -e 'use'
Test::Harness qw(&runtests $verbose) ; $verbose=0;
    runtests @ARGV;'
t/Require.t t/Trace.t t/X.t t/autoload.t t/balloo n.t
t/browseentry.t t/create.t t/dash.t t/fbox.t t/fileevent.t
t/fileselect.t t/ font.t t/geomgr.t t/list.t t/mega.t t/mwm.t
t/optmenu.t t/photo.t t/progbar.t t/ widget.t t/zzHList.t
t/zzPhoto.t t/zzScrolled.t t/zzText.t
t/zzTixGrid.t
t/Require..........ok
t/Trace............ok
...
```

```
t/zzText...........ok
t/zzTixGrid........ok
All tests successful.
Files=25,  Tests=904, 107 wallclock secs
(79.89 cusr +  4.99 csys = 84.88 CPU)
```

From this, you can see that the module performed 904 tests and that all were successful.

If you pass all the tests, you can move on to the installation step:

```
$ make install
...
Installing /home/oualline/local/lib/perl5/site_perl/5.005/i386-
➥linux/auto/Tk/pTk/extralibs.ld
Installing /home/oualline/local/lib/perl5/site_perl/5.005/i386-
➥linux/auto/Tk/Xlib/Xlib.so
Installing /home/oualline/local/lib/perl5/site_perl/5.005/i386-
➥linux/auto/Tk/Xlib/Xlib.bs
...
Installing /home/oualline/local/bin/ptksh
Writing /home/oualline/local/lib/perl5/site_perl/5.005/i386-
➥linux/auto/Tk/.packlist
/bin/sh: /home/oualline/local/lib/perl5/5.00503/i386-linux/
➥perllocal.pod: No such file or directory
make: [doc_site_install] Error 1 (ignored)
Appending installation info to /home/oualline/local/lib/perl5/
➥5.00503/i386-linux/perllocal.pod
....
```

Don't Worry About the Error

Don't worry about the error at the end. (On the other hand, if you're really a worrier, you can create an empty file named /home/oualline/local/lib/perl5/5.00503/i386-linux/ perllocal.pod and then do the install. The error will go away.)

At this point, you're finished and can start to use the new module.

In summary, the basic commands to install a module manually are

- Download
- Unpack
- perl Makefile.PL
- make
- make test
- make install

Using the CPAN Installer (UNIX and Linux)

When you install manually, you have to go through each step. Perl programmers don't like to do anything twice if they can help it, and that includes installing modules. So there is a Perl script designed to download and install modules called CPAN.

The CPAN script also has one additional advantage over manual installation; it automatically downloads and installs any prerequisite modules that are needed. Thus if you are installing the C Inline module and need the recursive decent parser, it automatically downloads and installs it.

The CPAN script comes with Perl. To start it, use the command

```
$ perl -MCPAN -e shell
```

> **For More Information**
>
> If you want to know what the -M and -e flags do, check out the document `perlrun` using the `perldoc` command. If you want to find out all about CPAN, you can use the command
> ```
> $ perldoc CPAN
> ```

> **Caution: Running CPAN with PERL5LIB**
>
> On occasion, I've experienced problems when running CPAN with the PERL5LIB environment variable set. If you experience problems, you might want to unset this variable and try again.

When you run CPAN for the first time, it asks you a number of questions to configure itself.

The first is "Are you ready for manual configuration?" If you answer "no," CPAN attempts to automatically configure everything using the default answers. Because some of these answers may not be correct, you should press Enter to select "yes," the default answer:

```
$ perl -MCPAN -e shell

CPAN is the world-wide archive of perl resources.
⇒It consists of about
100 sites that all replicate the same contents all around the globe.
Many countries have at least one CPAN site already. The resources
found on CPAN are easily accessible with the CPAN.pm module. If you
want to use CPAN.pm, you have to configure it properly.

If you do not want to enter a dialog now, you can answer 'no' to this
question and I'll try to autoconfigure. (Note: you can revisit this
dialog anytime later by typing 'o conf init' at the cpan prompt.)

Are you ready for manual configuration? [yes]
```

Next CPAN asks you for the location of the build and cache directory. The default works fine for most systems:

```
I see you already have a  directory
      /home/oualline/.cpan
Shall we use it as the general CPAN build and cache directory?

CPAN build and cache directory? [/home/oualline/.cpan]
```

The next few questions concern some configuration parameters for the cache and downloading. These questions include

```
Cache size for build directory (in MB)? [10]
Policy on building prerequisites (follow, ask or ignore)? [follow]
```

It's safe to accept the default for these questions.

The CPAN script needs some tools to do its work, so it now asks you where they are. Don't worry if you don't have all of them. CPAN can work around most of the missing files. On Microsoft Windows, you will need an unzip program and a make command, however:

```
Where is your gzip program? [/usr/bin/gzip]
Where is your tar program? [/bin/tar]
Where is your unzip program? [/usr/bin/unzip]
Where is your make program? [/usr/bin/make]
Where is your lynx program? [/usr/bin/lynx]
Where is your ncftpget program? [/usr/bin/ncftpget]
Where is your ftp program? [/usr/bin/ftp]
What is your favorite pager program? [/usr/bin/less]
What is your favorite shell? [/bin/csh]
```

Remember that during manual installation you had to execute a number of commands. CPAN executes them for you, but it needs to know what arguments to use. Because you are installing modules in your local directory, you need to give the `perl Makefile.PL` command the argument `PREFIX=/home/oualline/local`. No other arguments are needed:

```
Parameters for the 'perl Makefile.PL'
        command? [] PREFIX=/home/oualline/local
Parameters for the 'make' command? []
Parameters for the 'make install' command? []
```

The next question concerns how long CPAN waits for a `make` command to finish. Just accept the default (0—forever):

```
Timeout for inactivity during Makefile.PL? [0]
```

CPAN needs to know how you are connected to the outside world. Specifically, it needs to know whether you have an ftp or http proxy. If you do, your network administrator should know all about them and what parameter to supply for the next few questions. In this example, you are connected directly to the Internet (no proxies), so you just input the default answers:

```
Your ftp_proxy?
Your http_proxy?
Your no_proxy?
```

Now CPAN goes off and does some work. It goes out to the CPAN archive and fetches a list of "mirror" sites. These are sites that keep a copy (mirror) of the CPAN module library:

```
You have no /home/oualline/.cpan/sources/MIRRORED.BY
I'm trying to fetch one

Please, install Net::FTP as soon as possible.
⇒CPAN.pm installs it for you
if you just type
install Bundle::libnet


Trying with "/usr/bin/lynx -source" to get
ftp://ftp.perl.org/pub/CPAN/MIRRORED.BY
```

The system just got a list of places from which you can download modules. To help you select one near you, it needs to ask you a bunch of questions concerning your geographic location:

```
(1) Africa
(2) Asia
(3) Central America
(4) Europe
(5) North America
(6) Oceania
(7) South America
Select your continent (or several nearby continents) [] 5

(1) Canada
(2) Mexico
(3) United States
Select your country (or several nearby countries) [] 3
```

Now CPAN displays a list of sites that have copies of the Perl archive. You need to select one that's near you. That's difficult to do because the system gives you no clue as to where these places are. So just pick a random one and hope that the electrons don't have to make a long trip all the way across the country:

```
(1) ftp://archive.progeny.com/CPAN/
(2) ftp://carroll.cac.psu.edu/pub/CPAN/
...
(38) ftp://ruff.cs.jmu.edu/pub/CPAN/
```

```
(39) ftp://uiarchive.uiuc.edu/mirrors/ftp/ftp.cpan.org/pub/CPAN/
Select as many URLs as you like [] 27 37
```

Type in the index of a server near you. You can type in more than one separated by spaces. In this case if one is busy or down, CPAN will switch to the next one in the list.

The final question concerns a WAIT server. Because you haven't installed the CPAN::WAIT module and don't know what a WAIT server is, just use the default on this one:

```
WAIT support is available as a Plugin. You need the CPAN::WAIT module
to actually use it. But we need to know your favorite WAIT server. If
you don't know a WAIT server near you, just press ENTER.

Your favorite WAIT server?
  [wait://ls6.informatik.uni-dortmund.de:1404]
```

Finally you reach the cpan> prompt:

```
cpan shell -- CPAN exploration and modules installation (v1.48)
ReadLine support available (try ''install Bundle::CPAN'')

cpan>
```

Don't Install Bundle::CPAN

Do not try to install Bundle::CPAN as suggested at this point. It installs a ton of files and modules, most of which you don't need at this point.

Using CPAN

The cpan> prompt indicates that you are in the CPAN shell. You can issue the h command at this point to get a list of commands:

```
    cpan> h
command  arguments      description
a        string               authors
b        or          display bundles
d        /regex/     info    distributions
m        or          about   modules
i        none                anything of above

r        as          reinstall recommendations
u        above       uninstalled distributions
See manpage for autobundle, recompile, force, look, etc.

make                    make
test     modules,       make test (implies make)
install  dists, bundles, make install (implies test)
clean    "r" or "u"     make clean
readme                  display the README file
```

```
reload    index¦cpan    load most recent indices/CPAN.pm
h or ?                  display this menu
o         various       set and query options
!         perl-code     eval a perl command
q                       quit the shell subroutine
cpan>
```

You need to install the Tk module, so get some information about this module using the m Tk command:

```
cpan> m Tk
... lots of chatter omitted ..
Module id = Tk
    DESCRIPTION  Object oriented version of Tk v4
    CPAN_USERID  NI-S (Nick Ing-Simmons <nick@ing-simmons.net>)
    CPAN_VERSION 800.023
    CPAN_FILE    N/NI/NI-S/Tk800.023.tar.gz
    DSLI_STATUS  bmcO (beta,mailing-list,C,object-oriented)
    INST_FILE    (not installed)
```

Install the Tk module using the install Tk command. The CPAN module downloads the latest version of the module and then goes through the entire installation process including running the unpacking, Makefile generation, building, testing, and installation:

```
cpan> install Tk
Running make for N/NI/NI-S/Tk800.023.tar.gz

Trying with "/usr/bin/lynx -source" to get
    ftp://mirrors.kernel.org/pub/CPAN/authors/id/N/NI/NI-S/
➥Tk800.023.tar.gz

  CPAN: MD5 security checks disabled because MD5 not installed.
  Please consider installing the MD5 module.

Tk800.023/Bitmap/Bitmap.pm
Tk800.023/Bitmap/Bitmap.xs
...
```

After a lot of output and a long time, the system completes the installation, and you can get out with the quit (q) command:

```
cpan> q
Lockfile removed.
```

Using the Perl Package Manager (Microsoft Windows)

The Perl Package Manager (PPM) is another program designed to make the installation of programs easier. The ActiveState people who produced the Microsoft Windows port of Perl have an extensive archive of precompiled binaries. The PPM command knows how to download and install them.

To start the PPM command in interactive mode, use the following command:

```
C:> PPM
PPM interactive shell (2.1.5) - type 'help' for available commands.
PPM>
```

The help command displays a list of commands:

```
PPM> help
Commands:
    exit              - leave the program.
    help [command]    - prints this screen, or help on 'command'.
    install PACKAGES  - installs specified PACKAGES.
    quit              - leave the program.
    query [options]   - query information about installed packages.
    remove PACKAGES   - removes the specified PACKAGES
    search [options]  - search information about available packages.
    set [options]     - set/display current options.
    verify [options]  - verifies current install is up to date.
    version           - displays PPM version number
```

The search command searches for uninstalled modules. Use this command to search for the Tk module:

```
PPM> search Tk
Packages available from
http://ppm.ActiveState.com/cgibin/PPM/ppmserver.pl?urn:/
PPMServer:
Devel-ptkdb      [1.1074 ] Perl debugger using a Tk GUI
Log-Dispatch-Tk  [1.3    ] Text widget for Log::Dispatch
Tie-ListKeyedHash [0.41  ] A system allowing the use of
anonymous arrays
Tk               [800.022] Tk - a Graphical User Interface Toolkit
Tk-ACH           [0.03   ] Entry that reflects its state in the
                           color
...
```

To install the package Tk, issue the following command:

```
PPM> install Tk
Install package 'Tk?' (y/N): y
Installing package 'Tk'...
Bytes transferred: 1742381
Installing C:\Perl\site\lib\Tk\Config.pm
Installing C:\Perl\site\lib\Tk\tkGlue.def
Installing C:\Perl\site\lib\Tk\tkGlue.h
....
```

The result is that the precompiled Tk package is downloaded and installed.

Cookbook

This section presents step-by-step instructions for installing the Perl modules Tk and Devel::ptkdb. The steps presented here can be useful in installing other modules from CPAN or the ActiveState repository.

Linux

To install these modules to a Linux system, do the following:

1. Check to see whether you have the gcc compiler installed by using the following command:

```
$ which gcc
```

   If the command reports an error, install the Linux package containing the GNU C compiler from your Linux system distribution. (The package name depends on which distribution you have, but it is usually called "gcc-<something>")

2. Check to see whether you have installed the XFree86 development libraries. You'll need these to compile programs that use the XFree86 windowing system, such as the Perl module Tk. To see whether this package is installed, execute the following command:

```
$ ls /usr/X11R6/include/X11/Core.h
```

   If this file does not exist, install the Linux package containing the XFree86 development system.

3. Install every Perl related package you can find.

4. Check to see whether the module Tk has already been installed using the following command:

```
$ perl -e "use Tk;"
```

   If you get an error message, go to the next step. If the program prints nothing, the module Tk is already installed, and you can go on to step 6.

5. Install Tk as root using CPAN, by executing the following commands:

```
$ perl -MCPAN -e shell

......

cpan> install Tk
```

   If you cannot become root, check out the section "Dealing with Permission Problems" later in the chapter.

6. Check to see whether the module `Devel::ptkdb` has already been installed using the command

```
$ perl -e "use Devel::ptkdb;"
```

If no error is reported, you're done, and the required modules have been installed. If an error message is output, go on to the next step.

7. Install `Devel::ptkdb` as root using CPAN, by executing the commands

```
$ perl -MCPAN -e shell
```

```
......
```

```
cpan> install Devel::ptkdb
```

UNIX Installation (All Systems)

To install to a UNIX system, do the following:

1. Check to see whether you have a `gcc` compiler by using the command

```
$ gcc -v
```

If you do not get a "command not found" error, you're okay and may proceed with step 3.

2. Check to see whether you have a `cc` compiler with the command

```
$ which cc
```

If this command results in an error, you have not installed the C compiler. You'll need to install one. The free GNU C compiler (`gcc`) is available from `http://www.gnu.org/`.

If you are using an HP-UX system, make sure that you have a full C compiler on your system, not the crippled version that HP installs by default. (Check with your system administrator on this.)

3. Check for the `gzip` command by executing the following command:

```
$ gzip -v
```

If you get a "command not found" error, download and install the `gzip` program from `http://www.gzip.org`.

4. Did you install a personal copy of Perl or do you have permission to write into the Perl system directories? If yes, go through the steps in the following section "Installing Modules into the Perl Library." Otherwise, you'll need to go through "Installing Personal Perl Modules" later in the chapter.

Installing Modules into the Perl Library

To install modules into the Perl library, you need to follow these steps:

1. Check to see whether the module Tk has already been installed using the following command:

```
$ perl -e "use Tk;"
```

If you get an error message, go to the next step. If the program prints nothing, the module Tk is already installed, and you can go on to step 3.

2. Install Tk using CPAN, by executing the commands

```
$ perl -MCPAN -e shell
```

```
......
```

```
cpan> install Tk
```

If you run into an error, you may be behind a firewall. Check with your network administrator about the problem and check out the documentation in perldoc CPAN to see how to pierce a firewall. If you cannot get around the firewall problem, you'll need to install the Tk module manually.

3. Check to see whether the module Devel::ptkdb has already been installed using the command

```
$ perl -e "use Devel::ptkdb;"
```

If no error is reported, you're done. If an error occurred, proceed to the next step.

4. Install Devel::ptkdb as root using CPAN, by executing the commands

```
$ perl -MCPAN -e shell
```

```
......
```

```
cpan> install Devel::ptkdb
```

Installing Personal Perl Modules

Follow these steps to install personal Perl modules on UNIX-like systems:

1. Install Tk as using CPAN, by executing the commands

```
$ perl -MCPAN -e shell
```

```
......
```

```
cpan> install Tk
```

If you run into an error, you may be behind a firewall. Check with your network administrator about the problem and check out the documentation in `perldoc CPAN` to see how to pierce a firewall. If you cannot get around the firewall problem, you'll need to install manually.

2. Use the `find` command to locate the file `Tk.pm`:

```
$ cd <your perl installation directory>

$ find ./ -name "Tk.pm" -print

/home/oualline/perl/site_perl/5.005/i386-linux/Tk.pm
```

Set the `PERL5LIB` environment variable so that it points to the directory in which `Tk.pm` resides.

If you are a `csh` or `tcsh` user, the command is

```
$ setenv PERL5LIB /home/oualline/perl/site_perl/5.005/i386-linux
```

If you are an `sh`, `bash`, or `ksh` user, the command is

```
$ PERL5LIB=/home/oualline/perl/site_perl/5.005/i386-linux
$ export PERL5LIB
```

The exact pathname will probably be slightly different on your machine. (Unless your name is Oualline, and you are using the same version of Perl as I do on my Linux system.)

3. Install `Devel::ptkdb` as root using CPAN, by executing the commands

```
$ perl -MCPAN -e shell

......

cpan> install Devel::ptkdb
```

4. Locate the file in which `ptkdb.pm` resides using the `find` command:

```
$ cd <your perl installation directory>

$ find ./ -name "Tk.pm" -print

/home/oualline/perl/5.005/Devel/ptkdb.pm
```

Append the directory containing `Devel` (not `ptkdb.pm`) to the `PERL5LIB` environment variable.

If you are a `csh` or `tcsh` user, the command is

```
$ setenv PERL5LIB ${PERL5LIB}:/home/oualline/perl/5.005
```

To avoid having to repeat this command every time you log in or start a new window, you may want to put all the commands that set up your PERL5LIB environment variable in your .cshrc file.

If you are an sh, bash, or ksh user, the command is

```
$ PERL5LIB=${PERL5LIB}:/home/oualline/perl/5.005
$ export PERL5LIB
```

You may want to put the commands to set up your PERL5LIB environment variable in your .profile file so that they will be automatically executed when a new shell starts.

Microsoft Windows Module Installation

The latest version of ActiveState Perl comes with the two modules that you need (Tk, Devel::ptkdb), so you shouldn't need to install them manually. But if you do, here are the steps:

1. Open up a command prompt (MS-DOS) window.
2. Check to see whether the Devel::ptkdb module has been installed with the command:

```
C:\WINDOWS> perl -e "use Devel::ptkdb;"
```

If this command executes without errors, you're done. If there is an error, continue with step 3.

3. Start PPM with the command

```
C:\WINDOWS> PPM
```

4. Install the package Devel::ptkdb with the command

```
PPM> install Devel::ptkdb
```

This automatically installs the package Tk because it is a prerequisite of Devel::ptkdb.

If this command fails, you are probably behind a firewall. Check with your network administrator and check your PPM configuration as well as reading the documentation on PPM (perldoc ppm) to see what can be done about this problem.

Using the Perl Debugger

One of the more useful tools when it comes to exploring a language is the
debugger. This tool allows you to see real-world programs in action and
examine what they are doing.

First you need a Perl script. Listing 1.1 shows a program that computes the
average grade for a list of students.

Listing 1.1   *ave.pl* **(Line numbers added)**

```
 1  use strict;
 2  use warnings;
 3
 4  while (<DATA>)
 5  {
 6      if (/^#/)
 7      {
 8          next;
 9      }
10      my @grades = split /[ \t]+/, $_;
11      my $name = shift @grades;
12      my $ave = ($grades[0] + $grades[1] + $grades[2]) / 3;
13      print "Student $name Average $ave\n";
14  }
15
16  __DATA__
17  # Student      Grade   Grade   Grade
18  oualline       98      95      92
19  smith          75      84      99
20  jones          45      26      55
```

Spelling __DATA__
__DATA__ is spelled "<Underscore><Underscore>DATA<Underscore><Underscore>" This spelling is
not obvious in typeset.

Leave Out *warning* **Statement**
If you get the error

    Can't locate warnings.pm at . . . . .

you have an old version of Perl that predates version 5.6.0. In that case, you can leave out the line

use warnings;

This statement turns on runtime warnings in your program. If it's left out, your program will still
run, but you won't get any warnings when something stupid happens.

To run this script, use the command

```
$ perl ave.pl
Student oualline Average 95
Student smith Average 86
Student jones Average 42
```

The Command-Line Debugger

Two major debuggers are available for Perl: the command-line debugger, which comes with the standard Perl distribution; and a GUI-based debugger called ptkdb, which you learn how to install and use in the next section.

To start the command-line debugger, use the command

```
$ perl -d adv.pl
Default die handler restored.

Loading DB routines from perl5db.pl version 1.07
Editor support available.

Enter h or 'h h' for help, or 'man perldebug' for more help.

main::(ave.pl:4):       while (<DATA>)
main::(ave.pl:5):       {
DB<1>
```

Table 1.1 lists the basic debugger commands.

Table 1.1   **Basic Debugger Commands**

Command	Name	Explanation
l	line number	List the source file starting at the given line number.
b	line number	Set a break point.
s	single step	Single step through the code, stepping into subroutines.
n	next	Single step through the code, treating subroutine calls as one statement.
x	print variable	Print the value of a variable.

Debugger Documentation
You can discover many other commands by using the perldoc perldeb command.

Look at the source file and debug it first in the standard Perl debugger:

```
DB<1> l 4
4==>        while (<DATA>)
  DB<2> l
5        {
6:           if (/^#/)
7            {
8:               next;
9            }
10:          my @grades = split /[ \t]+/, $_;
11:          my $name = shift @grades;
12:          my $ave = ($grades[0] + $grades[1] + $grades[2])/3;
13:          print "Student $name Average $ave\n";
14       }
```

Next, single step through a few lines using the s command:

```
    DB<2> s
main::(ave.pl:6):           if (/^#/)
main::(ave.pl:7):           {
    DB<2> s
main::(ave.pl:8):               next;
```

There is a special variable called $_. In this program it contains the last input line read. To find out what's in this variable, use the x command. The result is the first line after the __DATA__ statement:

```
DB<3> x $_
0   "# Student\cIGrade\cIGrade\cIGrade\cJ"
```

Now go a few more steps:

```
    DB<4> s
main::(ave.pl:6):       if (/^#/)
main::(ave.pl:7):       {
    DB<4> s
main::(ave.pl:10):      my @grades = split /[ \t]+/, $_;
    DB<4> s
main::(ave.pl:11):      my $name = shift @grades;
```

Now look at the variable @grades:

```
DB<4> x @grades
0   'oualline'
1   98
2   95
3   92
```

The variable @grades is an array; the debugger displays all four elements in the array (numbered 0 through 3).

You're finished now, so exit the program with a q (quit) command:

```
DB<8> q
```

Using the *ptkdb* Debugger

There is a GUI-based debugger that is much easier to use for simple programs. However, it's not part of the Core distribution. You'll have to install the module

```
Devel::ptkdb
```

to use the debugger. (If you're installing manually, you'll also need to install the prerequisite module Tk.)

To debug the program with this debugger, start your program with the command

```
$ perl -d:ptkdb ave.pl
```

A debugging window appears, as shown in Figure 1.6.

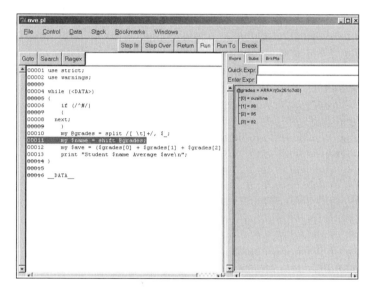

Figure 1.6   ptkdb debugger.

The left side of the screen shows the program. The current line is highlighted. As you can see in Figure 1.6, a few statements have already been executed.

The right side is used for displaying data. Figure 1.6 shows the result of typing @grades in the Enter Expr: blank and pressing Enter.

You may notice that line 8 is indented strangely. That's because the debugger does not handle tabs properly.

The Step In button single steps, going into subroutines. The Step Over button steps over them.

The Return button executes the program until the current function returns.

The Run button runs the system until the program finishes or until a breakpoint is hit.

To set a breakpoint, click on the line number where you want the breakpoint. (Don't click on the line, click on the line number.) Then select the Control, Set Breakpoint menu item.

There are many other commands as well. You can find out about them by executing the command

```
$ perldoc Devel::ptkdb
```

If you want to automatically use the ptkdb debugger as your default debugger, you'll need to set the environment variable PERL5DB.

On UNIX or Linux using the C shell (csh), use the command

```
$ setenv PERL5DB 'BEGIN {require "Devel/ptkdb.pm";}'
```

On UNIX or Linux using most other shells (sh, ksh, bash), use the command

```
$ PERL5DB='BEGIN {require "Devel/ptkdb.pm";}'
$ export PERL5DB
```

On Microsoft Windows, use the command

```
C:> set PERL5DB='BEGIN {require "Devel/ptkdb.pm";}'
```

Summary

In this chapter, you learned how to shake Perl to get information out of it. This includes not only how to use the perldoc command to find out about all the online documentation but also how to use CPAN to learn about modules and documentation stored in the main Perl archive.

By using modules and exploring the work of other people, you can make your programming job simpler. But you still have to do some programming yourself, so the next few chapters cover how to actually write Perl programs.

Exercises

1. Find out what the built-in function split does.

2. What modules are in the CPAN archive for dealing with dates?

3. Print the documentation for the File::Path module.

Resources

This section presents a list of the various online resources you can access to give you more information about what's been discussed in this chapter.

Online Documentation

- `perldoc perl`—An overview of the various online Perl documents.
- `perldoc CPAN`—The CPAN module, used for installing modules on UNIX and Linux.
- `perldoc PPM`—The Perl Package Manager, used for installation of modules on Microsoft Windows.
- `perldoc pod2html`—The pod2html command turns Perl style documentation into HTML. (This makes it easy to print nice-looking documentation.)
- `perldoc perldebug`—Information on the command-line debugger. This debugger is extremely powerful but somewhat cryptic.
- `perldoc Devel::ptkdb`—Information on the visual debugger. This debugger is simple to use but not all that powerful.

Module Repositories

- `http://cpan.perl.org`—The master Perl module archive. If it's not here, it probably is not published.
- `http://www.activestate.com`—Location of precompiled modules for Microsoft Windows.

Software

- `http://www.gnu.org`—The main web site of the Free Software Foundation. Among other things, you will find a free C compiler for UNIX and Linux called gcc.
- `http://www.gzip.org`—Contains the compression/decompression program gzip.
- `http://www.sfsu.edu/ftp/win/utils`—Location of PowerArc, a powerful compression and archiving program for Microsoft Windows. (This is a free program that provides the same functionality as the programs WinZip or Zip.)

- **http://www.borland.com**—Provides a free version of its C++ compiler and make tool for Microsoft Windows.
- **http://cygwin.com**—Provides a free set of UNIX-like tools for Microsoft Windows.
- **http://www.freshmeat.net**—A database containing information on many of the free software programs available, including many Perl programs.

2

Perl Basics

PERL AND C SHARE A LOT OF the same basic syntax. In this chapter, you learn how to write simple programs starting with, of course, "Hello World." Next you explore the basic Perl statements and operators that have C equivalents.

Finally, the chapter covers some simple I/O. When you have completed this chapter, you'll know enough to write some basic Perl programs. You won't know enough to solve all the world's problems, but you will know enough to get yourself in trouble.

Writing Your First Perl Program

This chapter starts with the Perl version of "Hello World." The program is fairly simple, yet it introduces some basic elements of Perl (see Listing 2.1).

Listing 2.1   *hello.pl*

```
use strict;
use warnings;

print "Hello World\n";
```

The first line,

```
use strict;
```

tells Perl to turn on strict syntax and variable checking. This line should begin every program you write. Without it, Perl relaxes the syntax rules and lets you do things you really shouldn't. (More on this later.)

The second line

```
use warnings;
```

turns on additional compile time and runtime warnings. These diagnostics can be very useful in spotting problems in your code.

The warnings directive is relatively new in Perl. If you are using an earlier version of Perl (pre-5.6.0), this directive won't work. You'll get an error: "Can't locate warnings.pm in @INC...". (To find out which version of Perl you are running, execute the command perl -v.) If that happens, upgrade your version of Perl or omit this directive.

Finally, you come to the heart of the program:

```
print "Hello World\n";
```

This prints the message

```
Hello World
```

Running a Perl Script as a Standalone Command

Frequently, you'll see Perl programs beginning with a line that looks something like:

```
#!/usr/bin/perl
```

This is actually not part of the Perl program itself, but a "magic string" that is used to turn this Perl script into something that can be executed as a standalone command. Because this string is highly installation dependent, it is not discussed here. Instead you'll find full details in Appendix B, "Turning Perl Scripts into Commands."

To run this program, use the command

```
perl hello.pl
```

If you are using an old version (pre 5.6) of Perl and want to turn on warnings, use the command

```
perl -w hello.pl
```

Now that you've gotten a Perl program to run, you can add on to this basic knowledge by adding in variables and expressions.

Variable Declarations and Simple Expressions

You start your exploration of Perl by looking at simple, single-value variables. Next you use these variables in some basic expressions. Almost all the concepts discussed here have equivalents in C, so learning them should not be too difficult.

Variables

Unlike most other languages, Perl doesn't have different variable types. There is only one type of data in Perl: the string. Perl lets you use numbers, but as far as Perl is concerned what you really have is a string of digits. Want to deal with characters? Then you're dealing with one-character strings. Want to handle binary? Then you're dealing with a string of 1s and 0s.

To declare a variable in Perl, use the directive `my`:

```
my $size = 42;      # The size of the box in inches
```

Take a close look at this statement. The statement begins with the keyword `my` indicating a local variable declaration. (You learn about global variables in Chapter 7, "Subroutines and Modules.") The name of the variable is `$size`. The dollar sign ($) indicates that this is a scalar variable. In other words, it holds a single value.

This statement initializes the value of the variable to 42. Because Perl is a string-oriented language, this is actually a two-character string. In fact, you could have written the statement as

```
my $size = "42";     # The size of the box in inches
```

Finally there is a comment. In Perl, comments begin with a hash mark (#) and continue to the end of the line.

If you do not initialize a variable, it is assigned the special value `undef`. This value is different from the empty string (`""`). If you try to use an initialized variable for comparison, printing, or arithmetic, Perl issues a warning (of course the warning is only issued if you turned on warnings with the `use warnings` statement or the -w flag). For example:

```
Use of uninitialized value at <file> line <line>.
```

Now see how you can use variable declarations in a simple program. On the weekends, I'm a real engineer at the Poway-Midland Railroad. A co-worker asked me how much power the locomotive produced. Listing 2.2 is a Perl program that answers this question.

The steam engine has 16-inch cylinders and operates at 120PSI.

Listing 2.2   *steam.pl*

```perl
use strict;
use warnings;

my $cylinder = 16;    # Cylinder size is 16 inches (diameter)
my $pressure = 120;   # Operating pressure in PSI

# Pressure at the cross head using the famous  pi r <squared>
my $effort = 3.14159 * ($cylinder / 2.0) ** 2;

print "Total pressure on the cylinder $effort\n";
```

This program introduces a couple of things. First is the exponent operator
(**).

Second, when Perl sees a string enclosed in double quotes ("), it interprets
any variables it finds in it. So when you tell Perl to print the answer, it looks
through the string for any dollar signs. If it sees any, it performs variable substi-
tution. If you want to put a dollar sign ($) inside a print statement, you need
to escape it. For example:

```perl
print "Total cost \$5,000\n";
```

prints

```
Total cost $5,000
```

Declare a Variable Anywhere

Perl lets you declare a variable anywhere. The scope of the variable is from the point it is declared
to the end of the file. If the variable is declared inside a curly bracket block ({}), the scope of the
variable ends at the end of the block.

Common Mistake: Using printf

Perl has both a print function, which prints strings, and a printf function, which acts very much
like the C printf function.

One common mistake made by most C programs is to over use the Perl printf statement. For
example:

```perl
printf "Total pressure on the cylinder %f\n", $effort;
```

Although this statement works, it's inefficient and not as clear as writing

```perl
print "Total pressure on the cylinder $effort\n";
```

continues

The problem with `printf` is that the function must interpret the string looking for format characters and converting the arguments to formatted text. This is a slow process.

Use `printf` only where you need precise control over the formatting of the variables—for example, if you are printing a check register and the columns must line up:

```
printf "%3d: %-20s %5.2f\n", $sequence, $description, $amount;
```

Simple Arithmetic and String Operators

Perl and C share a common set of operators. All the C arithmetic operators do the same thing in Perl. These operators include the following:

+ Addition

- Subtraction

* Multiplication

/ Division

% Modulo

<< Left Shift

>> Right Shift

++ Increment

-- Decrement

¦ Bitwise or

& Bitwise and

^ Bitwise exclusive or

~ Bitwise not (invert)

?: Conditional

In addition, Perl has a few new operators that C does not. These are

. String concatenation

```
my $full_name = $first . " " . $last; # See note below
```

** Exponentiation

```
my $gross = 12**2
```

x Repeat (Repeats a string a given number of times)

```
my $no = "no " x 3;
print "$no\n";      # prints "no no no"
```

The expression:

```
my $full_name = $first "" $last;
```

uses explicit concatenation to create the result. It's much simpler to use the string interpretation method described in the next section.

So when it comes to arithmetic, Perl is not that much different from C. However, Perl's power comes from what it can do with strings, as you'll see in later chapters.

Quoting Rules

There's one type of expression that you haven't learned about yet—the expressions evaluated when a string is interpreted. For example, the statement

```
my $full_name = "$first $last";
```

actually has a couple of implied concatenation operations. In this case, the system concatenates the variable $first, a space, and the variable $last together and assigns the result to $full_name.

A number of characters have special meaning inside double quotes ("). These are the scalar variable names, which begin with $, array names, which begin with @ (more on this in Chapter 3, "Arrays"), and escape sequences, which start with \.

For example:

```
my $size = 42;          # Size of a dimension
my $name = "width";     # Name of the dimension
my $title = "$name\t$size";
```

In this case, the value of $title is assigned the following value:

```
width<tab>42
```

But what happens if you want to put text after a variable name? Suppose that you want to say "42inches" rather than just "42." You can't write the expression as

```
my $title = "$name\t$sizeinches";
```

This won't work because Perl looks for a variable called $sizeinches. The solution is to separate the variable from the rest of the string by enclosing the name in curly brackets ({}) as follows:

```
my $title = "$name\t${size}inches";
```

If you don't want Perl to interpolate your strings, use single quotes ('). The only things that Perl considers special inside single quotes are the escape characters \' and \\.

For example:

```
print 'The amount is 800   ($HK) 100 ($US) \n';
```

> **Warning**
> The previous example contains an error: The author expected the escape \n to print a newline.
> Because Perl does not interpret things inside single quotes (except \' and \\), \n does not print new-
> line. Instead it prints "backslash n."

Numeric Constants

Perl lets you define numbers using the same syntax rules as C. Octal numbers begin with "0", hexadecimal numbers with "0x", and floating point numbers use a decimal point, or the "E" notation (for example, 1E33). Hexadecimal numbers begin with a zero and a lowercase x. The prefix 0X does not signify a hexadecimal number.

Perl does allow you to use the underscore in numbers if you want. For example:

```
my $cost = 1_333_832;     # Something costs a lot
```

Now that you've got variables, constants, and expressions down, you can look at I/O and control statements.

Reading Input

You can read input from the "standard in" using the following statement:

```
$variable = <STDIN>;
```

This reads an entire line, up to and including the newline (just like the C fgets function).

Listing 2.3 shows an example.

Listing 2.3   *name1.pl*

```
use strict;
use warnings;
my $name;                            # Name of the user
print "Enter name: ";
$name = <STDIN>;
print "Hello $name. How are you?\n";  # Send name to STDOUT
```

The output of this program looks like this:

```
Enter name: Steve
Hello Steve
. How are you?
```

The problem is that when you read the name, you get "Steve\n", instead of "Steve". That's because the statement

```
$name = <STDIN>;
```

reads everything you type and puts it in $name—everything! If you type "Steve<Enter>", that's what gets put in $name. In Perl terms, the variable $name has the value "Steve\n".

But what you really want is "Steve", so you need to strip off the last character. This problem is so common that Perl has a special function called chomp whose job is to strip newlines off the ends of strings.

Listing 2.4 shows the program revised to make it work properly.

Listing 2.4   *name2.pl*

```
use strict;
use warnings;
my $name;          # Name of the user
print "Enter name: ";

$name = <STDIN>;
chomp($name);

print "Hello $name. How are you?\n";
```

The *if* Statement and Relational Operators

The if/else statement looks pretty much like the C version of the if/else statement:

```
if (condition) {
    # body of the if
}
```

and

```
if (condition) {
    # body of the if
} else {
    # body of the else
}
```

The expression must be enclosed in (), and most of the relational operators are the same. About the only difference is that fact that the curly braces are required. In other words, the following is illegal:

```
if ($size == 20)
    print "Size is 20\n";    # Illegal -- no {}
```

The *elsif* Statement

The `elsif` statement is a shorthand for "else if." For example:

```
if ($size == 1) {
    # operators running when $size is equal to 1
} elsif ($size == -1) {
    # operators running when $size is equal to -1
} elsif ($size == 0) {
    # operators running when $size is equal to 0
} else {
    die("Illegal size value");
}
```

The `die` function prints an error message and aborts the program.

Conditional Operators

Perl has a rich set of conditional operators. In fact, there are two major sets of operators—one for numbers and one for strings. Table 2.1 lists the simple relational operators.

Table 2.1   **Simple Relational Operators**

Numeric	String	Meaning
==	eq	Equal
!=	ne	Not equal
<	lt	Less than
<=	le	Less than equal
>	gt	Greater than
>=	ge	Greater than or equal

The string version of the operators compares two strings much like the C function `strcmp`. The numeric version of the operators compares two values as if they were numbers.

Listing 2.5 shows how this works.

Listing 2.5   *cond.pl*

```
use strict;
use warnings;

if ("19" <= "101") {        # TRUE (numeric compare)
    print "19 <= 101\n";
}
```

continues

Listing 2.5 **Continued**

```
if ("19" le "101") {        # FALSE (string compare)
    print "19 le 101\n"
}

if ("able" eq "baker") {    # FALSE (string compare)
    print "able eq baker\n";
}

if ("able" == "baker") {    # TRUE (numeric compare),
                            # but warning issued
    print "able == baker\n";
}
```

The last if deserves a closer examination. The problem is that it uses the numeric version of the equality operator (==) rather than the string version (eq). The result is that "able" is converted to a number. The result of this conversion is 0. (That's because Perl looks at the first character. It's not a digit, so Perl does the best it can and returns the number 0.) Similarly "baker" goes through a similar conversion, and the result is 0. Because 0 == 0, the conditional is true.

So you have to worry not only about the old C problem of = versus ==, but also about the Perl problem of == versus eq.

This is one place where turning on warnings helps you discover problems in the code. Normally, Perl silently converts non-numeric values such as "able" into numbers. With warnings turned on, this sort of conversion results in a warning message being issued:

```
Argument "able" isn't numeric in eq at <file> line <line>.
```

Comparison Operators

The operator <=> (numeric) and cmp (string) return −1 if the first value is less than the second, 0 if they are equal, and 1 if the first value is bigger.

Common Mistake: = Versus ==

In C programming, one of the most common mistakes that new programmers make is using = rather than ==. Perl lets you make the same mistake. The following code is supposed to check whether $answer is 55, but it doesn't:

```
if ($answer = 55)        # WRONG
```

Instead, the code assigns $answer the value 55 and then checks the result to see whether it's true. The proper way to do this test is

```
if ($answer == 55)        # RIGHT
```

To novice programmers it may seem like I'm over emphasizing the = versus == problem. However, I can assure you that if you haven't made this mistake, you will. (Experienced programmers will read this, chuckle, and say, "Been there. Done that!")

Common Mistake: Using == for Strings

As mentioned previously, C programmers are used to using == to check whether two values are equal. For example:

```
if ("Sam" == "Joe") {    # WRONG
```

However, Perl has two equal operators—string equal (eq) and numeric equal (==). The preceding example uses numeric equal. When "Sam" is converted to a number, the result is 0. The same thing happens when "Joe" is converted. Because 0 == 0, the comparison is true.

When two strings are compared, you need to use the string equal operator (eq):

```
if ("Sam" eq "Joe") {    # RIGHT
```

The *defined* Function

The defined function tests to see whether a variable has a value. Listing 2.6 shows an example.

Listing 2.6   *define.pl*

```
use strict;
use warnings;

my $name = "Sam";    # A defined variable
my $value;           # A undefined variable

if (defined($name)) {
    print "The name is defined as $name\n";
}

if (not defined($value)) {
    print "but the value is not defined\n";
}
```

Normally, a variable becomes defined when you assign it a value. You can make it undefined by setting it to the special value undef:

```
use strict;
use warnings;
my $name = "Sam";      # $name is defined
```

```
$name = undef;              # $name is now undefined

if (not defined($name)) {
    print "No name is defined\n";
}
```

An alternative way of undefining a variable is to call the undef function:

```
undef($name);
```

or

```
undef $name;
```

> **Common Mistake: Using undef as a Function**
>
> In the following code fragment, the programmer wanted to print a message if the variable is unde-
> fined. But he made a mistake:
>
> ```
> if (undef($value)) {      # ERROR here
>     print "Value is not defined\n";
> }
> ```
>
> This does not work because the undef function does not test the value of the variable for unde-
> fined. Instead it sets the value of the variable to undefined and returns undefined in the process.
>
> The correct way to check whether a variable is not defined is to use the following code:
>
> ```
> if (not defined($value)) {      # This works
>     print "Value is not defined\n";
> }
> ```

The Definition of Truth

Perl has an unusual definition of what's true and what's not:

- An undefined variable is false.
- An empty string is false as well.
- The value "0" is false. (Exact match!)
- Anything else (a non-empty string or a number that's not zero) is true.

For example, the values undef, "0", and "" are false. The values "sam", "1", and
"55" are true.

> **String "00"**
>
> One of the more unusual true values is the string "00". Take a look at how Perl treats this value:
>
> 1. Is it undefined? If it is, it's false. Not undefined.
>
> 2. Is it the empty string? If it is, it's false. Not the empty string.
>
> 3. Is it the same as the string "0"? If it is, it's false. Because "0" is not equal to "00", it's not the same as "0".
>
> 4. Then it must be true.
>
> This string is defined, not empty, and not the string "0," so it is true.

> **What Is Truth Anyway?**
>
> For a long time, people have been searching for the meaning of truth. However the legal profession has created a precise definition of this philosophical term.
>
> "Truth is anything the judge says it is. An absolute truth is anything 5 out of 9 Supreme Court Justices agree upon."

Simple Dividing Program

Listing 2.7 contains a program that divides two numbers. To make sure that nothing goes wrong, a check is provided to make sure that you don't divide by zero.

One problem with this program is that it doesn't check the input to make sure that it's numeric. The technique for doing this is covered later in Chapter 4, "Regular Expressions."

Listing 2.7   *divide.pl*

```
# Divided one number by another
use strict;
use warnings;

print "Enter a number: ";
my $num1 = <STDIN>;
chomp($num1);

print "Enter a second number: ";
my $num2 = <STDIN>;
chomp($num2);

# We should check $num1 and $num2 to make sure that
# they were numeric.  We'll learn how in a later
# chapter.
```

continues

Listing 2.7   **Continued**

```
if ($num2 == 0) {
    print "ERROR: Can't divide by zero\n";
} else {
    my $result = $num1 / $num2;
    print "$num1 / $num2 = $result\n";
}
```

Looping Statements

Perl has a `while` statement that's very similar to C's. The basic syntax is

```
while (condition) {
    # Body of the loop which is executed when "condition" is true
}
```

The `last` statement exits a loop, much like a C `break` statement. For example, Listing 2.8 computes the square of the first 10 integers.

Listing 2.8   *square.pl*

```
use strict;
use warnings;

my $number = 1;    # The number we are looking at
my $square;        # The square of the number

while (1) {
    $square = $number ** 2;
    print "$number squared is $square\n";
    ++$number;
    if ($number > 10) {
        last;
    }
}
```

To start a loop over, use the `next` statement. This is the equivalent of the C statement `continue`.

The *for* Statement

The `for` statement in Perl works much like the C version. It has three parts: an initialization statement, a limit expression, and an increment statement. Listing 2.9 shows an example.

Listing 2.9 *square.pl*

```
use strict;
use warnings;

my $number;
my $square;

for ($number = 0; $number <= 10; $number++) {
    $square = $number ** 2;
    print "$number squared is $square\n";
}
```

Simple I/O

This section shows you how to do simple I/O. In Chapter 9, "Advanced I/O," you learn how to do more complex I/O. In this section, you learn how to read and write files, thus unlocking a whole new set of programming possibilities.

Reading Files

To open a file for reading, use the open function. For example, to open the file data.txt use the statement

```
open IN_FILE, "<data.txt";
```

This statement opens a file named data.txt for reading and associates it with the file variable IN_FILE. The "<" is a special character that indicates that you want to read this file.

The open function returns true if the open worked, and undef if it did not. You can check the result using an if statement:

```
if (not (open IN_FILE, "<data.txt")) {
    print "Error: Could not open data.txt\n";
    exit (8);
}
```

The more typical Perl approach is to use the following statement:

```
open IN_FILE, "<data.txt" or die("Could not open data.txt");
```

The open function attempts to open the file. If it is successful, it returns true, and the rest of the or statement is not evaluated. If it returns false, the statement after the or is executed. This is a die call which aborts the program with a nice error message.

You already know how to read the file `<STDIN>`. Reading the file `<IN_FILE>` is done the same way:

```
$line = <IN_FILE>;
```

If there is no more data to read, `<IN_FILE>` returns `undef`. So to check for the end of file, use the statement

```
if (not defined($line)) {
    # EOF reached
```

When you're finished with the file, close it using the following statement:

```
close (IN_FILE);
```

Common Mistake: Failing to chomp

The following program is supposed to read in a series of numbers, stopping when it sees a blank line. Or at least that's what it's supposed to do. But for some reason, it never exits the loop.

It has been confirmed that there is a blank line in the data file, so what's wrong? Here is the program:

```
use strict;
use warnings;

my $number;

open IN_FILE, "<data.txt" or
  die("Could not open data.txt
for reading");
while (1) {
    $number = <IN_FILE>;
    if ($number eq "") {
        last;
    }
    # ... do something with the number
}
```

Remember that when the program reads a line, the entire line, including the newline, is read in as well. Thus when the program sees an empty line, the value of $number is "\n", not the empty string "".

You need to put in a chomp function to trim the newline from the end of line:

```
    $number = <IN_FILE>;
    chomp($number);
```

In fact, unless you really know what you are doing, it's a good idea to put a chomp after each input statement. It's a nice habit to get into.

Writing a File

To open a file for writing, use the output redirect operator (">"). For example, to open `ppp.log` for writing, use the statement

```
open OUT_FILE, ">ppp.log" or die("Could not create ppp.log");
```

Writing to a file is done with the `print` statement. For example:

```
print OUT_FILE "Starting Log File";
```

Note that there is no comma after the filename.

Copying a File

Listing 2.10 contains a program that copies a file called `in_file.txt` to `out_file.txt`.

Listing 2.10   *copy.pl*

```
use strict;
use warnings;

open IN_FILE, "<in_file.txt" or die("Could not open in_file.txt");
open OUT_FILE, ">out_file.txt" or
  die("Could not create
out_file.txt");

my $line;

while (1) {
    $line = <IN_FILE>;
    if (not defined($line)) {
        last;
    }
    print OUT_FILE $line;
}
close (IN_FILE);
close (OUT_FILE);
```

Summary

In this chapter, you learned about simple variables and basic control structures. This gives you the ability to write simple programs. The next few chapters build on this basic framework and unlock the real power of Perl.

Exercises

1. Write a program to compute the area of a triangle.
2. Create a program that reads in a first name and a last name and outputs the name in the form "Last, First."
3. Read in a set of numbers and average them.
4. Given a series of numbers, write a program that prints the largest and smallest values.
5. Write a four-function calculator. This program takes an operator (one line of input) and a value (another line) and outputs a result. Hint: Use the string equality operator; check for the entered operator. A simple run is shown here:

```
Zero now is in stack

Enter operator: +
Enter value: 100
Result: 100

Enter operator: *
Enter value: 2
Result: 200

Enter operator: /
Enter value: 4
Result: 50
```

Resources

Online Documentation

- **perldoc -f chomp**—Information on the chomp function.
- **perldoc -f undef**—How undef works.
- **perldoc -f defined**—Information on the defined test operator.
- **perldoc perlsyn**—Basic syntax information.
- **perldoc perlop**—Information on the Perl operators.
- **perldoc perlopentut**—A tutorial on how to use simple I/O.

3

Arrays

Now that you've mastered simple scalars, you can go on and group data together in arrays. Perl's arrays are both simple and complex. Perl makes arrays simple because it automatically handles all the memory allocation associated with arrays. Thus you don't have to worry about making sure that the dimensions are right.

The complexity comes from the rich set of operators that you can use to manipulate arrays. These provide considerable power when it comes to array handling.

Basic Arrays

In Perl, all array variable names begin with @. For example:

```
my @list;   # An array of numbers
```

You can declare and initialize the array in one step:

```
my @list = ("Sam", "Joe", "Fred", "Sue");      # An array of names
```

Perl uses zero-based indexing just like C, but with a slight twist. The elements of the array are not

```
@list[0], @list[1], @list[2], @list[3]    # Not!
```

Instead, they are

```
$list[0], $list[1], $list[2], $list[3]
```

There is a good, if somewhat obscure, reason for this. Anything that begins with a dollar sign ("$") results in a scalar. Anything that begins with an at sign ("@") is an array. Finally, as you learn later, anything beginning with a percent sign ("%") is something called a *hash*.

Because you are dealing with an array of strings (strings are scalars), you need to put the "$" in front of any element reference. As you'll see in Chapter 6, "Hashes, References, and Complex Data Structures," if you have an array of arrays, then you put a "@" in front of an element reference.

> **Scalars ($) and Arrays (@) have Different Namespaces**
>
> The scalar namespace is kept separate from the array namespace. Thus it is possible to have an array called @list and a scalar called $list. (In terms of style, this is really stupid.)
>
> It is possible to have code like the following:
>
> ```
> # Please don't name things like this
> my $foo = 1;    # A scalar
> my @foo = (10, 20, 30); # An array
> print "Scalar is $foo\n";
> print "First element of the array is $foo[0]\n";
> ```
>
> However, it's not good programming practice to name two variables by the same name even if they do differ by a prefix.
>
> Array elements can be used just like any ordinary scalar:
>
> ```
> my $average = ($list[0] + $list[1] + $list[2] + $list[3]) / 4;
> ```

Finally, elements can even be printed using an ordinary print statement:

```
print "The first element is $list[0]\n";
```

Determining the Number of Elements in an Array

The special variable name $#array returns the index of the last element of the array. In other words, it returns the number of elements in the array minus 1.

For example, the following code prints all the elements of an array:

```
my @array = (1, 2, 3, 4);
for (my $index = 0; $index <= $#array; $index++) {
    print "array[$index] = $array[$index]\n";
}
```

This program outputs the following:

```
array[0] = 1
array[1] = 2
array[2] = 3
array[3] = 4
```

Notice that the whole expression $array[$index] is interpreted even though it's inside a string.

Common Mistake: Using C Style Iteration

C programmers use the following code to iterate over an array:

```
// C Code
#define ARRAY_SIZE 3
int array[ARRAY_SIZE] = {1, 3, 5};
// ...
    for (int i = 0; i < ARRAY_SIZE; i++)
        printf("array[%d] = %d\n", i, array[i]);
```

The key item in this example is the conditional (i < ARRAY_SIZE). Most C programmers are used to using the less than sign (<) in this context.

This doesn't work in Perl. Perl uses the less than or equal (<=) conditional. If you use the wrong conditional, you omit the last element:

```
# We mistakenly use the C style conditional
for (my $index = 0; $index < $#array; $index++) {
    print "array[$index] = $array[$index]\n";
}
```

Common Mistake: Assuming that (*$#array == 0*) Means an Empty Array

Remember that the expression $#array returns the index of the last element of the array. For a one-element array, $#array returns 0. An empty array causes $#array to yield –1.

Array Example

Listing 3.1 contains a program that finds the largest and smallest element in an array.

Listing 3.1   *array.pl*

```
use strict;
use warnings;

# Array to examine
my @array = (45, 98, 20, 12, 83, 64, 98, 33, 99);
```

continues

Listing 3.1   **Continued**

```
my $biggest;   # Biggest element in the array
my $smallest;  # Smallest element in the array

# Assume that the first element is the biggest / smallest
$biggest = $array[0];
$smallest = $array[0];

# Loop through the rest of the elements of the array
# checking for the biggest and smallest
for (my $index = 1; $index <= $#array; $index++) {
    if ($array[$index] > $biggest) {
        $biggest = $array[$index];
    }
    if ($array[$index] < $smallest) {
        $smallest = $array[$index];
    }
}
print "Biggest is $biggest, smallest $smallest\n";
```

Array Expressions

Elements of an array can be assigned and used just like ordinary scalars. But you can assign a value to the entire array at one time by using an array expression.

An *array expression* is just a list of scalars enclosed in parentheses. For example:

```
@array = (1, $data, "sam");
```

An array expression also can consist of a single array:

```
@array_dest = @array_source;
```

You can combine scalars with arrays. The following expression adds two elements ($prefix1 and $prefix2) to an array (@message) and assigns the resulting array to @full_message:

```
@full_message = ($prefix1, $prefix2, @message);
```

Printing Arrays

You can print arrays the same way that you print scalar variables. For example:

```
my @array = ("Tom", "Dick", "Harry");
print "The names are: @array.\n";
```

This prints the following:

```
The names are: Tom Dick Harry.
```

Arrays with Holes in Them

Consider the following code:

```
my @array = (1);
$array[5] = 4;
```

You know that `$array[0]` is 1 and that `$array[5]` is 4. But what about elements 1, 2, 3, and 4? Perl fills in the "hole" in the array with undefined values. So the elements of the `@array` are `(1, undef, undef, undef, undef, 4)`.

The Quote Word (*qw*) Operator

A previous example initialized an array with a set of strings using the following statement:

```
my @array = ("Tom", "Dick", "Harry");
```

You can simplify this with the qw operator. (qw stands for "quote words.") The same statement using this notation looks like

```
my @array = qw(Tom Dick Harry);
```

Common Mistake: Commas in *qw* List

Notice that the words for the qw operator are not separated by commas. If you put commas in, they become part of the word. For example, the statement

```
my @words = qw(alpha, beta, gamma);
```

assigns the element `$words[0]` the value "alpha," (comma included), the second element gets "beta," and so on.

This error is so common, that when warnings are enabled (use warnings;), Perl issues a warning if your qw list contains commas.

Manipulating the Array Ends

Listing 3.2 shows a program that reads a list of numbers from the user and creates an array out of them.

Listing 3.2   *read1.pl*

```
# Note: This program is inefficient
use strict;
use warnings;

my @array = ();    # The list of numbers we have read

while (1) {
```

continues

Listing 3.2 **Continued**

```
    print "Input number or <Enter> to finish: ";
    my $answer = <STDIN>;
    chomp($answer);

    if ($answer eq "") {
        last;
    }
    @array = (@array, $answer);
}
```

The problem is the following line:

```
@array = (@array, $answer);
```

This takes the array @array and the scalar $answer and combines them into an array expression. This array expression is then assigned to @array. Because you are computing a new array and doing an entire replacement, this is inefficient.

A more efficient way of doing things is to use the Perl push function. It adds an element on to the end of an array. So you can replace the array assignment statement with a push statement:

```
push(@array, $answer);
```

The pop function is the opposite of push. It takes the last element off the list and returns its value. For example:

```
@array = (1, 3);
push(@array, 5);            # @array is now (1, 3, 5)
my $element = pop(@array);
#  @array is now (1, 3)
#  $element is $5
```

If you want to remove an element from the *start* of an array, use the shift operator. For example:

```
my @array = (1, 2, 3);
while ($#array >= 0)
{
    my $first = shift @array;
    print "$first ";
}
print "\n";
```

This program prints "1 2 3".

The unshift function is the opposite of shift. It adds an element on to the beginning of an array:

```
my @array = (5, 7);
unshift(@array, 9);
print "@array\n";
```

This code prints "9 5 7".

Figure 3.1 illustrates how the functions push, pop, shift, and unshift work.

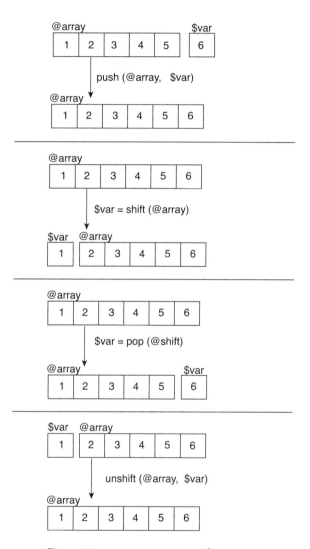

Figure 3.1 push, pop, shift, and unshift.

> **Naming Schemes**
>
> The names push, pop, shift, and unshift may seem like an unusual collection of words to use
> for array manipulation. These names have a bit of history behind them. The push and pop opera-
> tors come from the classical terms used for stack manipulation.
>
> The term shift comes from shell programming. Perl borrows much of its syntax from the UNIX
> Bourne shell and its successor the Korn shell and the Bourne Again shell.
>
> As for unshift, it seems the obvious choice for the name of something that's the reverse of shift.

Dealing with Parts of an Array

Perl contains a wealth of features that let you deal with part of an array. For
example, Perl lets you index an array not only with a single index, but also
with a set of indices. To make this specification easier, the range operator (..)
can be used to specify a whole set of indices.

The splice function lets you extract or replace a whole set of values
within an array.

Using a Set of Indices

You know that the notation @array is used to specify an entire array, and the
expression $array[$index] specifies a single value.

You can specify a set of indices separated by commas. For example:

```
my @new_array = @array[1,3,5]
```

The following expression swaps the first two elements of an array:

```
@array[1,0] = @array[1, 0];
```

Here's another example, where you set the first and last elements of an array
to −1:

```
@array[0, $#array] = (-1, -1);
```

The Range Operator

Suppose that you want to assign something to the first three elements of an
array without changing the rest of the array. One way to do this is to use the
comma (,) operator:

```
@array[0,1,2] = (0, 0, 0);
```

But suppose that you want to zero the first 10 elements. You could write out
all the numbers from 0 to 9, or you could use the range operator to specify a
range of values:

```
@array[0..9] = ((0) x 10);
```

(You can also use the x operator to repeat the 0 ten times.)

The *splice* Function

The `splice` function allows you to remove or replace part of an array. The simplest form of this function looks like the following:

```
splice @array, $offset;
```

This deletes the elements in the array starting at *offset* and going to the end of the array.

For example:

```
my @array = (0, 1, 2, 3, 4, 5);
splice(@array, 3);
print "@array\n";
```

This prints "0 1 2" (elements from 3 on removed). If the *offset* is negative, the number of elements is counted from the end of the array rather than the start. For example, if you apply the following to the original array

```
splice(@array, -2);
```

you get "0 1 2 3" (two elements dropped from the end).

The *splice* Function's Return Value

The `splice` function returns different things depending on whether it's used in the array context or the scalar context. *Array context* means that the result is assigned to an array, or the function is used in a place where you would expect an array. Similarly, a *scalar context* is where the result is assigned to a scalar or used as if it were a scalar.

When used in the array context, the `splice` function returns the elements deleted. For example:

```
my @array = (0, 1, 2, 3, 4, 5);
my @result = splice(@array, 3);    # Array context
print "@result\n";
```

This prints the removed elements "3 4 5".

In the scalar context, it returns the last element removed. For example:

```
my @array = (0, 1, 2, 3, 4, 5);
my $result = splice(@array, 3);    # Array context
print "$result\n";
```

Because three elements were removed, this prints "5".

Additional *splice* Arguments

By default, `splice` deletes all the elements from the `offset` to the end of the array. The `splice` function allows you to supply an additional argument, `length`, which tells `splice` how many elements to delete:

```
@new_array = splice @array, $offset, $length
```

For example:

```
my @array = (0, 1, 2, 3, 4, 5);
splice(@array, 3, 2);
print "@array\n";
```

This example deletes two elements starting with the third element and prints "0 1 2 5".

Finally, `splice` lets you supply a set of elements to be inserted into the array at `offset`:

```
@new_array = splice @array, $offset, $length, REPLACEMENTS
```

(`REPLACEMENTS` can be a list of scalars or an array expression.)

For example, replace one element of an array with a new value:

```
my @array = (0, 1, 2, 3, 4, 5);
splice(@array, 3, 0, "sam", "joe", "mac");
print "@array\n";
```

This command goes to element #3 (`offset`), deletes one element (`length`), and inserts three new elements ("sam", "joe", and "mac") before element #3. The result is

```
0 1 sam joe mac 4 5
```

This example uses three scalars as replacement elements. You could just as easily have used an array or array expression:

```
my @new_stuff = qw(sam joe max);
splice(@array, 3, 0, @new_stuff);
```

Figure 3.2 illustrates how the various forms of `splice` work.

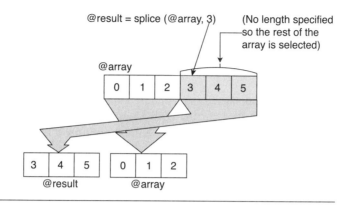

@result = splice (@array, 3)   (No length specified so the rest of the array is selected)

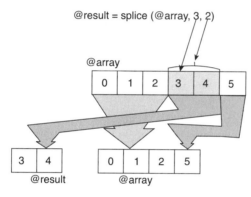

@result = splice (@array, 3, 2)

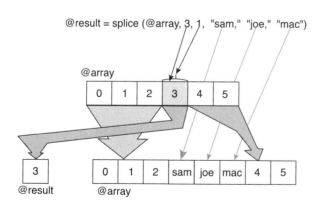

@result = splice (@array, 3, 1, "sam," "joe," "mac")

Figure 3.2   The splice function.

The *split* and *join* Functions

The split function is one of the most useful functions in Perl. It splits up a string and turns it into an array. This makes it extremely useful when it comes to parsing things such as Excel export files, UNIX or Linux configuration files, or other similar text files.

For example, suppose that you have an inventory data file where the colon (:) separates each record. A typical entry might look like the following:

```
#10 screws:1000:500:Universal Screw Company
```

(This record has a listing for #10 screws. Currently 1000 are in stock. When the number reaches 500, you'll reorder more from the Universal Screw Company.)

Now turn this record into an array. You do this by using the split function:

```
@array = split /:/, $record;
```

The first argument to the split function tells it what delimiter to use to split the string. This case uses a colon (/:/). The second argument is the string to be split. In this case, it's the database record.

The first argument is enclosed in slashes (/) because it is a regular expression. (See Chapter 4, "Regular Expressions," for a more detailed explanation of it.)

Balancing a Checkbook

Suppose that you want to balance your checkbook. The checking information is kept in a file. Each line is a single check record consisting of a date, whom the check was made out to, and an amount. The fields are separated by a tab.

The program must read in this data and produce a report. Listing 3.3 contains the program.

Listing 3.3   *check.pl*

```
use strict;
use warnings;

my $total = 0;    # Current running total of all the checks

while (1) {
    my $line = <STDIN>;

    # STDIN may be redirected, check for EOF
    if (not defined($line)) {
        last;
    }
```

```
    # Check for end of input
    chomp($line);

    if ($line eq "") {
        last;
    }

    my @check_info = split /\t/, $line;
    # $check_info[0] = Date
    # $check_info[1] = Description
    # $check_info[2] = Amount
    $total += $check_info[2];
    printf "%-8s: %-20s %6.2f  Total: %5.2f\n",
        $check_info[0], $check_info[1], $check_info[2], $total;
}
```

Note that when an end of file is detected on the standard input, when you do a read:

```
    my $line = <STDIN>;
```

the result ($line) is undefined.

A typical input file might look like this:

```
01/01/01--->Rent Payment ---->500.00
01/01/01--->Car Payment ----->$86.29
01/08/01--->Grocery store---->$26.95
01/15/01--->Dog Groomer------>$19.95
```

(---> denotes a tab.)

When you run this program, you must redirect the standard input to the data file. A typical run looks like:

```
$ perl check.pl <check.txt
01/01/01: Rent Payment          500.00  Total: 500.00
01/01/01: Car Payment            86.29  Total: 586.29
01/08/01: Grocery store          26.95  Total: 613.24
01/15/01: Dog Groomer            19.95  Total: 633.19
```

Common *split* Expressions

Some common split expressions are listed in Table 3.1.

Table 3.1 **Common *split* Expressions**

Expression	Explanation
/\t/	Tab separated (One of Excel's export format.)
/ +/	One or more spaces

continues

Table 3.1   **Continued**

/\s+/	One or more whitespaces—that is, spaces or tabs
/,/	Comma
/,\s*/	Comma, which may be followed by zero or more whitespaces
/\n/	Newline (Useful when your string contains a bunch of lines and you want to separate it into an array of individual lines.)

Common Programming Mistake: split /\s*/

Many people wrongly use the regular expression /\s*/ to split up a line where the fields are separated by spaces (\s in Perl terms). For example, the code in Listing 3.4 is designed to split a full name into the first name and the last name:

Listing 3.4   *name.pl*

```perl
use strict;
use warnings;
my $full_name = "Steve Oualline";

my @name = split /\s*/, $full_name;  # WRONG WRONG

for (my $index = 0; $index <= $#name; $index++) {
    print "$index: $name[$index]\n";
}
```

The regular expression /\s*/ tells split to split the line where a whitespace character (\s) occurs zero or more times (*). The key word here is "zero." If you look at the string "Steve Oualline", there are zero spaces between the "S" and "t" of "Steve". The split function sees that. It matches the delimiter specification and splits the "S" off from the "t".

So the result of the split is not

```
0: Steve          # This does not happen
1: Oualline
```

but instead, you get

```
0: S
1: t
2: e
3: v        # And so on
```

If you want to split a space delimited record, use the regular expression /\s+/, which means look for a whitespace character (\s) one or more times (+).

The *join* Function

The `join` function is the reverse of the `split` function. It takes the elements of an array and joins them together. The general form of the `join` function is

```
$result = join ($string, @array);
```

For example, say that you want to write a file that can be imported by Microsoft Excel. The simplest import file is one in which the fields are separated by tabs. So to turn an array into a line that Microsoft Excel can use, you need the Perl statement

```
my $line = join ("\t", @data);
```

Sorting an Array

The `sort` function sorts an array. By default, the `sort` function sorts in ASCII order. For example:

```
my @array = qw(John Mark Ann);
my @sorted = sort @array;
print "@sorted\n";
```

This prints the following:

```
Ann John Mark
```

To sort an array in numerical order, use the statement

```
@result = sort {$a <=> $b}, @unsorted;
```

Note that this code uses an advanced feature of `sort` that is discussed in further detail in Chapter 7, "Subroutines and Modules."

Multiple Dimension Arrays

Perl does not have a multiple dimension array. It can do a pretty good job of faking one through the use of anonymous references. (References are discussed in Chapter 6.)

For example:

```
my @matrix = (
    [ 1,  2,  3],
    [11, 12, 13],
    [21, 22, 23]
);

$matrix[2][2] = "Sam";
```

Notice that square brackets are used ([]) to declare the rows of the matrix.

At this point in the game, you can pretend that Perl has multiple dimension arrays. For almost everything you'll write, Perl does the right thing. But for a more detailed description of what's going on, you have to wait for Chapter 6.

The @ARGV Variable

The special variable @ARGV contains the command-line arguments for the program. For example, if you run a script with the command

```
$ perl doit.pl alpha beta gamma
```

Then

```
$ARGV[0] = "alpha";
$ARGV[1] = "beta";
$ARGV[2] = "gamma";
```

To get the number of arguments, use the notation $#ARGV (there is no argc). Note that unlike in C programming, the first argument is not the name of the program. If you need the name of the program, it's assigned to the variable $0.

The *English* Module

Remembering cryptic names such as $0 may be a little difficult. To make things easier, someone wrote the module English. This module lets you use more descriptive names such as $PROGRAM_NAME. All the special variables (both English and cryptic) are documented in the Perl documentation page perlvar.

Summary

Perl provides all the power of C arrays with none of the headaches. (You don't have to worry about dimensions, going off the end, resizing, and so on.)

But Perl goes far beyond what you can do with C. For example, Perl has array expressions as well as scalar ones. Also there is a rich set of array manipulation functions such as shift, unshift, push, pop, and splice. Thus Perl lets you perform complex array operations with a few simple operators.

Perl also provides a rich set of operations for examination and manipulation of strings as you see in Chapter 4.

Exercises

1. The "hosts" file on most machines consists of a set of lines.

    (The "hosts" file is located in /etc/hosts on UNIX and Linux machines; in C:\WINDOWS\HOSTS on Windows 95 and Windows 98 machines; and in C:\WINDOWS\SYSTEM32\DRIVERS\ETC\HOSTS on Windows NT, 2000, and XP.

You may not find a HOSTS file on all Microsoft Windows machines, but
you will find one on all UNIX and Linux machines. A bit of advice for
Windows users: if you don't manage to locate a HOSTS file, try to find
HOSTS.SAM.)

Each line lists an IP address, a host name, and an optional set of aliases. A
typical hosts file looks like the following:

```
192.168.0.1     www.pfc.com pcf.com
192.168.0.2     micky micky.pfc.com mailhost
192.168.0.3     loghost secure.pcf.com
127.0.0.1       localhost
```

Ignore the fact that a real "hosts" file can have comment lines that begin
with "#".

Write a program that takes as input the "hosts" file and writes out a
report listing each host and its address. For example:

```
www.pfc.com     192.168.0.1
pfc.com         192.168.0.1
micky           192.168.0.2
micky.pfc.com   192.168.0.2
mailhost        192.168.0.2
....
```

For added credit, sort the output.

2. You have a list of bug reports in the following form:

    status<tab>*date-opened*<tab>*description*

    Write a program that reads this list and writes out all the records whose
    status is "OPEN".

    For bonus work, write out only those records that have been open more
    than 45 days. To do this, you have to find a date parsing module on
    CPAN and learn about the built-in function time.

3. A teacher keeps his student data in a simple text file of the following
    form:

    student   grade1 grade2 grade3 ....

    Write a program to produce a grade average. Note: You don't know the
    number of grades ahead of time, but you can assume that all grades are
    listed.

4. Write a program that takes a list of numbers and splits them into two
    lists. The lower half of the numbers goes in one list, and the upper half
    goes in another.

Write a program that reads in a list of scores (all in the range of 0–100). Drop off the top and bottom 5 percent and then compute the median of the remainder.

Note that the median is not the average. It's the value for which half the values are higher, and half are lower.

Resources

This section presents a list of the various online resources you can access to give you more information about what's been discussed in this chapter.

Online Documentation

- `perldoc English`—Documentation on the `English` module.
- `perldoc perlvar`—A list of Perl's built-in variables.
- `perldoc -f join`—Function reference for `join`.
- `perldoc -f splice`—Function reference for `splice`.
- `perldoc -f split`—Function reference for `split`.

Modules

- `English`—Module to provide nice names (understandable) for some cryptic Perl built-in variable names. (Part of the core Perl distribution.)

4

Regular Expressions

THIS CHAPTER EXAMINES ONE OF THE MOST powerful features of Perl—regular expressions. Regular expressions are extremely useful when it comes to examining and manipulating strings.

Basic Regular Expressions

Suppose that you have a configuration file in which any line beginning with # is a comment. You want to read the file and throw away comments. How do you tell which lines are comments?

The answer is to use Perl's regular expression operators. A *regular expression* is a powerful pattern matching tool. It enables you to match, and replace if needed, virtually any text you can imagine. Regular expressions are enclosed in slashes (//). The slashes are similar to the double quotes ("") used for strings. This chapter starts with a simple regular expression and builds up to more complex comment matching ones. The first regular expression is

/#/

This matches any string with a hash character (#) anywhere within the string. For example, it matches

```
# Starts with a hash
There is # in the middle
One at the end #
Two # in the # line
```

but it does not match the string

```
No hash today
```

The operator =~ checks to see whether a string (on the left-hand side) matches a regular expression on the right-hand side. For example, the expression

```
"A # line" =~ /#/
```

evaluates to true. Putting it all together, to check a line to see whether it has a hash mark in it, you need the following expression:

```
if ($line =~ /#/)
```

Listing 4.1 contains a program that checks a set of strings to see whether they are comments.

Listing 4.1   *comment.pl*

```
use strict;
use warnings;

my @strings = (
    "# Starts with a hash",
    "This one's got nothing",
    "There is # in the middle",
    "One at the end #",
    "Two # in the # line",
    "No hash");
my $i;

for ($i = 0; $i <= $#strings; $i++) {
    if ($strings[$i] =~ /#/) {
        print "COMMENT: $strings[$i]\n";
    } else {
        print "CODE:    $strings[$i]\n";
    }
}
```

When run, this program prints

```
COMMENT: # Starts with a hash
CODE:    This one's got nothing
COMMENT: There is # in the middle
COMMENT: One at the end #
COMMENT: Two # in the # line
CODE:    No hash
```

In the regular expression /#/, the # character is called an *atom*. It matches the character "#". Letters and digits are atoms that match themselves. For example, if you want to see whether a line contains the word "Error," you can use the statement

```
if ($line =~ /Error/)
```

Back to the comment eliminator—there's a problem with the code. It matches any line that contains a # anywhere in the line. You want to match only lines that begin with the # character.

For that, you need to tell Perl that the # must appear at the beginning of the line. The ^ character is used to anchor a pattern at the beginning of a line. So /#/ means match # anywhere, and /^#/ means match # only if it occurs at the beginning of a line.

So to check for a comment, you need the statement

```
if ($line =~ /^#/)
```

So this expression will match

```
# This is a test
```

but will not match

```
SRC=ccm.c
    # Indented comment (not caught yet)
A line with a # in the middle
```

But what if you want to check for empty lines as well? The $ character matches the end of a line. So if you want to check for an empty line, use the following statement:

```
if ($line =~ /^$/)
```

This matches any line that has a beginning (^) followed immediately by an ending ($). Because the only way you can have the beginning of the line in the same place as the end is when the line is empty, this matches empty lines.

Vim (Vi Improved) and Regular Expressions

The *Vim* editor (a Vi clone available from `http://www.vim.org`) is extremely useful when it comes to learning regular expressions. When you search in Vim (using the `/`, `?`, or related commands), the search string you specify is a regular expression very similar to the regular expression used by Perl.

Vim has an option called *highlight search*. When you do a search with this option enabled, all matching strings are highlighted. Thus if you don't know exactly what the regular expression `/the+/` will match, you edit the file with Vim, search for "the+", and see what's highlighted.

To turn on the highlight search option, execute the Vim command:

`:set hlsearch`

Modifiers

Suppose that you want to make your comment structure a little more flexible. You want to let the user type a few spaces before the # in a comment. The following lines are all considered comments:

```
#  This is a comment
<space># This is too
<space><space><space># And this is also
```

Note that I've spelled out a space as `<space>` in this example, because real spaces are difficult to see on the page. I mean real spaces.

To match this, you need to tell Perl that a comment has the following characteristics:

- Beginning of line
- Zero or more spaces
- A #

Now to translate these rules into Perl: Rule one is "Beginning of a line." That's "^" in Perl speak.

Zero or more spaces is trickier. A single space is easy to do—that's " ". But you need a modifier to tell Perl that the space can be repeated zero or more times. For that, use the star (*) modifier. So zero or more spaces translates to " *".

Finally, there's the # itself.

So the full regular expression is

```
if ($line =~ /^ *#/)
```

This successfully matches the three comment lines.

Character Sets

One problem with the current approach is that it only takes into account leading spaces. But what happens if someone decides to start a comment line with a <tab>? The regular expression won't work.

You need to tell Perl that a line may start with a combination of spaces or tabs. By enclosing a set of characters in square brackets ([]), you tell Perl to match any one of the enclosed characters. For example, if you want to match a space or tab, use the expression [\t] (\t is the escape sequence for tab).

So the new regular expression is

```
if ($line =~ /^[ \t]*#/)
```

This matches

```
# Hash at the beginning of the line
    # 4 spaces before the hash
        # A tab starts this line
```

This expression is starting to get a little complex. It would be a good idea to comment it. So the expression, including comments looks like the following:

```
#                +---------- Beginning of line (^)
#                |+++++----- Space or tab ( ) and (\t)
#                |||||||+---- Repeated 0 or more times (*)
#                ||||||||+--- The character #
if ($line =~ /^[ \t]*#/)
```

Commenting regular expressions like this serves several purposes. First it helps you organize your thoughts. Thinking about what you are doing can be a big help when creating regular expressions. (It's not a bad lesson for life either!)

But also, it helps you make sure that you include all the elements you expected to. Because of the compact nature of regular expressions, it's easy to leave out something.

Finally, it leaves notes around for the people who come after you and maintain the code. Because regular expressions are both dense and cryptic, these notes will be extremely useful to the poor slob who inherits your code.

More on the Character Set Operator ([])

The character set operator matches any character enclosed in the square brackets ([]). For example, to match the lowercase vowels, you can use the expression /[aeiou]/. Suppose that you want to match the word "the". The regular expression would be /the/. But the word can be capitalized. That means that you want to look for "The" or "the". The regular expression for this is /[tT]he/.

Although this matches "the" or "The", it does not match "THE". For that you need /[tT][hH][eE]/. (Yuck!)

Also you can specify a range of characters. For example, [a-z] matches any single lowercase letter.

Now you'll design a regular expression to see whether a variable contains a number. A number consists of one or more digits. So breaking things down into components, your regular expression is

- ^—Match the start of the line (that way the regular expression won't skip junk at the beginning of the line).
- [0-9]—Match a single digit.
- [0-9]*—Zero or more additional digits.
- $—Match the end of the string. (The number can't have any trailing garbage.)

The regular expression is /^[0-9][0-9]*$/.

So this matches things like

```
0
14
568
333
000
0524
```

but does not match

```
x45       # Does not begin with a digit
45x       # Last digit is not at end of line.
45x45     # Letter in the middle breaks the string of digits.
```

The modifier + acts like the *, only it tells Perl to repeat the previous atom *one* or more times. Thus with a +, your new regular expression is /^[0-9]+$/.

Whitespace (\s)

Back to the comment matching statement—you need to make one final change. Currently, the expression [\t] matches whitespace. It's simpler and easier to use escape code (\s) instead. This is a special regular expression atom that matches one whitespace character. So your final comment matching code looks like the following:

```
#                +------- Beginning of line (^)
#                |++----- Match whitespace
#                |||+---- Repeated 0 or more times
#                ||||+--- The character #
if ($line =~ /^\s*#/)
```

Using Grouping to Split a Line

So far, you've created regular expressions that can determine whether a line is a blank line or a comment line. But what about a line that's half data and half comment? For example:

```
CC = gcc        # Use the gnu compiler
```

Suppose that you want to separate this line into its two components, executable code and a comment. For this you use the grouping operator (parentheses).

First, you want to match the noncomment part of the line. That's everything, up to but not including the #. When a character range begins with a caret (^), it tells Perl to match all the characters except for those in the range. So if you want to match anything except a #, you use the expression [^#].

Similarly, you can use the caret (^) and a range to exclude a range of characters. For example, the expression [^0-9] matches everything *except* a digit.

> ### The Two Meanings of
>
> Note that /^[a-z]/ is different from /[^a-z]/. In fact, the character caret (^) means different things in the two expressions. In the first one, /^[a-z]/, the caret (^) is outside any range specification ([ ]), so it means "start of line." So /^[a-z]/ means "start of line" (^) followed by a lowercase letter ([a-z]).
>
> In the second case, /[^a-z]/, the caret (^) is inside the range specification ([ ]), so it means "anything except the following." So /[^a-z]/ means match a single character that's not a lowercase letter.
>
> The dollar sign ($) has a similar double meaning. Outside a range specification ([ ]), it means "match end of line." Inside it means the literal character dollar sign.

The comment then starts with # and continues on for the end of the line.

To capture the two parts of the line, put parentheses around the first part and another set of parentheses around the second. The data matched by the regular expression contained in the first parentheses will be placed in the special Perl variable $1. The result of the second match will be put in $2.

The following shows how this works:

```
#                    ++++---------- Any character except #
#                    ||||+--------- Repeated 0 or more times (*)
#                    +||||+-------- Put the enclosed in $1
#                     ||||||||
#                     ||||||||
#                     |||||||| #------ The character hash (#)
#                     |||||||| |+----- Any character (.)
#                     |||||||| ||+---- Repeated 0 or more times (*)
#                     |||||||||+|||+--- Put the enclosed in $2
if ($line =~ /([^#]*)(#.*)/) {
    $code = $1;
    $comment = $2;
```

Now see how this operates on your test statement:

```
CC = gcc        # Use the gnu compiler
```

The first part of the regular expression says match everything except a #:

```
[^#]*
```

This matches the underlined part of the line:

```
CC = gcc        # Use the gnu compiler
```

Because this portion of the regular expression is enclosed in the first set of parentheses, the matching string is put in the variable $1. So $1 is now "CC = gcc   ."

The next part of the regular expression tells Perl to match a # (#) followed by any character (.) repeated zero or more times (*), followed by the end of line ($):

```
#.*$
```

The second string is enclosed in the second set of parentheses, so the matching string gets placed inside the variable $2.

```
CC = gcc        # Use the gnu compiler
```

In this case, $2 becomes "# Use the gnu compiler".

Dealing with Alternatives (|) and Limited Matches

Regular expressions work in almost all cases. There is a problem, however, if you have a line like

```
MACRO = "String with # in it"    # Comment
```

In this case, you don't want to break the line at the first # since it's in the middle of a quoted string. So how do you write a regular expression that excludes it?

The solution is to refine the regular expression so that you consider the elements command to be

- Any character other than #
- A quoted string
- Either one, or both repeated zero or more times

This introduces a new operator or (|). This causes Perl to match either one of two different values. The two values in this case are any character other than a # or " ([^#"]) or a quoted string (".*"). Note that you exclude the quotation mark from the first element because it's taken care of in the second.

The new regular expression looks like

```
#                    +----------------------- Match start of line
#                    ¦ +++++----------------- Match all except # or "
#                    ¦ ¦¦¦¦¦+---------------- Repeat 0 or more times (*)
#                    ¦ ¦¦¦¦¦¦
#                    ¦ ¦¦¦¦¦¦
#                    ¦ ¦¦¦¦¦¦¦+-------------- Match either pattern (¦)
#                    ¦ ¦¦¦¦¦¦¦¦
#                    ¦ ¦¦¦¦¦¦¦¦+------------- Match "
#                    ¦ ¦¦¦¦¦¦¦¦¦+------------ Any character (.)
#                    ¦ ¦¦¦¦¦¦¦¦¦¦+----------- Repeat 0 or more times (*)
#                    ¦ ¦¦¦¦¦¦¦¦¦¦¦+---------- Match "
#                    ¦ ¦¦¦¦¦¦¦¦¦¦¦¦
#                    ¦ +¦¦¦¦¦¦¦¦¦¦¦¦+--------- Group the following and
#                    ¦ ¦¦¦¦¦¦¦¦¦¦¦¦¦¦            put into $2
#                    ¦ ¦¦¦¦¦¦¦¦¦¦¦¦¦¦+-------- Repeated 0 or more times (*)
#                    ¦+¦¦¦¦¦¦¦¦¦¦¦¦¦¦¦+-------- Put the encoded in $1
#                    ¦¦¦¦¦¦¦¦¦¦¦¦¦¦¦¦¦
#                    ¦¦¦¦¦¦¦¦¦¦¦¦¦¦¦¦¦ #------ The character hash (#)
#                    ¦¦¦¦¦¦¦¦¦¦¦¦¦¦¦¦¦ ¦+----- Any character (.)
#                    ¦¦¦¦¦¦¦¦¦¦¦¦¦¦¦¦¦ ¦¦+---- Repeated 0 or more times (*)
#                    ¦¦¦¦¦¦¦¦¦¦¦¦¦¦¦¦¦+¦¦¦+--- Put the enclosed in $3
if ($line =~ /^((([^#"]*¦".*")*)(#.*)/)
```

You have to use the grouping operators (()) to get the expression to work. But that causes you to put the statement in $1 and the comment part in $3. You want it in $2, so you have to tell Perl "group these, but don't put the result in a $<number> variable." You do that by changing the grouping operator (...) to (?:....). The result is

```
              +++¦¦¦¦¦¦¦¦¦¦¦¦¦+-------- Group (but no $n placement)
if ($line =~ /^((?:[^#"]*¦".*")*)(#.*)/)
```

But there's still a problem. What happens when you see a line like

```
MACRO = "String"    #  "String" used
```

The regular expression ".*" tries to match as much as possible. The result is that it matches

```
MACRO = "String"    #  "String" used
```

You want it to match only the first part. A solution to this is to follow the star (*) with a question mark (?). The question mark (?) tells Perl to match as little as possible. So the revised expression is

```
              +------------ Match any character (.)
              ¦+----------- repeat 0 or more times (*)
              ¦¦+---------- as little as possible (?)
              ¦¦¦+--------- Match quote (")
if ($line =~ /^((?:[^#"]*¦".*?")*)(#.*)/)
```

This change tells Perl that the string stops when the first double quote (") is seen.

Conditionals

Now add a final refinement to the code. You want to match strings that contain an escaped double quote (\") in them, such as

```
MACRO = "string with \" in it"  # Comment
```

Now when you look for a string, you want to match "all the text from one double quote to another, but don't match double quotes with an escape in front of them."

Fortunately, Perl has a "don't match if" operator. Actually, the Perl term for this is "negative lookbehind assertion."

So your string consists of

- A starting quote (")
- Zero or more inside characters (.*)
- An ending quote (") that works only if
- It is not preceded by a \ (?<!\\)

The updated expression is

```
                        ++--------- Character (\\)
                        ||          (The thing not to match)
                    ++++||+-------- Match next (") if
                    ||||||||        enclosed (\) does not
                    ||||||||        occur here.
                    ||||||||+------ Match double quote (")
                    |||||||||
if( $line =~ /^((?:[^#"]*|".*?(?<!\\)")*)(#.*)/)
```

Now take the revised expression and use it in a program that parses `Makefiles` and parses the lines into their various parts. Listing 4.2 contains the results.

Listing 4.2   *make.pl*

```perl
use strict;
use warnings;

my $line;
while ($line = <STDIN>) {
    # No \n because it's already in $line
    print "Line: $line";

    if ($line =~ /^\s*#/) {
        next;
    }
    #                      +--------------------------------- Match start of line
    #                      |    +++++----------------------- Match all except # or "
    #                      |    ||||||+---------------------- Repeat 0 or more times (*)
    #                      |    ||||||
    #                      |    ||||||
    #                      |    ||||||+--------------------- Match either pattern (¦)
    #                      |    ||||||#
    #                      |    ||||||#+-------------------- Match "
    #                      |    ||||||#¦+------------------- Any character (.)
    #                      |    ||||||#¦¦+------------------ Repeat 0 or more times (*)
    #                      |    ||||||#¦¦¦+----------------- As little as possible (?)
    #                      |    ||||||#¦¦¦¦+++++------------ Lookback conditional
    #                      |    ||||||#¦¦¦¦^¦¦¦¦             Must not be preceded by:
    #                      |    ||||||#¦¦¦¦^¦¦¦¦++---------- The character \
    #                      |    ||||||#¦¦¦¦^¦¦¦¦¦^+--------- Match "
    #                      |    ||||||#¦¦¦¦^¦¦¦¦¦^¦
    #                      | +++¦||||||#¦¦¦¦^¦¦¦¦¦^¦+-------- Group the following but
    #                      | |||||||||#¦¦¦¦^¦¦¦¦¦^¦|         put do not put into $n ( (?: )
    #                      | |||||||||#¦¦¦¦^¦¦¦¦¦^¦|+------- Repeated 0 or more times (*)
    #                      |+||||||||#¦¦¦¦^¦¦¦¦¦^¦||+------ Put the enclosed in $1
    #                      |^||||||||#¦¦¦¦^¦¦¦¦¦^¦||
    #                      |^||||||||#¦¦¦¦^¦¦¦¦¦^¦||^ +----- The character hash (#)
    #                      |^||||||||#¦¦¦¦^¦¦¦¦¦^¦||^ |+---- Any character (.)
    #                      |^||||||||#¦¦¦¦^¦¦¦¦¦^¦||^ ||+--- Repeated 0 or more times (*)
    #                      |^||||||||#¦¦¦¦^¦¦¦¦¦^¦||^+|||+-- Put the enclosed in $3
    elsif ($line =~ /^((?:[^#"]*¦".*?(?<!\\)")*)(#.*)/) {
        print "Type: Command with Comment\n";
        print "Command: $1\n";
        print "Comment: $2\n";
    } else {
        print "Type: Command only\n";
    }
    print "\n";
}
```

It's interesting to note that this example has 24 lines of comments for one line of code. When you deal with something as compact and as powerful as regular expressions, comments like this occur.

The designers of Perl recognized that complex regular expressions can be difficult to explain, so they added a feature that allows you to comment them. The x modifier tells Perl to ignore spaces (escaped spaces are still valid) and to allow comments beginning with #.

To turn an ordinary regular expression into an extended one, you need to escape any space or # characters. The first # occurs in a character range ([^#"]), so it does not have to be escaped. The second one, in the #.* subexpression, does. So the new regular expression is

```
if( $line =~ /^((?:[^#"]*¦".*?(?<!\\)")*)(\#.*)/x )
```

Now you can add comments and whitespace to make the thing clearer:

```
if( $line =~
    /^                      # Match beginning of the line
      (                     # Put enclosed in $1
         (?:                # Group the enclosed expression
             [^#"] # A series of characters excluding # and "
                   # (i.e. everything except a comment or
                   # string)
           *       # Repeated zero or more times
           ¦       # command *OR* string
           "       # String, starts with "
           .       # Match any character (inside string)
           *?      # Zero or more times, but as
                   # little as possible.
           (?<!    # Don't match if the next quote
                   # is preceded by a
                \\ # Backslash
           )       # End negative assertion
           "       # Quote (string end)
                   # Must not have \ in front of it
         )         # End of command or string
         *         # Repeat expression 0 or more times
      )            # End of $1 (command part)

      (            # Put enclosed in $2
         \#        # Begin with #
         .*        # Any charter zero or more times
      )            # End of $2
    /x )           # Allow comments in the regular expression
```

Now are these 29 lines of comment regular expression easier to read than the line regular expression with its 24 lines of comments? Not that much really. It seems that no matter how you arrange a mess, it still looks like a mess.

Probably the only major advantage of the extended version of the regular expression is the fact that to comment it, you didn't have to draw all those vertical bars (¦).

Common Mistake: Putting / in a Regular Expression Comment

Take a look at the following extended regular expression:

```
if ($line =~ /
    \/\/          # C / C++ Single line comment Start
    .*            # Goes to the end of line
    /x )          # End of extended regular expression
```

At first glance, everything looks okay. The regular expression begins with / and ends with /x, so it is an extended regular expression. But there's a problem.

When Perl sees this, it doesn't know it's an extended regular expression, so it parses things until it finds the end of the expression. The first slash is the slash in the comment:

```
\/\/          # C / C++ Single line comment Start
```

Perl sees this and, because it doesn't know that this is an extended regular expression yet, concludes that the / in "C / C++" is the end of an ordinary regular expression.

For this reason, you can't use / in a regular expression comment.

Using the Regular Expression Debugging Package

Regular expressions use a code all their own. This makes them tricky to write and debug. However, you can use a few tricks to make your life easier.

First, the best way of debugging a regular expression is to avoid making a mistake in the first place. This is difficult, especially for a novice, but if you design and comment your regular expressions, you'll reduce errors before you even start.

But in spite of how clever or careful you are, some errors will get through. In that case, you can use Perl's regular expression debugging module. Regular expression debugging is turned on with the line

```
use re 'debug';
```

It is turned off with the statement

```
no re 'debug';
```

When debug is turned on, Perl outputs some debugging messages whenever a regular expression is compiled. Take a look at how this works with a simple regular expression /#/. The result of the compilation is

```
Compiling REx `#'
size 3 first at 1
   1: EXACT <#>(3)
   3: END(0)
anchored `#' at 0 (checking anchored isall) minlen 1
```

The first line tells you what is being compiled. The second tells you how large the compiled result is and which node starts the expression (in this case #1).

The next two lines are the parsed version of the regular expression. Each line consists of a single element of the expression called a node. In this case, the expression consists of two nodes, an exact match for the character # and the end of the expression:

```
1: EXACT <#>(3)
3: END(0)
```

The number at the beginning of each line is an identification number. The number at the end of each line indicates the next node to be evaluated. This is usually the next node for simple regular expressions, but things can jump around if you have moderately complex code.

Finally, one final line displays optimizer information:

```
anchored `#' at 0 (checking anchored isall) minlen 1
```

This line can safely be ignored.

But the compilation of a regular expression is only part of the job. Perl also must perform matches. With debugging enabled, you can watch the progress of matching the string `# Starts with a hash`. For example, the first comparison results in

```
Guessing start of match, REx `#' against `# Starts with a hash'...
Found anchored substr `#' at offset 0...
Guessed: match at offset 0
```

In this example, the optimizer guessed that the string matches the regular expression at offset 0. (In other words, the thing figured out that the first character of `# Starts with a hash` is `#`.) Now you go from the simple to the complex. Take a look at what happens when you turn on debugging for the `make` regular expression in Listing 4.2. The result of the compilation can be seen in the following debug output:

```
Compiling REx `^((?:[^#"]*¦".*?(?<!\\)")*)(#.*)'
size 44 first at 2
   1: BOL(2)
   2: OPEN1(4)
   4:   CURLYX {0,32767}(33)
   6:     BRANCH(17)
   7:       STAR(32)
   8:         ANYOF[\0-!$-\377](0)
  17:     BRANCH(31)
  18:       EXACT <">(20)
  20:       MINMOD(21)
  21:       STAR(23)
  22:         REG_ANY(0)
```

```
23:        UNLESSM[-1](29)
25:          EXACT <\>(27)
27:          SUCCEED(0)
28:          TAIL(29)
29:        EXACT <">(32)
31:      TAIL(32)
32:      WHILEM[1/1](0)
33:    NOTHING(34)
34: CLOSE1(36)
36: OPEN2(38)
38:    EXACT <#>(40)
40:    STAR(42)
41:      REG_ANY(0)
42: CLOSE2(44)
44: END(0)
floating `#' at 0..2147483647 (checking floating) anchored(BOL) minlen 1
```

Take a look at what each of these nodes means.

This line

```
1: BOL(2)
```

matches the beginning of the line. (This is generated by the ^ character.)

The next line

```
2: OPEN1(4)
```

opens (OPEN) group 1.

The following line repeats what follows 0 to 32767 times:

```
4:    CURLYX {0,32767}(33)
```

Note that 33 is the next token. That means that the CURLYX matches up to the NOTHING node at 33. So what the CURLYX applies to is the (?:[^#"]*|".*?(?<!\\)") part of the regular expression. (Note: The CURLYX is generated because of the * at the end of this expression. Although * means 0 to infinity, Perl translates this into 0 to 32767.)

This line indicates that you can make a choice:

```
6:    BRANCH(17)
```

You can choose this branch or the selection that starts at node #17.

These lines

```
7:        STAR(32)
8:          ANYOF[\0-!$-\377](0)
```

are Perl's way of saying [^#]*. The ANYOF indicates a match of any of the selected characters. Perl takes the exclude specification ([^#]) and turns it into an include specification ([\0-!$-\377]) that includes everything but #. This is modified by the STAR (*) specification

You may wonder why the next node after the STAR is #32. That's because it's the end of the alternate branch starting at node #17.

In line 17

```
17:      BRANCH(31)
```

again you have a new branch that might be taken. This one includes all the nodes from 17 to 29 (the node before 31).

In this branch

```
18:      EXACT <">(20)
```

you are looking for a double quote (").

This line

```
20:      MINMOD(21)
```

indicates that the next set of operators is to match as little as possible (triggered by the *? operator).

The following two lines

```
21:      STAR(23)
22:        REG_ANY(0)
```

show the parsed version of .*—anything (REG_ANY), repeated zero or more times (STAR).

These lines

```
23:      UNLESSM[-1](29)
25:        EXACT <\>(27)
```

are the negative assertion (?<!\\), which tells Perl to fail the following (EXACT <\>) matches.

If it doesn't fail, this portion of the expression succeeds:

```
27:      SUCCEED(0)
```

This is a nop:

```
28:      TAIL(29)
```

It's inserted to allow people from outside a place to branch into the function (for example, node 17).

This is an exact character match:

```
29:      EXACT <">(32)
```

This line is another node used as a branch destination:

```
31:      TAIL(32)
```

These lines

```
32:      WHILEM[1/1](0)
33:    NOTHING(34)
```

perform curly brace matching (WHILEM) if the rest matches (NOTHING). This defines an anchor point for the expression.

This line

```
34: CLOSE1(36)
```

closes the $1 processing.

This line starts the $2 processing:

```
36: OPEN2(38)
```

The expression for $2 starts with a #:

```
38:   EXACT <#>(40)
```

Then a series of any characters (REG_ANY) zero or more times (STAR):

```
40:   STAR(42)
41:     REG_ANY(0)
```

This line closes $2:

```
42: CLOSE2(44)
```

This line is the end:

```
44: END(0)
```

Tracking the Execution of the Match

Now look at what happens when you try the following string against the big regular expression in Listing 4.2:

```
CC = gcc   # Code and comment
```

First, the optimizer tries a few guesses. Because # is key to this regular expression, it first sees whether it can find it, and it does. It then sees whether the first part (CC = gcc) matches the first part of the regular expression. For example:

```
Guessing start of match, REx `^((?:[^#"]*¦".*?(?<!\\)")*)(#.*)' against `CC =
⇒gcc   # Code and comment\n'...
Found floating substr `#' at offset 11...
Guessed: match at offset 0
Matching REx `^((?:[^#"]*¦".*?(?<!\\)")*)(#.*)' against `CC =
⇒gcc   # Code and comment\n'
```

The system now parses the first part of the expression:

```
Setting an EVAL scope, savestack=15
 0 <> <CC = gcc   #>  ¦  1:  BOL
 0 <> <CC = gcc   #>  ¦  2:  OPEN1
 0 <> <CC = gcc   #>  ¦  4:  CURLYX {0,32767}
 0 <> <CC = gcc   #>  ¦ 32:    WHILEM[1/1]
                         0 out of 0..32767  cc=7b0419c0
```

At this point, the system sees the ¦ symbol and realizes that it has two different possible options, so it saves its current location and tries the first branch:

```
Setting an EVAL scope, savestack=24
  0 <> <CC = gcc   #>   ¦  6:         BRANCH
Setting an EVAL scope, savestack=24
```

Now it tries to match using the regular expression [^#]*:

```
  0 <> <CC = gcc   #>   ¦  7:             STAR
  ANYOF[\0-!$-\377] can match 11 times out of 32767...
```

Turns out that this matches 11 characters. But you're not finished. If the other match is longer, it will win, so Perl needs to evaluate it too:

```
Setting an EVAL scope, savestack=24
 11 <cc   > <# Code >   ¦ 32:          WHILEM[1/1]
                             1 out of 0..32767  cc=7b0419c0
```

The second branch starts here:

```
Setting an EVAL scope, savestack=33
 11 <cc   > <# Code >   ¦  6:             BRANCH
Setting an EVAL scope, savestack=33
 11 <cc   > <# Code >   ¦  7:             STAR
  ANYOF[\0-!$-\377] can match 0 times out of 32767...
```

The preceding doesn't match anything. Then it proceeds on:

```
Setting an EVAL scope, savestack=33
 11 <cc   > <# Code >   ¦ 32:          WHILEM[1/1]
 2 out of 0..32767  cc=7b0419c0
 empty match detected,try continuation...
```

So the match fails. But the first branch succeeded, so clean up and use that one to determine what portion matches:

```
 11 <cc   > <# Code >   ¦ 33:             NOTHING
 11 <cc   > <# Code >   ¦ 34:             CLOSE1
```

Now take care of the second part of the regular expression, which matches from the # to the end:

```
 11 <cc   > <# Code >   ¦ 36:             OPEN2
 11 <cc   > <# Code >   ¦ 38:             EXACT <#>
 12 <c  #> < Code a>    ¦ 40:             STAR
                        REG_ANY can match 17 times out of 32767...
```

Finally, with a little more cleanup, you're finished:

```
Setting an EVAL scope, savestack=33
 29 <and comment> <\n>   ¦ 42:             CLOSE2
 29 <and comment> <\n>   ¦ 44:             END
  Match successful!
```

So the string matches.

Debug Summary

Regular expressions are complex and tricky. The debug output is supposed to
make things better, but it can itself sometimes be just as difficult to read as the
expression it's trying to clarify.

A full discussion of the debug output for regular expressions can be found
in the online document `perldoc perldebguts`.

For those of you who want to see the regular expression matching system
working really hard, the following listing contains the output of the program
dissecting a line that contains not only a quoted string but also one with a \"
in it.

Those of you who really want to get into the true guts of the regular
expression parser can go through this listing as it goes through many different
branches and backtrack while parsing this string.

```
QSTR = "Str with \" quote" # Quoted string

Guessing start of match, REx `^((?:[^#"]*|".*?(?<!\\)")*)(#.*)'
➥against `QSTR = "Str with \" quote" # Quoted string\n'...
Found floating substr `#' at offset 27...
Guessed: match at offset 0
Matching REx `^((?:[^#"]*|".*?(?<!\\)")*)(#.*)' against `QSTR =
➥"Str with \" quote" # Quoted string\n'
  Setting an EVAL scope, savestack=15
  0 <> <QSTR = "Str >   |  1:   BOL
  0 <> <QSTR = "Str >   |  2:   OPEN1
  0 <> <QSTR = "Str >   |  4:   CURLYX {0,32767}
  0 <> <QSTR = "Str >   | 32:     WHILEM[1/1]
                        0 out of 0..32767  cc=7b0419c0
  Setting an EVAL scope, savestack=24
  0 <> <QSTR = "Str >   |  6:       BRANCH
  Setting an EVAL scope, savestack=24
  0 <> <QSTR = "Str >   |  7:         STAR
  ANYOF[\0-!$-\377] can match 7 times out of 32767...
  Setting an EVAL scope, savestack=24 <"Str wi>   | 32:          WHILEM[1/1]
                        1 out of 0..32767  cc=7b0419c0
  Setting an EVAL scope, savestack=33
  7 <TR = > <"Str wi>   |  6:           BRANCH
  Setting an EVAL scope, savestack=33
  7 <TR = > <"Str wi>   |  7:             STAR
  ANYOF[\0-!$-\377] can match 0 times out of 32767...
  Setting an EVAL scope, savestack=33
  7 <TR = > <"Str wi>   | 32:             WHILEM[1/1]
  2 out of 0..32767  cc=7b0419c0
  empty match detected, try continuation...
  7 <TR = > <"Str wi>   | 33:             NOTHING
  7 <TR = > <"Str wi>   | 34:             CLOSE1
  7 <TR = > <"Str wi>   | 36:             OPEN2
  7 <TR = > <"Str wi>   | 38:             EXACT <#>
```

```
                                              failed...
                                              failed...
                                              failed...
    7 <TR = > <"Str wi>    ¦ 18:                  EXACT <">
    8 <R = "> <Str wit>    ¦ 20:                  MINMOD
    8 <R = "> <Str wit>    ¦ 21:                  STAR
Setting an EVAL scope, savestack=33
    8 <R = "> <Str wit>    ¦ 23:              UNLESSM[-1]
    7 <TR = > <"Str wi>    ¦ 25:                  EXACT <\>
                                              failed...
    8 <R = "> <Str wit>    ¦ 29:                  EXACT <">
                                              failed...
                              REG_ANY can match 1 times out of 1...
    9 < = "S> <tr with>    ¦ 23:              UNLESSM[-1]
    8 <R = "> <Str wit>    ¦ 25:                  EXACT <\>
                                              failed...
    9 < = "S> <tr with>    ¦ 29:                  EXACT <">
                                              failed...
                              REG_ANY can match 1 times out of 1...
   10 <= "St> <r with >    ¦ 23:              UNLESSM[-1]
    9 < = "S> <tr with>    ¦ 25:                  EXACT <\>
                                              failed...
   10 <= "St> <r with >    ¦ 29:                  EXACT <">
                                              failed...
                              REG_ANY can match 1 times out of 1...
   11 < "Str> < with \>    ¦ 23:              UNLESSM[-1]
   10 <= "St> <r with >    ¦ 25:                  EXACT <\>
                                              failed...
   11 < "Str> < with \>    ¦ 29:                  EXACT <">
                                              failed...
                              REG_ANY can match 1 times out of 1...
   12 <"Str > <with \">    ¦ 23:              UNLESSM[-1]
   11 < "Str> < with \>    ¦ 25:                  EXACT <\>
                                              failed...
   12 <"Str > <with \">    ¦ 29:                  EXACT <">
                                              failed...
                              REG_ANY can match 1 times out of 1...
   13 <Str w> <ith \" >    ¦ 23:              UNLESSM[-1]
   12 <"Str > <with \">    ¦ 25:                  EXACT <\>
                                              failed...
   13 <Str w> <ith \" >    ¦ 29:                  EXACT <">
                                              failed...
                              REG_ANY can match 1 times out of 1...
   14 <tr wi> <th \" q>    ¦ 23:              UNLESSM[-1]
   13 <Str w> <ith \" >    ¦ 25:                  EXACT <\>
                                              failed...
   14 <tr wi> <th \" q>    ¦ 29:                  EXACT <">
                                              failed...
                              REG_ANY can match 1 times out of 1...
   15 <r wit> <h \" qu>    ¦ 23:              UNLESSM[-1]
   14 <tr wi> <th \" q>    ¦ 25:                  EXACT <\>
                                              failed...
```

```
15 <r wit> <h \" qu>     ¦ 29:                  EXACT <">
                                               failed...
                         REG_ANY can match 1 times out of 1...
16 < with> < \" quo>     ¦ 23:                  UNLESSM[-1]
15 <r wit> <h \" qu>     ¦ 25:                  EXACT <\>
                                               failed...
16 < with> < \" quo>     ¦ 29:                  EXACT <">
                                               failed...
                         REG_ANY can match 1 times out of 1...
17 <with > <\" quot>     ¦ 23:                  UNLESSM[-1]
16 < with> < \" quo>     ¦ 25:                  EXACT <\>
                                               failed...
17 <with > <\" quot>     ¦ 29:                  EXACT <">
                                               failed...
                         REG_ANY can match 1 times out of 1...
18 <ith \> <" quote>     ¦ 23:                  UNLESSM[-1]
17 <with > <\" quot>     ¦ 25:                  EXACT <\>
18 <ith \> <" quote>     ¦ 27:                  SUCCEED
                                               could match...
                                               failed...
                         REG_ANY can match 1 times out of 1...
19 <th \"> < quote">     ¦ 23:                  UNLESSM[-1]
18 <ith \> <" quote>     ¦ 25:                  EXACT <\>
                                               failed...
19 <th \"> < quote">     ¦ 29:                  EXACT <">
                                               failed...
                         REG_ANY can match 1 times out of 1...
20 <h \" > <quote" >     ¦ 23:                  UNLESSM[-1]
19 <th \"> < quote">     ¦ 25:                  EXACT <\>
                                               failed...
20 <h \" > <quote" >     ¦ 29:                  EXACT <">
                                               failed...
                         REG_ANY can match 1 times out of 1...
21 < \" q> <uote" #>     ¦ 23:                  UNLESSM[-1]
20 <h \" > <quote" >     ¦ 25:                  EXACT <\>
                                               failed...
21 < \" q> <uote" #>     ¦ 29:                  EXACT <">
                                               failed...
                         REG_ANY can match 1 times out of 1...
22 <\" qu> <ote" # >     ¦ 23:                  UNLESSM[-1]
21 < \" q> <uote" #>     ¦ 25:                  EXACT <\>
                                               failed...
22 <\" qu> <ote" # >     ¦ 29:                  EXACT <">
                                               failed...
                         REG_ANY can match 1 times out of 1...
23 <" quo> <te" # Q>     ¦ 23:                  UNLESSM[-1]
22 <\" qu> <ote" # >     ¦ 25:                  EXACT <\>
                                               failed...
23 <" quo> <te" # Q>     ¦ 29:                  EXACT <">
                                               failed...
                         REG_ANY can match 1 times out of 1...
24 < quot> <e" # Qu>     ¦ 23:                  UNLESSM[-1]
23 <" quo> <te" # Q>     ¦ 25:                  EXACT <\>
                                               failed...
```

```
24 < quot> <e" # Qu>      ¦ 29:                    EXACT <">
                                               failed...
                          REG_ANY can match 1 times out of 1...
25 <quote> <" # Quo>      ¦ 23:                    UNLESSM[-1]
24 < quot> <e" # Qu>      ¦ 25:                    EXACT <\>
                                               failed...
25 <quote> <" # Quo>      ¦ 29:                    EXACT <">
26 <uote"> < # Quot>      ¦ 32:                    WHILEM[1/1]
                                  2 out of 0..32767   cc=7b0419c0
Setting an EVAL scope, savestack=46
26 <uote"> < # Quot>      ¦  6:                    BRANCH
Setting an EVAL scope, savestack=46
26 <uote"> < # Quot>      ¦  7:                    STAR
                          ANYOF[\0-!$-\377] can match 1 times
⇥out of 32767...
Setting an EVAL scope, savestack=46
27 <ote" > <# Quote>      ¦ 32:                    WHILEM[1/1]
                                  3 out of 0..32767

Setting an EVAL scope, savestack=59
27 <ote" > <# Quote>      ¦  6:                    BRANCH
Setting an EVAL scope, savestack=59
27 <ote" > <# Quote>      ¦  7:                    STAR
                          ANYOF[\0-!$-\377] can match 0 times
⇥out of 32767...
Setting an EVAL scope, savestack=59
27 <ote" > <# Quote>      ¦ 32:                    WHILEM[1/1]
                                  4 out of 0..32767

⇥cc=7b0419c0

                                              empty match detected,
⇥try continuation...
27 <ote" > <# Quote>      ¦ 33:                    NOTHING
27 <ote" > <# Quote>      ¦ 34:                    CLOSE1
27 <ote" > <# Quote>      ¦ 36:                    OPEN2
27 <ote" > <# Quote>      ¦ 38:                    EXACT <#>
28 <te" #> < Quoted>      ¦ 40:                    STAR
                          REG_ANY can match 14 times out of 32767...
Setting an EVAL scope, savestack=59
42 <uoted string> <\n>    ¦ 42:                    CLOSE2
42 <uoted string> <\n>    ¦ 44:                    END
Match successful!
```

Regular Expression Element Summary

In this section, you saw how to use all the different elements of a regular expression, including the following:

- **Atoms**—These can be simple things such as letters, digits, and other single charters, or they can be a character range such as [A-Z] or [AEIOU].

  They can also be any other regular expression that has been turned into a group by () or related operators.

- **Ranges**—A range is a set of charters enclosed in [ ].

- **Anchors**—Anchors serve to position a pattern on the line. You've used the beginning of line (^) anchor to make sure that your regular expression is at the right place. Other anchors include things such as the end of line ($) and word boundaries (\B).

- **Modifiers**—Modifiers tell Perl how many of an item to expect. You used the * (zero or more times) modifier extensively in this example. Another common modifier is +, which stands for "one or more times."

- **Grouping**—Grouping occurs when you want to split a line and get the result in the $n Perl variables.

- **Conditionals**—Conditionals give Perl a "match if" capability. You used one to "match # if it's not escaped" ((?<!\\)#).

By putting together all these elements, you can easily build up a very powerful string-matching capability.

Regular Expression Construction

You should remember a few things when you create regular expressions:

- **Start slowly**—Regular expressions are complex and tricky. Start with something simple and build on it later.

- **One step at a time**—Because one character out of place in a regular expression can change the whole meaning of the operation, you should build slowly on what works to make sure that what you are doing is right.

- **Test often**—What you think you've written and what you really wrote can easily be different. Make sure that you check things out carefully at each stage of the construction. (Vim is extremely helpful when it comes to verifying regular expressions.)

- **Comment verbosely**—Every character in a regular expression has its own meaning. It was put there for a purpose. When you construct it, write down the purpose by sticking it in a comment. It's easy for even the programmer who wrote it to forget why a regular expression was constructed the way it was, so write down everything and stick that information in the comments. The programmer's life you save may be your own.

- **Check the documentation regularly**—A ton of things can go into a regular expression. To make sure that you are using the right ones, and to make sure that you aren't missing things, check out the online documentation (perlre) regularly. There may be something inside that will surprise you.

Finally, now is a good time to take a break and depressurize. You've probably never had such a concentrated session of powerful and cryptic syntax thrown at you at one time. Take a break, let the concepts settle in a little, and continue after a cup of coffee.

Substitutions

At one job site where I worked, I encountered a number of problems caused by improperly formatted `Makefiles`. The problems were caused by

- **Lines that began with eight spaces rather than a tab**—The `make` program is picky about this and insists on a tab.
- **Lines that ended in a continuation character (\) followed by whitespace**—This means that although the line looked like it was continued, it wasn't.

To get things working, I turned to Perl to solve the problem by writing a `Makefile` fixing script.

The script read the `Makefile` one line at time and wrote out a corrected `Makefile`. I then used the Perl `s//<flag>` operator to perform a substitute edit on the line.

The general form of it is

```
$line =~ s/<old>/<new>/<flag>;
```

where `<old>` is the text to replace, `<new>` is what to replace it with, and `<flags>` are flags affecting the replacement. One of the most common flags is g, which tells Perl to perform the replacement as many times as possible. (The default is to replace only once.) Another common flag is i, which tells Perl to ignore case when performing the match.

So to correct a line that begins with eight spaces, use the command

```
$line =~ s/^        /\t/;
```

Note that if the line does not begin with eight spaces, it remains unchanged.

In this expression, the ^ anchors the expression to the beginning of the line.

To correct the other problem, (whitespace after a continuation character), you need the following command:

```
#                       Change
#           ++---------- The character backslash
#           ||++-------- Any whitespace character (\s)
#           ||||+------- Repeat one or more times
#           |||||                to
#           ||||| ++--- The character backslash
$line =~ s/\\\s+/\\/;
```

Listing 4.3 contains the full `Makefile` fixing program.

Listing 4.3 *fix_make.pl*

```
use strict;
use warning;

while (1) {
    my $line = <STDIN>;
    if (not defined($line)) {
        last;
    }
    chomp $line;

    $line =~ s/^        /\t/;
    $line =~ s/\\\s*/\\/;

    print "$line\n";
}
```

The *grep* Function

The `grep` function searches through a list of strings and returns an array of the strings that match a regular expression. (UNIX users will notice that this function works very much like the system `grep` command. Microsoft Windows users will find that it works like a very souped-up `FIND` command.)

The general form of the function is

```
grep /expression/, list
```

where `/expression/` is the regular expression to check, and `list` is a list of strings to examine.

For example, if you want to find any lines with the word "TODO:" in them, you can use the statement:

```
my @todo_lines = grep /TODO:/, @file_lines;
```

Summary

This chapter covered one of the most powerful features of Perl—regular expressions. As you can see from the examples in this chapter, regular expressions allow you to do some very sophisticated examination and manipulation of strings. This is, again, part of the strength of Perl as a language.

Exercises

1. Write a script to take a list of names in the format

    `last, first`

    and write it out as

    `first last`

2. Write a script that searches a file for lines that contain an error message. You can assume that all error messages begin with the string "`Error:`".

3. The last line of a typical United States postal address is of the form

    `City, State zip`

    Note that the state can be a two-letter abbreviation, or a full state name. The ZIP Code can be nine digits or ZIP+4 (that is, 92126-1234).

    Write a program that splits these fields apart and prints them individually.

4. A bug reporting system contains a status log line. The status log line contains an entry for each change made to the bug report. A typical entry looks like

    ```
    OPENED by sdo on 19-Aug-00, VERIFIED by khou on 30-Aug-00,
    ASSIGNED by fred on 31-Aug-00, FIXED by arun on 01-Sep-00,
    TESTED by james on 01-Sep-00, CLOSED by ckunard on 02-Sep-00
    ```

    Note that this is all one big, ugly line.

    Although this entry contains every possible status, some bugs may contain fewer entries. For example:

    ```
    OPENED by sdo on 19-Aug-00
    ```

    Write a program that goes through a status log and determines whether any entries have been CLOSED without being TESTED.

    Bonus: Download one of the date parsing modules from CPAN and use it to determine the number of days between the time a report is opened until the time it is closed.

5. (UNIX/Linux only): Write a program that reads the file `/etc/password` into an array. It then lets the user type in a username and displays the full name for that user.

6. The following is the file from a web server:

```
213.243.150.121 - - [17/Feb/2002:04:17:39 -0800] "GET /vim-cook.html
➥HTTP/1.1" 200 34154
213.243.150.121 - - [17/Feb/2002:04:17:40 -0800]
➥"GET /favicon.ico HTTP/1.1" 404 217
213.243.150.121 - - [17/Feb/2002:04:18:16 -0800]
➥"GET /favicon.ico HTTP/1.1" 404 217
213.243.150.121 - - [17/Feb/2002:04:19:45 -0800]
➥"GET /favicon.ico HTTP/1.1" 404 217
151.38.61.85 - - [17/Feb/2002:04:20:48 -0800] "GET
/default.ida?NNNNNNNNNNNNNNNNNNNNNNNNNNNNNNNNNNNNNNNNNNNNNNNNNNNNNNNNNNNNN
➥NNNNNNNNNNNNNNNNNNNNNNNNNNNNNNNNNNNNNNNNNNNNNNNNNNNNNNNNNNNNNNNNNNNNNNNNN
➥NNNNNNNNNNNNNNNNNNNNNNNNNNNNNNNNNNNNNNNNNNNNNNNNNNNNNNNNNNNNNNNNNNNNNNNNN
➥NNNNNNNNNNNNNNNN%u9090%u6858%ucbd3%u7801%u9090%u6858%ucbd3%u7801%u9090%u
➥6858%ucbd3%u7801%u9090%u9090%u8190%u00c3%u0003%u8b00%u531b%u53ff%u0078%u
➥0000%u00=a  HTTP/1.0" 404 205
64.152.75.64 - - [17/Feb/2002:04:44:22 -0800]
➥"GET /robots.txt HTTP/1.0" 200 27
64.152.75.64 - - [17/Feb/2002:04:44:23 -0800]
➥"GET /col/vote.html HTTP/1.0" 200 3847
64.152.75.121 - - [22/Feb/2002:17:11:04 -0800]
➥"GET /10/.vimrc HTTP/1.0" 200 519
63.224.129.221 - - [22/Feb/2002:17:14:39 -0800]
➥"GET / HTTP/1.0" 200 3329
204.210.62.170 - - [22/Feb/2002:17:15:21 -0800]
➥"GET /scripts/root.exe?/c+dir HTTP/1.0" 404 210
204.210.62.170 - - [22/Feb/2002:17:15:25 -0800]
➥"GET /MSADC/root.exe?/c+dir HTTP/1.0" 404 208
204.210.62.170 - - [22/Feb/2002:17:15:28 -0800]
➥"GET /c/winnt/system32/cmd.exe?/c+dir HTTP/1.0"
➥404 218
204.210.62.170 - - [22/Feb/2002:17:15:31 -0800]
➥"GET /d/winnt/system32/cmd.exe?/c+dir HTTP/1.0"
➥404 218
204.210.62.170 - - [22/Feb/2002:17:15:42 -0800] "GET
➥/scripts/..%255c../winnt/system32/cmd.exe?/c+dir HTTP/1.0" 404 232
204.210.62.170 - - [22/Feb/2002:17:15:54 -0800] "GET
➥/_vti_bin/..%255c../..%255c../..%255c../winnt/system32/cmd.exe?/
➥c+dir HTTP/1.0" 404 249
204.210.62.170 - - [22/Feb/2002:17:15:57 -0800] "GET
➥/_mem_bin/..%255c../..%255c../..%255c../winnt/system32/cmd.exe?/
➥c+dir HTTP/1.0" 404 249
204.210.62.170 - - [22/Feb/2002:17:16:00 -0800] "GET
➥/msadc/..%255c../..%255c../..%255c/..%c1%1c../..%c1%1c../..%c1%1c../
➥winnt/system32/cmd.exe?/
➥c+dir HTTP/1.0" 404 265
204.210.62.170 - - [22/Feb/2002:17:16:03 -0800] "GET
➥/scripts/..%c1%1c../winnt/system32/cmd.exe?/c+dir HTTP/1.0" 404 231
204.210.62.170 - - [22/Feb/2002:17:16:09 -0800] "GET
➥/scripts/..%c0%2f../winnt/system32/cmd.exe?/c+dir HTTP/1.0" 404 231
204.210.62.170 - - [22/Feb/2002:17:16:16 -0800] "GET
➥/scripts/..%c0%af../winnt/system32/cmd.exe?/c+dir HTTP/1.0" 404 231
```

```
204.210.62.170 - - [22/Feb/2002:17:16:19 -0800] "GET
↳/scripts/..%c1%9c../winnt/system32/cmd.exe?/c+dir HTTP/1.0" 404 231
204.210.62.170 - - [22/Feb/2002:17:16:25 -0800] "GET
↳/scripts/..%%35%63../winnt/system32/cmd.exe?/c+dir HTTP/1.0" 400 215
204.210.62.170 - - [22/Feb/2002:17:16:28 -0800] "GET
↳/scripts/..%%35c../winnt/system32/cmd.exe?/c+dir HTTP/1.0" 400 215
204.210.62.170 - - [22/Feb/2002:17:16:31 -0800] "GET
↳/scripts/..%25%35%63../winnt/system32/cmd.exe?/c+dir HTTP/1.0" 404 232
204.210.62.170 - - [22/Feb/2002:17:16:34 -0800]
↳"GET /scripts/..%252f../winnt/system32/cmd.exe?/c+dir HTTP/1.0" 404 232
128.107.253.38 - - [22/Feb/2002:17:17:02 -0800]
↳"GET /col/cpm.html HTTP/1.1" 200 7632
208.216.180.101 - - [22/Feb/2002:17:23:57 -0800]
↳"GET /vim-cook.html HTTP/1.1" 200 34154
195.101.94.101 - - [22/Feb/2002:17:48:18 -0800]
↳"GET /10vimrc HTTP/1.1" 404 213
24.98.106.254 - - [22/Feb/2002:17:48:28 -0800] "GET / HTTP/1.0" 200 3329
193.214.115.198 - - [22/Feb/2002:18:08:17 -0800]
↳"GET /robots.txt HTTP/1.0" 200 27
211.157.101.42 - - [22/Feb/2002:18:12:14 -0800] "GET / HTTP/1.0" 200 3329
66.150.40.66 - - [22/Feb/2002:18:18:16 -0800] "HEAD / HTTP/1.1" 200 0
193.214.115.198 - - [22/Feb/2002:18:30:12 -0800]
↳"GET /vim-cook.html HTTP/1.0" 304 -
```

As you can see, someone is trying to access things like "favicon.ico" and "cmd.exe". This is the result of hackers trying to break into this server.

The format of this file is

```
[<date>] [<problem-type>] [client <ip-address>] <Status Message>
```

Write a program that extracts the client address from each entry trying to access cmd.exe and produces a sorted list of the IP addresses of the people trying to hack into this machine.

Resources

Regular Expression Elements

Table 4.1 presents a short list of the regular expression elements discussed in this chapter. For a full list of the extensive set of Perl regular expression operators, see the online documentation perldoc perlre.

Table 4.1   **Regular Expression Elements Discussed in the Chapter**

Element	Meaning
`<character>`	Match the given character. Works on letters, digits, and a few symbols. (Most symbols have a special meaning.)
`^`	Match the beginning of the line.
`$`	Match the end of the line.
`*`	Repeat zero or more times.
`+`	Repeat one or more times
`[xyz]`	Match any of the characters "x", "y", or "z". (Only one character in the string is matched.)
`[a-m]`	Match any character from "a" to "m".
`[^xyz]`	Match any character except "x", "y", or "z".
`\s`	Match a whitespace character.
`\S`	Match any character that's not whitespace.
`\d`	Match a digit.
`.`	Match any single character.
`(...)`	Put characters that match the enclosed regular expression in the variable `$1`. The next ( )'s data is placed in `$2` and so on.
`x¦y`	Match "x" or "y".
`*?`	Repeat zero or more times, but match as little as possible. (The default is to match as much as possible.)
`(?:....)`	Treat the enclosed regular expression as a single atom but do not put the enclosed text in `$1`, `$2`, and so on.
`(?<!...)`	Negative assertion. In other words, the text cannot match "..." at this point.

Debugging Tokens

Table 4.2 presents a list of the debugging tokens available as part of Perl's regular expression debugging module:

Table 4.2   **Debugging Tokens in the Debugging Module**

Token	Meaning
BOL	Match the beginning of the line.
BRANCH	Beginning of a choice. Two subexpressions follow. Either one can cause a match.
CLOSE	Close a () subexpression.
CURLYX	Match the expression from *m* to *n* times.
EXACT	Match the string exactly
MINMOD	Match the minimum number of times (default is maximum).
NOTHING	Match the empty string. (Used as a placeholder for branching.)
SUCCEED	End of the match. The match succeeded.
STAR	Match 0 or more times.
UNLESSM	Fail if the following matches.
WHILEM	Do CURLYX processing if the rest matches.

Online Documentation

- **perldoc perlre**—Perl's online documentation on regular expressions.
- **perldoc perlop**—Documents Perl's operators such as the s/// operation.
- **perldoc perldebguts**—Debugging information concerning the internals of Perl. This document contains a reference on all the codes output by the regular expression debugger.

5

Perl's New Syntax

THE PERL LANGUAGE CONTAINS MANY FEATURES you don't find in C or C++.
This chapter shows you those features, which include many new control and
looping statements, some special variables, and other aspects of the language.

This chapter is divided into two sections. The first section shows you the
most useful new features of Perl. The second section contains some of the
more obscure and less-used features that you may find in some Perl code.
Although you'll probably never use statements like these, you should be aware
of the syntax so that you can understand other Perl programs you might come
across.

New and Useful Syntax

This section describes Perl statements that have no C or C++ counterpart and
are useful besides.

The *foreach* Statement

Chapter 3, "Arrays," used the following statement to go through all the elements of an array:

```
for ($index = 0; $index <= $#array; $index++)
{ my $element = $array[$index]; }
```

The same statement can be written more easily as a `foreach` statement:

```
foreach $element (@array)
```

The `foreach` statement loops through each element in the list. The variable `$element` is assigned the value of each element as Perl goes through the list.
For example:

```
my @array = (qw(One Two Three));

print "The array contains ";
foreach my $element (@array) {
    print "$element ";
}
print "\n";
```

This code fragment prints the elements of the array. Notice that you are able to declare the variable `$element` inside the `foreach` statement. The output of this program is

```
The array contains One Two Three
```

Incidentally, the entire loop could have been replaced with one statement:

```
print "The array contains @array\n";
```

Note that the `$element` variable is actually a reference to the array element (see Chapter 6, "Hashes, References, and Complex Data Structures," for information on references). This means that any change to `$element` changes the element in the array.

The *$_* Variable

In C and C++, people generally use the variable i as the "handy-dandy, all-purpose, very temporary integer." In Perl, that honor goes to the predefined variable `$_`. In addition to being a handy temporary value, this variable is used as the default for many of Perl's functions and statements.

For example, if no variable is supplied in the `foreach` statement, `$_` is implied. For example, the following two statements are equivalent:

```
foreach $_ (@array)
foreach (@array)
```

The $_ variable serves as the default in the following cases:

- It is the default value when doing a pattern match expression:

```
if ($_ =~ /^#/) {      # is the same as
if (/^#/)
```

- Unless a variable is specified, an input statement will store the result on a read in $_:

```
$_ = <STDIN>;  # is the same as
<STDIN>;
```

- If no variable is specified for chomp, then $_ is used:

```
chmop($_);      # is the same as
chomp;
```

- It is the default string for split:

```
my @words = split /\s+/, $_;   # Is the same as
my @words = split /\s+/;
```

- A standalone s/xx/yy/ statement modifies it by default:

```
$_ =~ s/manager/idiot/g;   # is the same as
s/manager/idiot/;
```

- It is the default argument for many arithmetic functions, such as sin, cos, and log:

```
my $angle = sin $_;   # is the same as
my $angle = sin;
```

- It is the default value for the print function:

```
print $_;    # is the same as
print;
```

Note that the use of $_ can lead to some compact code. For example, Listing 5.1 shows a program that removes all the trailing whitespace from the standard in and writes the results to standard out.

Listing 5.1   *trailing.pl*

```
use strict;
use warning;

while (<STDIN>) {
    s/\s+$//;
    print;
}
```

As a rule, if you want to write clear and readable programs, you don't want to have hidden variables or defaults. After all, if you see a statement like

```
chomp;
```

how can you tell whether the programmer wanted the program to change $_ or whether he just forgot to put in the variable name? To avoid confusion, it is advised that you include a variable and not let things default.

"Here-Doc" Syntax

Suppose that you want to print a bunch of lines. One way to do it is with a bunch of `print` statements:

```
print "Help text:\n";
print "Command line is:\n";
print "datecheck [options] <file> [<file>...]\n";
print "Where:\n";
print "    [options] are to be defined\n";
```

Another way of doing it is to print using a single long string:

```
print "Help text:
Command line is:
datecheck [options] <file> [<file>...]
Where:
    [options] are to be defined\n";
```

A third solution is to use the "here-document" syntax. This syntax tells Perl that a long, multiline string that follows the here-document statement should be printed as it was entered until the closing marker is found. In other words, I've put the string *here* in the script itself. The string starts on the line following the statement and continues on until a special keyword is found.

The syntax of a here-doc string is *<<Keyword*. The *<<* signals that a here-document string follows. The *Keyword* tells Perl that the string stops when you see a line with just *Keyword* on it.

For example:

```
print <<EOF;
Help text:
Command line is:
datecheck [options] <file> [<file>...]
Where:
    [options] are to be defined
EOF
```

This example uses the keyword `EOF`. This is the traditional keyword used for almost all here-doc strings, but any other word can be used.

In this case, a here-doc string is used for a `print` statement, but you could have just as easily used it in an assignment statement:

```
my $error_msg = <<EOF;
Error: Syntax error on line $line, no such keyword $key
Please check spelling and try again.
EOF
```

Perl expands variable names in a here-doc string just like it does in any other double-quoted (") string. So in this example, `$line` will be replaced by the value of the variable `$line`, and the variable `$key` will be interpreted as well.

If you do not want variables interpreted, you need to tell Perl to treat this string as if it were in single quotes ('). This is done by putting the keyword in single quotes:

```
print <<'EOF';
Total cost is $6,250.00
Shipping is $450 more
EOF
```

Common Mistake: Forgetting the ;

If you are a shell or csh programmer, the here-doc syntax is familiar to you. But remember that a Perl here-doc string just replaces a normal string in the statement. It doesn't replace the rest of the line. You still need the semicolon (;) to end the line. For example:

```
# Incorrect
print <<EOF
Phase one is now complete.
Phase two is beginning.
EOF
```

Although this looks correct to shell programmers, the missing semicolon (;) causes Perl to complain.

The *die* Function

Frequently in a program, you'll encounter a fatal error. When this occurs, print an error message and abort the program.

Perl has a convenient function to do that, called `die`. The usage is simple enough:

```
die("We can not go on");
```

When run, the following prints:

```
We can not go on at test.pl line 4.
```

So the function not only prints the error message but also tells the user where in the script the error occurred. This makes the `die` function very useful for all those error conditions that cause your program to stop.

The Special File <>

The UNIX `cat` command takes a list of files as its arguments:

```
cat [file] [file] [....]
```

It then goes through each file in order and sends them to the standard out. If no file is specified, it copies standard in to standard out.

The `cat` command is like many other UNIX commands, such as `sort`, `grep`, and `uniq`, which take a list of files as their arguments. If no files are specified, they operate on standard in.

This type of program is so common that Perl has a special file called <> to facilitate the construction programs like this.

The <> file is defined as follows:

- If there are arguments in @ARGV, <> treats each argument as a filename and reads them in order.

- If @ARGV is empty, <> reads standard in.

Listing 5.2 contains the Perl version of the `cat` command.

Listing 5.2   *cat.pl*

```
use strict;
use warnings;

my $line;    # Current input line
while ($line = <>) {
    print $line;
}
```

That's all there is to it. If you run the program as

```
$ perl cat.pl file1.txt file2.txt
```

the program will read and print all the lines in `file1.txt` and then go to `file2.txt` and read and print all the lines in that file as well.

If you run the program as

```
$ perl cat.pl
```

then the script reads from standard in (in this case the keyboard) and writes anything it sees to standard out. In other words, what you type gets typed right back at you.

Getting the Name of the Current File

The name of the file currently being processed by the <> file is contained in the variable $ARGV.

The File Test Operators

In C and C++, you need to call the library function access to determine whether a file exists, or whether you can read or write it. In Perl, these operations are built in. The operator -f checks to see whether a file exists and whether it is an ordinary file. For example:

```
if (-f "file.bak") {
    die("file.bak exists.  Delete before running this script");
}
```

Some other common file test operators are as follows:

-r —File is readable.

-w —File is writable.

-x —File is executable.

-d —File is a directory.

For a full list of all the Perl file operators, see the online document using the following command:

```
$ perldoc -f -X
```

In other words, these operators are considered functions, and their documentation is filed under the function name -X.

The *redo* Operator

The next operator starts a loop over at the top. The redo operator starts a loop over without reevaluating the conditional. For example:

```
use strict;
use warnings;
my $i; # Loop index

my $flag = 0;    # True if we've been here before

for ($i = 1; $i <= 5; $i++) {
    print "$i ";
    if (($flag == 0) and ($i == 3)) {
        $flag = 1;
        redo;
    }
}
print "\n";
```

This function prints

```
1 2 3 3 4 5
```

Suppose that you want to read in a list of names and store them in an array. You want to be nice to the user, so you will ignore blank lines. The code looks like the following:

```
for (my $index = 1; $index <= 10; $index++) {
    print "Enter name number $index: ";
    my $result = <STDIN>;
    chomp($result);

    # If the user typed a blank line, give him
    # another chance
    if ($result eq "") {
        redo;
    }
    $name_list[$index-1] = $result;
}
```

The Translate (*tr*) Operator

The translate operator (tr) translates one set of characters to another. For example:

```
$hex =~ tr/abcdef/ABCDEF/;
```

This changes each letter "a" in the string to "A," each "b" to "B," and so on. Character ranges may be specified, such as

```
$name =~ tr/[a-z]/[A-Z]/;
```

I work on a Linux system, but I have to deal with many people who use Microsoft Windows systems. One problem that I have is that Windows users tend to put bad characters in filenames. For example, a Windows user thinks nothing about a filename like the following:

```
Chapter 1 (Fixed) edited by "Sam's Brother".doc
```

On Linux, such a filename is difficult to type on the command line. It's not impossible if you escape all the special characters, but it is messy.

A solution to this problem is creating a short program that renames bad filenames to good ones and eliminates special characters. The heart of the program is a translate statement that changes all bad characters into

```
$new_name = $old_name;
$new_name =~ tr/!()[]$%'"?<>`/............../;
```

Arrays on the Left Side of the =

Perl is a little unusual in that it lets you put array expressions on both sides of the = operator. For example:

```
($first, $middle, $last) = @array;
```

This is the equivalent of

```
$first = $array[0];
$middle = $array[1];
$last = $array[2];
```

Another use for this syntax is to swap two variables without the use of a temporary value:

```
($first, $second) = ($second, $first);
```

Perl's Darker Corners

Perl's designers have stated that their philosophy in designing Perl is "There's more than one way to do it." My philosophy is a little different: "There is only one clearest way to do it."

Unfortunately, if you examine some of the existing Perl scripts, you'll discover that Perl has a very rich and sometimes confusing set of syntax elements. This section describes some of the slightly more obscure statements so that you'll know what they do when you come across them.

The *unless* Statement

The unless statement is a shorthand for if not. For example, the following two statements are the same:

```
if (not defined ($title))
unless (defined ($title))
```

But why use two different words (unless and if) where one will do? There is no need for you to remember both of them. Just stick with the if not, and don't worry about the unless.

The Dangling *if* and *unless* Statements

Normally the if and the unless statements precede the statements they control; but Perl lets you use the if and unless statements as a sort of postscript. For example, the following statement prints a debug message if the variable $debug is true:

```
print "The current file is $file\n" if ($debug);
```

This is the equivalent of saying

```
if ($debug) {
    print "The current file is $file\n";
}
```

The dangling `if` syntax can be a bit confusing. It's like saying "I want you to perform this operation, but maybe not." Same thing goes for the dangling `unless`. I suggest you stick to the traditional `if`. It might seem boring, but you'll make your code clear and easy to understand for other programmers.

The __DATA__ File

A Perl program normally ends when you read the end of the file. You can, however, put in a special directive:

```
__DATA__
```

This directive tells Perl that what follows is not a part of the script but is a special place in your script for your data that can be read as an ordinary file using the `<DATA>` file handle.

For example:

```
use strict;
use warnings;

while (<DATA>) {
    print $_;
}
__DATA__
Hello, this is the data file
and it will be printed by this program.
```

Note that there's nothing that you can do with a data file that can't be done with a proper set of initialization statements.

Summary

Perl has a very rich syntax. This chapter covered all the features you don't find in C and C++. It filled in the gaps, and you should now be familiar with all the major Perl syntax elements.

From here, you'll learn about some of Perl's more advanced data structures as well as how to organize Perl programs into subroutines, packages, and objects.

Exercises

1. Write a program that encodes a file using the *rot13* encoding scheme. In this scheme, each letter in the alphabet is replaced by the letter 13 places to the right. For example, "a" becomes "n," "b" becomes "o," "n" becomes "a," "o" becomes "b," and so on.

    Note that uppercase letters always map to uppercase letters, and lowercase letters always map to lowercase letters.

2. A programmer uses the symbol QQQ to indicate debugging or temporary code. Write a program that searches files for this indicator and prints out any lines on which this symbol occurs. The program should print the filename followed by the line.

    The program should work for all the files on the command line. If no files are specified, <STDIN> should be used.

3. Update the program in Exercise 2 to search for an arbitrary regular expression specified on the command line. (This is much like the grep command.)

4. Write a program that reads a file and locates all the hexadecimal numbers. These are the numbers like 0x12AB. Hexadecimal numbers can use uppercase or lowercase letters. Rewrite all the numbers you find so that they use a lowercase "x" and uppercase "ABCDEF." For example:

```
0x12AB      -> 0x12AB
0X12ab      -> 0x12AB
0x12Ab      -> 0x12AB
```

    Create a program that takes a set of files on the command line and writes out a three-section report consisting of (1) A list of the read-only file, (2) A list of the writable files, and (3) A list of the directories.

Resources

Online Documentation

- **perldoc perlsyn**—Contains a brief description of Perl's syntax.
- **perldoc perlvar**—Describes Perl's built-in variables, such as $_, $ARGV, and @ARGV.
- **perldoc -f -X**—The file test operators are filed in this obscure place. They are in the function documentation under a function called -X.

6

Hashes, References, and Complex Data Structures

THIS CHAPTER COMPLETES YOUR STUDY OF THE basic Perl data types with an examination of *associative arrays*, better known as *hashes*. Unlike ordinary arrays, hashes enable you to use a string as an index rather than a number.

This chapter also covers references. A *reference* is similar to a C pointer in that it points to other data. (Actually, there are some differences between the two, but for now, you can consider them about the same.)

Finally, the chapter combines all the data structures along with your knowledge of references to create complex data structures. As you will see, nested data structures in Perl are a little trickier than they are in C or C++.

Hashes

A hash is an array in which you index the data with a string rather than a number. For example:

```
my %flags;
$flags{start} - "MN_START";
$flags{end} = "MN_TERMINATE";
$flags{middle} = "CONNECTED";
```

There are a few bookkeeping details to take care of first. A hash name begins with a percent sign (%). An element of a hash is a scalar, so it begins with a dollar sign ($). Whereas simple arrays use square brackets ([ ]) to index the array, hashes use curly brackets ({}).

The index of a hash is called a *key*. In this example, the keys are start, end, and middle. The result of a hash indexed by a key is a *value*. In this example, the values are "MN_START", "MN_TERMINATE", and "CONNECT".

Finally, this example indexes %flags with a *bare word*, which is a word not enclosed in quotes—for example, start. In this context, the bare word is treated as a string. This means that the following statements are identical:

```
$flags{"start"} = "MN_START";
$flags{'start'} = "MN_START";
$flags{start} = "MN_START";
```

Now you'll see an example of how to use hashes. Listing 6.1 contains a program designed to correct common spelling mistakes. In other words, when it reads a word such as "beleive", it replaces it with "believe".

To simplify things (including the program), the input file contains one word per line.

To solve the spelling problem, the program constructs a hash. The hash's keys are the misspelled words, and the values are the correctly spelled words.

Listing 6.1   *spell.pl*

```
use strict;
use warnings;

my %fix_words;    # Hash containing bad words and their fixes
$fix_words{beleive} = "believe";
$fix_words{adminstration} = "administration";
$fix_words{skool} = "school";

my $line;
while ($line = <STDIN>) {
    chomp($line);        # Remove newline

    # Is there a fix for the word?
    if (defined ($fix_words{$line}))
    {
        # yes - print it
        print "$fix_words{$line}\n";
    }
    else
    {
        # No - print the word
        print "$line\n";
    }
}
```

This example initialized the hash the hard way. If you wanted to initialize it at declaration time, you could have used the syntax

```
my %fix_words = (
    beleive => "believe",
    adminstration => "administration",
    skool => "school"
);
```

Printing Out an Entire Hash

Listing 6.2 contains a short password file from a Linux system.

Listing 6.2 *passwd*

```
xfs:x:100:233:X Font Server:/etc/X11/fs:/bin/false
peg:x:117:100:Peg Kover:/home/peg:/bin/tcsh
wong001:x:118:100:Chi Mui Wong:/home/wong001:/bin/csh
www:x:200:100:WWW Service:/home/httpd:/bin/tcsh
oualline:x:203:100:Stephen Oualline:/home/oualline:/bin/tcsh
shari:x:503:503:Shari Shivers:/home/shari:/bin/bash
```

The file contains password records, one per line. Each record contains entries for the username, password (always "x"), a couple of ID numbers, the full name of the user, and other garbage. You want to read this file and print all the usernames and the full name of the user.

Start by reading in the file and storing the username and full name in a hash:

```
my %pw_hash;    # Full name of the user indexed by account name
open IN_FILE, "<passwd" or die("Could not open password");
my $line;    # Line from the password file
while ($line = <IN_FILE>) {
    # The fields of the password entry
    my @fields = split /:/, $line;
    $pw_hash{$fields[0]} = $fields[4];
}
close (IN_FILE);
```

Now you have a hash whose values are the full usernames and whose keys are the account names. How do you print it?

The solution is to use the keys function. This function looks at a hash and returns a list containing all the key values. So to print out the array, you need the code

```
foreach my $cur_key (keys %pw_hash) {
    print "$cur_key => $pw_hash{$cur_key}\n";
}
```

Simple Reading and Writing of Hashes

Listing 6.3 contains a simple program that reads in a hash from a file. The format of the file is

```
key: value
```

Note that this format limits the keys and values used in the hash to one liners.

Listing 6.3 *read_hash.pl*

```perl
use strict;
use warnings;

my %hash;    # The hash to read
open IN_FILE, "<hash.txt" or die("Could not open hash.txt");
my $line;    # Current line
while ($line = <IN_FILE>) {
    $line =~ /([^:]*): (.*)/;
    $hash{$1} = $2;
}
# ... a set of operators and functions
close (IN_FILE);
```

Writing out a hash is simple as well. Listing 6.4 contains a program that writes out a simple hash.

Listing 6.4 *write_hash.pl*

```perl
use strict;
use warnings;

my %hash = (
    sam => 45,
    joe => 57,
    mac => 68
);

open OUT_FILE, ">hash.out" or die("Could not write to hash.out");
foreach my $cur_key (sort keys %hash) {
    print OUT_FILE "$cur_key: $hash{$cur_key}\n";
}
close (OUT_FILE);
```

Reading and Writing More Complex Hashes

These programs work fine for hashes whose keys and values are limited to single lines. But what if you want to work with more complex values?

That's where the module `Storable` comes in. (It's not part of the standard Perl distribution, so you may have to download and install it.)

To use this module, you'll need to put the following line in your code:

```
use Storable qw(nstore retrieve);
```

This line tells Perl that you are going to use the module `Storable` and use the functions `nstore` and `retrieve` in it. (Other functions are in this package, but you're not using them now.)

The `nstore` function stores a hash in a file. For example:

```
my $status = nstore \%hash, "file.dat";
```

This example uses the function `nstore` to store a hash named `%hash` into a file named `file.dat`. If `nstore` succeeds, it returns a value of true. If there is a problem, `$status` will be undefined.

Checking to See Whether a Word Is in a List

This section shows you how to write a program that allows only a selected group of people access to privileged commands. One way to do this is to put the list of special people in an array and write a loop that walks through the array:

```
my $user = "oualline";    # User name (hardcoded for this example)
# List of people who are allowed privileges
my @power_users = qw(
    oualline
    fred
    wong
    jones
);
my $privileged = 0;  # Assume that the user is not privileged
#
# Loop through each power user and check to see if
# $user is one of them.
#
foreach my $cur_user (@power_users)
{
    if ($cur_user eq $user) {
        $privileged = 1;    # We are a power user
        last;
    }
}
```

But loops are costly, and you can use a hash to make things easier. First turn the array into a hash whose keys are the users and whose values are 1:

```
my %power_users = (
    "oualline" => 1,
    "fred"     => 1,
```

```
        "wong"      => 1,
        "jones"     => 1
);
```

Now to check to see whether someone is a power user, all you need is a single statement:

```
if (defined($power_users{$user})) {
    $privileged = 1;
}
```

or if you want to be really compact, you can use the statement

```
$privileged = defined($power_users{$user});
```

Using the *map* Function

The privileged user checking code is limited by the fact that the list of users is written into the program. It would be nice if you could read the list of users from a file and turn them into a hash. For example:

```
open IN_FILE, "<user_list.txt" or die("Could not open
user_list.txt");
my @user_array = <IN_FILE>;
chomp(@user_array);
close (IN_FILE);

my %power_users;
foreach my $cur_user (@user_array) {
    $power_users{$cur_user} = 1;
}
```

You can make this loop more efficient by using the map function:

```
my %power_users = map +($_ => 1), @user_array;
```

This function tells Perl to repeat the expression enclosed in the parentheses (+($ => 1)) for each element in the @user_array. (In this context, $_ is the current element of the array.)

Thus if the @user_array contains "sam", "joe", and "mac", the map function expands the statement into

```
my %power_users = ("sam" => 1, "joe" => 1, "mac" => 1);
```

So the program can now be optimized as

```
open IN_FILE, "<user_list.txt" or die("Could not open
user_list.txt");
my @user_array = <IN_FILE>;
chomp(@user_array);
close (IN_FILE);

my %power_users = map +($_ => 1), @user_array;
```

If you do decide to make things so compact, please put in a few comments so that anyone maintaining your code can understand what's going on.

Perl's Syntax Subtleties and the map Function

Only read this sidebar if you're interested in the subtleties of the Perl syntax.

The general form of the map function is

```
map expression, array
```

where *expression* is an expression repeated for each element of the array. In the preceding example, the expression is ($_ => 1). So why the + before it?

The problem is that when Perl sees a function call, it expects a set of parameters to follow. These parameters might not be enclosed in parentheses. Thus the following two statements are equivalent:

```
print "This is a ", "test\n";
print ("This is a ", "test\n");
```

The other problem is that Perl lets you use the comma (,) operator to string together two statements. For example:

```
$i = 1, $j = 2;
```

Consider the following statement:

```
%power_users = map ($_ => 1), @user_array;
```

Does Perl treat this as a function call with two parameters or statements joined by the comma operator? The two statements would be a function call with one parameter:

```
map ($_ => 1)
```

and an array:

```
@user_array
```

The rule Perl follows is that if the first character after a function is an open parenthesis, a parameter list follows. That means that Perl treats the first item ($_ => 1) as the entire parameter list to the map function.

To fool Perl into thinking that map has two parameters, you need to add a unary plus (+) in front of the expression. The unary plus does nothing to the expression, but it does cause Perl to parse this statement as a map function call with two parameters:

```
%power_users = map +($_ => 1), @user_array;
```

Perl is full of interesting syntax subtleties like this. Fortunately, the programs in this book avoid most of them.

Deleting an Element from a Hash

You know how to put things into a hash, but how do you remove one? You might think that it can be done by assigning undef to the hash element, but this technique doesn't quite do the job. For example, look at the following statement:

```
$hash{sam} = undef;
```

This statement does not remove the element sam from the hash. It leaves the element in place, with the value undef. The key sam is still in the hash.

To actually remove the element sam from the hash, use the delete function:

```
delete ($hash{sam});
```

Arrays and Hashes

You can assign a hash to an array. If you assign a hash to an array, you get an array whose elements are *key*, *value*, *key*, *value*, ... For example:

```
my %hash = (
    sam => 45,
    joe => 57,
    mac => 68
);
my @array = %hash;
print "@array\n";
```

This example may print

```
joe 57 mac 68 sam 45
```

You may have noticed that the keys are not in order. That's because in a hash, the key order is not defined. The output could just as easily have been

```
joe 57 sam 45 mac 68
```

It also is possible to assign an array to a hash. The result is a hash whose first key is $array[0] and first value is $array[1]. The second key is $array[2], and the second value is $array[3]. This continues until the system runs out of elements. If you specify an odd number of elements, a warning is issued.

For example:

```
my @array = qw(sam 45 joe 57 mac 68);
my %hash = @array;
```

results in the same hash you had in the previous example.

References

A reference is simply a Perl equivalent of a C pointer. Actually, Perl references do much more than C pointers, but for now, it's easiest to think of them as pointers.

The backslash character (\) indicates a reference. The equivalent operator in C is address of (&). The following example creates a reference to a simple variable:

```
my $variable = 1;
my $reference = \$variable;    # Reference to a variable
$$reference = 2;
print "$variable\n";    # Prints 2
```

In this example, $reference is a reference to a scalar—$variable. To get to the actual scalar being referenced, you need to add another $ to the expression—$$reference. Think of ($) as a (*) C operator being used with a C pointer.

The following example gets a little bolder and defines a reference to an array:

```
my @array = qw(red white blue);
my $ref = \@array;
```

The elements of the array are

```
$array[0], $array[1], $array[2]
```

or if you access them through the following reference:

```
$$ref[0], $$ref[1], $$ref[2]
```

To get the number of the last element in an array, you use the expression $#array. When using a reference, you would use $#$ref instead.

You can use the push, pop, shift, and unshift commands on references as well as normal arrays. For example:

```
push(@$ref, "new-value");
```

References to hashes follow a similar pattern. You make the reference with the backslash (\) operator and then use $ref in place of the variable name everywhere:

```
my %hash = ( red => 1, blue => 2, green => 3);
my $ref = \%hash;

print "Red's value is $hash{red}\n";
print "Blue's value is $$ref{blue}\n";
```

The following code fragment prints all the values in a hash:

```
foreach my $cur_key (keys %$ref)
{
    print "$cur_key: $ref->{$cur_key}\n";
}
```

There is, however, one bit of syntactic sugar that you can use with hashes. Instead of referencing an element of the hash with the awkward `$$ref{value}`, you can write this expression as `$ref->{value}`. This is similar to C syntax, which lets you write `(*struct_ptr).value` and `struct_ptr->value`. For example:

```
print "Green's value is $ref->{green}\n";
```

Anonymous References

Unlike C or C++, Perl doesn't have a heap where you can explicitly allocate things. Instead, variables are created using *anonymous references*. For example, you already know how to create a reference to a named data array:

```
my @array = ("red", "white", "blue");
my $ref = \@array;
```

An anonymous reference looks much like this, only you don't use `@array`:

```
my $ref = ["red", "white", "blue"];
```

The square brackets (`[]`) tell Perl to create a new array, and return a reference to it.

The square brackets also can be used to create a copy of an array and return an anonymous reference to it:

```
my $copy_ref = [@array];
```

In C and C++, you have to explicitly free any memory you allocate. In Perl it's done automatically. Perl maintains a reference count for each variable. This is a count of the number of references that "point" to it. When the reference count goes to zero, the variable is automatically deallocated. For more on this topic, see the New Riders book *Win32 Perl Programming: Standard Extensions, 2nd edition*, by Dave Roth.

You also can create references to anonymous hashes. This is done through the use of the curly bracket (`{}`) operators. Here's an example:

```
my $ref = { red => 1, blue => 2, green => 3};
```

Again, this operator can be used to create a copy of a hash and return an anonymous reference to it:

```
my $copy_ref = {%hash};
```

Translating C Data Structures into Perl

Perl and C have vastly different ways of dealing with data structures. In C, you can generate complex data structures and precisely control their layout. Perl's data structures are both simpler (you can't nest data structures) and more complex (anonymous references). Yet despite these differences, it's easy to translate almost any C data structure into Perl. Some of the internals and the details may be different, and the syntax is vastly different, but it can be done.

Hashes as Structures

Perl does not have a built-in data type similar to a C structure, but you can make do with a hash. For example, suppose that you need a structure to hold the date. In C, this would be written as

```
struct date {      /* C Code */
    int day;
    int month;
    int year;
} today = {
    5, 10, 2001
};
```

This can be easily translated into a Perl hash as follows:

```
my %today = {    # Perl code
    day => 5,
    month => 10,
    year => 2001
};
```

But there are a few differences between Perl's hashes and C's structures. The first is that whereas the fields in a C structure are ordered, the elements of a Perl hash are unordered. In other words, Perl guarantees that you have something with a day, month, and year in it, but does not tell you anything about how it's put together.

Second, you can add and remove elements from a hash, whereas the fields in a C structure are fixed.

Arrays of Hashes

Perl does not allow you to nest data structures directly, so you can not have an array whose elements are hashes. But you can come up with a good approximation by using references.

Suppose that you want to declare the Perl equivalent of a C array of dates. In C, this is

```
struct date date_array[100];   /* C array of dates */
```

In Perl, the declaration is

```
my @date_array;
```

Not too impressive. But now populate it with a few dates:

```
$date_array[0] = { month => 7, day => 4, year => 1776};
$date_array[1] = { month => 12, day => 7, year => 1941};
```

Notice that you have to use the curly brackets ({}) to make this an anonymous reference.

Reading In an Array of Dates

Perl is an ideal language for reading in a set of data, munching it, and writing a report. You'll see this in action.

The program constructed in this example reads a set of dates into an array of hashes. Now that you have the data, you need to do something with it. This example writes out a report listing all the years for which you have dates.

The program starts by opening the file and doing the necessary book-keeping:

```
open IN_FILE, "<dates.txt" or die("Could not open dates.txt");
my @date_array = ();    # The dates we have read in

my $line;    # Line from the input file
```

Now read and parse each line:

```
while ($line = <IN_FILE>) {
    chomp($line);
    # Date is of the form mm/dd/yyyy (WARNING: This format is USA specific)
    my @date_parts = split /\//, $line;
```

At this point, you should have an array containing the month, day, and year. Turn this into a hash and stuff it into date_array:

```
my %date_hash = (
    month => $date_parts[0],
    day => $date_parts[1],
    year => $date_parts[2]);
    push (@date_array, {%date_hash});
```

Notice that you use the curly brackets ({}) in the push statement. This turns the %date_hash into an anonymous hash reference.

After you finish reading the data, you need to process it. You need to figure which years are represented by the data. This is done by constructing a hash whose keys are the years, and the values are always 1:

```
my %year_hash;
foreach my $cur_date (@date_array) {
```

```
        $year_hash{$cur_date->{year}} = 1;
    }
```

If you wanted to be really efficient, you could replace this section of code with a single map call:

```
    my %year_hash = map +($_->{year} => 1), @date_array;
```

The only thing left is to store the data and print a report:

```
    foreach my $cur_year (sort keys %year_hash)
    {
        print "$cur_year\n";
    }
```

The full program appears in Listing 6.5.

Listing 6.5   *date.pl*

```
use strict;
use warnings;

open IN_FILE, "<dates.txt" or die("Could not open dates.txt");
my @date_array = ();    # The dates we have read in

my $line;    # Line from the input file

while ($line = <IN_FILE>) {
    chomp($line);
    # Date is of the form mm/dd/yyyy
    # (WARNING: This format is USA specific)
    my @date_parts = split /\//, $line;
    if ($#date_parts != 2) {
        print STDERR "Bad input line $line";
    }
    my %date_hash = (
        month => $date_parts[0],
        day => $date_parts[1],
        year => $date_parts[2]);
    push (@date_array, {%date_hash});
}
close IN_FILE;
# Now let's figure out which years are present
my %year_hash;

foreach my $cur_date (@date_array) {
    $year_hash{$cur_date->{year}} = 1;
}
# Print out the years
foreach my $cur_year (sort keys %year_hash)
{
    print "$cur_year\n";
}
```

Arrays of Arrays

Chapter 3, "Arrays," showed you how to construct a two-dimensional array. For example:

```
my @matrix = (
    [11, 12, 13],
    [21, 22, 23],
    [31, 32, 33]
);
```

From this, you can see that `@matrix` is not really a two-dimensional array but rather an array of references to an array of integers. In other words, in C terms, what you've declared is

```
int r1[3] = {11, 12, 13};    /* C code */
int r2[3] = {21, 22, 23};
int r3[3] = {31, 32, 33};
typedef int* int_ptr;
int_ptr matrix[3] = {r1, r2, r3};
```

To get the number of rows in the array, use the expression `$#array`. To get the number of columns, use the expression `$#{$array[0]}`. Use curly brackets (`{}`) to make sure that Perl understands how to properly parse this expression.

But `$#{$array[0]}` gets the size of only the first row of the array. Believe it or not, in Perl you can construct a matrix where each row has a different number of columns:

```
my @matrix = (
    [11, 12, 13],
    [21, 22, 23, 24, 25, 26, 27],
    [31, 32, 33, 34]
);
```

Take a look at the various sizes of the elements of this data structure:

`$#matrix`	2	Number of rows—1
`$#{$matrix[0]}`	2	Number of columns—1 for row #0
`$#{$matrix[1]}`	6	Number of columns—1 for row #1
`$#{$matrix[2]}`	3	Number of columns—1 for row #2

From this, you can see how Perl can be so simple and complex at the same time. Because of the way Perl uses references, even a simple matrix can have hidden meaning.

Printing Complex Data Structures

Sometimes, such as when you're creating a program like `date.pl`, you'll need to print out a complex data structure. You can do this in the debugger, or you can use the module `dumpvar.pl` to display the data.

To use this module, you need to put the following line near the top of your program, just after the `use` lines:

```
require "dumpvar.pl";
```

Now when you want to print a variable, just use the function call:

```
dumpValue(reference);
```

where *reference* is a reference to the variable to dump. For example, to print out the `@date_array` variable in human readable format, use the following command:

```
dumpValue(\@date_array);
```

Copying Data Structures

Suppose that you want to make a duplicate of a data structure, such as an array of hashes, as in `@date_array` shown previously. You could use an assignment statement such as

```
my @new_array = @date_array;    # Won't work as expected
```

Because this array contains a set of references, the references (pointers) are copied, not the data. This is not what you want because if you change some of the data in `@new_array`, you'll change the data in `@date_array`. What you want is a new copy of all the data, not just the references.

For that purpose, you need to go back to the `Storable` module. The function `dclone` clones a complex data structure, making copies of all the references. It takes one argument, a reference to the data to clone, and returns a reference to a copy of the data.

So replace the assignment statement with a `dclone` call:

```
use Storable qw(dclone);
# .....
my $new_array_ref = dclone(\@date_array);
```

Summary

Data structures are one of the most difficult things for beginning Perl programmers to master. However, because you are a C programmer and already know the basics, it's easy to translate your C knowledge into Perl. True, Perl has its own way of doing things, but with a little work, you can easily create complex and wonderful data structures in Perl.

Exercises

1. For this first exercise, you'll need a set of daily stock prices. You can get them from `http://quote.yahoo.com`.

   To get this information, follow these steps:

   1. Open up `http://quote.yahoo.com`. (No www!)
   2. Select a stock symbol (for example "RHAT") and click Get.
   3. In the More Info. box, click Chart.
   4. A table of information is displayed in which there is a chart. Below the table, click on the Historical quotes: daily button.
   5. The display now contains a list of historical quotes. Save this file as a text file, edit out the junk, and you've got a table of stock prices.

   Write a program that reads the stock data and stores it in an array of hashes. Print the results to make sure that you got things right.

2. Change problem #1. Remove the printing of the data and instead compute the average stock price, as well as the high and low values for the period.

3. Change problem #2. Compute the daily gain or loss for the stock. Print a report with the records sorted so that the days with the biggest gains come out first, and the days with the biggest losses come out last.

4. Download Redhat's stock prices in comma-separated format for Microsoft Excel from
   `http://table.finance.yahoo.com/table.csv?a=1&b=1&c=2001&d=12&e=31&f=2002&s=RHAT&y=0&g=d` for the year 2001 and do the three previous exercises for this file.

5. Change Problem #4. Find the dates when a daily gain or loss was 10 percent higher than the average gain/loss during the previous 10 business days (hint: 10 previous records).

Resources

Online Documentation

- **perldoc perldata**—Information on Perl's data structures.
- **perldoc -f delete**—Function to delete the element of a hash.

Modules

- **Storable**—A Perl module to store and retrieve complex data structures from files.
- **dumpvar.pl**—An undocumented module that dumps out variables.

7

Subroutines and Modules

YOU NOW KNOW ENOUGH PERL TO BE able to write a moderately complex program. At this point, you need to start organizing your code into subroutines.

Perl lets you put a collection of subroutines together into *packages*. A package designed to hold reusable code is called a *module*.

In this chapter, you'll learn how to produce modules as well as how to create your own module library.

Subroutines

Suppose that you want to write a subroutine to compute the difference between two time values. Start your subroutine definition like this:

```
sub timediff($$) {
```

The sub keyword signals the start of a subroutine. In this case, the subroutine is named timediff. The function takes two scalar parameters. This is indicated by the parameter list ($$).

The method Perl uses to pass parameters is unique: passing by special variable. When a function is called, Perl assigns the parameters to the array @_. You now need to get the parameters out of the @_ array and into something you can use.

One simple way of doing this is to use the shift function to "shift" the parameters out of @_ and into simple variables:

```
my $start_time = shift;     # Time the event started
my $end_time = shift;     # Time the event finished
```

Now comes the body of the function, which computes an answer and stores it in $result. This value can be returned to the caller with the return statement:

```
return ($result);
}
```

So the complete (mostly) function looks like

```
sub timediff($$) {
    my $start_time = shift;     # Time the event started
    my $end_time = shift;     # Time the event finished

    # Something amazing happens
    # $result = the answer

    return ($result);
}

# Sample call
$elapsed = timediff($end_time, $start_time);
```

More on Parameter Specification

The $ in a parameter specification indicates a scalar variable. In the preceding example, the function timediff($$) takes two scalar variables.

This tells Perl that when it sees a function call such as

```
my minutes = timediff("1:30", "2:40");
```

to execute the following code:

```
@_ = ("1:30", "2:40");
-- call timediff --
    $minutes = -- value returned by timediff --
```

Other specifications can be used in a parameter list. A \@ indicates an array parameter. For example, the function swap_array(\@\@) can be called with

```
swap_array(@first, @last);
```

Perl automatically converts the arrays to array references and puts them in the parameter list. So the parameter passing code that Perl executes behind your back looks like this:

```
@_ = (\@first, \@last);
-- call swap --
```

Now see how this would affect the way you write the function:

```
sub array_swap(\@\@) {
    my $array1 = shift;      # Reference to @first
    my $array2 = shift;      # Reference to @second
```

Similarly, the \% parameter flag indicates a hash parameter that's turned into a hash reference when the subroutine is called.

Finally, there's the & flag, which indicates a function reference.

Array and Hash Parameters

The flag @ in a parameter list specification tells Perl that an array is to be passed and to *not* automatically convert it to a reference. For example:

```
sub sum_array(@)
```

In this case, Perl assigns the entire array to the parameter variable @_. A typical call might look like

```
my $sum = sum_array(@foo);
```

The parameter passing code generated by Perl is equivalent to

```
@_ = (@foo);     # Notice the absence of a backslash
```

To get the parameter out of @_ and into a real array, use code like this:

```
sub sum_array(@)
{
    my @array_to_sum = @_;
```

There are some limitations on this type of parameter: You can use it only once in a parameter specification, and it must be last.

Here's another example of a subroutine that takes two scalar arguments and an array parameter:

```
sub sum_slice_array($$@)
{
    my $start_index = shift;    # Index of the first element to sum
    my $end_index = shift;      # Index of the last element to sum
    my @array_to_sum = @_;      # The array containing the data to sum
```

Compare these two subroutines:

```
sub sum_slice_ref($$\@)
```

```
sub sum_slice_array($$@)
```

The first, sum_slice_ref, uses a reference for the array specification. This means that passing the array in is a little more efficient.

But it means that the function call is limited to passing in a single array. For example:

```
sum_slice_ref(1, 3, @array);     # Legal
sum_slice_ref(1, 3, @start, @middle, @end);     # Illegal
```

On the other hand, when you use the @ parameter specifier, Perl takes all the leftover parameters and stuffs them in one array. Thus the following are legal:

```
sum_slice_array(1, 3, @array);     # Legal
sum_slice_array(1, 3, @start, @middle, @end);     # Legal
```

The code generated for that last call looks like

```
@_ = (1, 3, @start, @middle, @end)
-- call to slice_array --
```

The % specification works similarly. You can use it to specify a hash at the end of a parameter specification. In this case, Perl converts the hash into an array (@_), but you can convert it right back again at the beginning of your function.

Variable-Length Parameter Lists

Suppose that you want a function that takes an optional third parameter. You can do this by using the ; to separate the mandatory from the optional parameters:

```
sub draw_rectangle($$;$) {
    my $width = shift;     # Mandatory
    my $height = shift;    # Mandatory
    my $color = shift;     # Optional
```

This can be called as

```
draw_rectangle(10, 20, "green");
```

or

```
draw_rectangle(40, 86);
```

But how can you tell whether the subroutine was called with the optional parameter? The answer is if the optional parameter is missing, it gets the value undef. For example, suppose that you want a default color to be black, which will be used if the color's not specified. You would write

```
if (not defined($color)) {
    $color = "black";
}
```

Note that all parameters after the semicolon are optional. Thus the function

```
sub compute_sum($;$$$) {
```

can take 1, 2, 3, or 4 parameters. (But not 5.)

Parameter Specification Summary

Perl has a simple, yet rich parameter syntax. Table 7.1 shows a summary of the various specification characters.

Table 7.1   **Parameter Specification Characters**

Specification	Explanation
$	Scalar
\@	Array (converted to reference)
\%	Hash (converted to reference)
&	Function reference
@	Array (must be last)
%	Hash (must be last)
;	Indicates that optional parameters follow

Alternate Parameter Passing Methods

There is nothing magic about the `shift` method used to get the parameters out of @_ and into variables. The method is simple, clear, and easy to use; that's why it's the preferred method of this author.

But you can convert @_ to variables in many other ways. One of the more common ways is to use an array assignment statement. For example:

```
sub distance($$$$)
{
    my ($x1, $y1, $x2, $y2) = @_;
```

This example assigns an array on the left-hand side to an array on the right-hand side, and everything works.

This system has the advantage of assigning all your parameters at once. However, the `shift` method is a little simpler and easier to comment.

Function with No Parameter Specification

There's a third way of specifying function parameters: the empty specification. For example:

```
sub do_it {
```

This tells Perl that the function takes any number of parameters of any type. In other words, absolutely no type checking is done. Also no automatic conversion of arrays to array references or hashes to hash references is done. All the parameters are concatenated together, dumped in @_, and that's it.

This form of parameter passing should be avoided. By using a parameter specification, you give Perl the capability to do valuable parameter checking. Leave out the parameter specification, and you invite chaos.

The *local* Declaration

The `local` keyword needs to be discussed because it's so commonly misused in subroutines. It does not mean create a local variable. The `my` keyword does that job. Instead, it has a more complex meaning.

A `local` declaration does the following:

- Saves the global definition of a variable.

- Lets you change the variable as much as you want.

- When the local variable goes out of scope, it restores the global definition.

For example, take a look at the following code:

```perl
print "$#ARGV arguments present\n";
{
    local @ARGV;
    my $first = shift @ARGV;
    print "$#ARGV arguments present now\n";
}
print "$#ARGV arguments restored\n";
```

This is the equivalent of saying

```perl
print "$#ARGV arguments present\n";
my @save_argv = @ARGV;
{
    my $first = shift @ARGV;
    print "$#ARGV arguments present now\n";
}
@ARGV = @save_argv;
print "$#ARGV arguments restored\n";
```

The bottom line is that `local` is a very tricky keyword that should only be used in limited circumstances. It is presented here so that you can recognize it when you see it in other people's code.

You should not use it at this stage. Instead, you should use the `my` declaration to declare your local variables. Note that `local` is one of the most misused keywords in Perl. Frequently, people will inappropriately use `local` when they really should use `my`.

Packages

You've now learned how to organize your code into subroutines. A collection of related subroutines is called a package. The statement

```
package call;
```

indicates to Perl that from now on all functions and variables are to be part of the package call. A Perl package is similar to a C++ class. Each variable and function exists in a namespace local to the class or package. Suppose that in this package you define a variable and a function:

```
my $in_call = 0;
sub start() {
    # ...
```

This defines a variable and function that can be used somewhere within the package. For example:

```
$in_call = 1;
```

But outside the package the program must use the scope operator (::) to access these names. For example, the variable $in_call in the package call is referred to by the name $call::in_call. Similarly, if you want to invoke the subroutine from outside the package, you need to use the name call::start().

The default package (the one that's implied if you don't specify a package directive) is named main.

Listing 7.1 illustrates how packages affect naming.

Listing 7.1   *package_ex.pl*

```
# Note: This example is artificial
# Most of the time packages are in
# separate files.
use strict;
use warnings;

my $calling = 0;     # Are we calling
                     # (Defines $main::calling)
package call;

my $in_call = 0;     # Are we in a call
                     # (Defines variable $call::in_call)

# Subroutine call::start()
sub start() {
    $in_call = 1;    # We are calling
                     # (Uses $call::in_call)
```

continues

Listing 7.1   **Continued**

```
}

package main;      # We are the main program

$calling = 1;      # We are calling
start();           # ERROR: No main::start()
call::start();     # OK, calls the correct start
```

Creating a Package File

By convention, Perl programmers put each package in a file of its own. For example, the package call would be placed in the file call.pm. For reasons that will be explained later, the file must end with the statement

```
1;
```

If the module or the package is in the current or Perl directory, you can use it by putting the following line in your program:

```
use call;
```

Providing an External Interface

A module is divided into two parts: a public interface that describes the functions and data to be provided (.h file) and a private implementation section (.c file).

In Perl, both parts are contained in a single file. So far, you've seen how to create functions and data. To create a public interface, you have to use the Exporter module.

Suppose that you want to write a module that reads in a bunch of numbers and lets the user compute a moving average on them:

```
read_data($file);   # Read the file
my @raw_data;       # Array containing the stock data
@result = moving_average($elements);
                    # Return a moving average
                    # that spans $elements array elements.
```

The module starts with the usual package statement:

```
package average;
```

You now need to define the interface. This starts with a statement to bring in the Exporter module:

```
require Exporter;
use vars qw(@ISA @EXPORT);
@ISA = qw(Exporter);
```

The @ISA array is part of Perl's object-oriented syntax, discussed in Chapter 8, "Object-Oriented Programming." For now, all you need to know is that it is required.

Now you need to tell Perl what functions and variables you are exporting:

```
@EXPORT = qw(read_data @raw_data moving_average);
```

Next, declare any global variables you want to export:

```
use vars qw(@raw_data);
```

Now implement the functions contained in the module:

```
sub read_data() {
    # ...
}
sub moving_average($) {
    # ...
}
```

Finally, at the end of the module, you need a statement to tell Perl that the module loaded successfully. This is done by returning a 1 to the module that invoked "average" module with the statement

```
1;
```

Listing 7.2 contains the nearly complete module.

Listing 7.2   *average.pm*

```
use strict;
package average;
#
# Comments explaining how to use the package
# should be put here.
#
use vars qw(@ISA @EXPORT @raw_data);
require Exporter;
@ISA = qw(Exporter);
@EXPORT = qw(&read_data @raw_data moving_average);

#############################################
# read_data($file_name) -- Read the data
#    from the file.  Data is stored in the
#    global variable @raw_data
#
# Returns:
#    undef -- Error
#    1 -- Success
#############################################
sub read_data($)
{
```

continues

Listing 7.2 **Continued**

```perl
    my $file = shift;     # The file to read

    open DATA_FILE, "<$file" or
        return (undef);
    @raw_data = <DATA_FILE>;
    chomp(@raw_data);
    close(DATA_FILE);
    return (1);     # Success
}

############################################
# sum(@array) -- Sum the elements of an array
#     and return the result
############################################
sub sum(@)
{
    my @array = @_;     # The array to sum
    my $the_sum = 0;    # Result so far

    foreach my $element (@array) {
        $the_sum += $element;
    }
    return ($the_sum);
}
############################################
# moving_averge($increment)
#
# Compute a moving average
#
# Returns:
#     Array containing the moving average
############################################
sub moving_average($)
{
    my $increment = shift;    # Increment for average
    my $index;                # Current item for average
    my @result;               # Averaged data

    for ($index = 0;
        $index <= $#raw_data - $increment;
        $index++) {
        my $total = sum(@raw_data[$index..$index + $increment -1]);
        push (@result, $total / $increment);
    }
    return(@result);
}

# Tell Perl we loaded successfully
1;
```

To use this package, first place the package file in the same directory as your script and then insert a single command in the program:

```
use average;
```

Listing 7.3 contains a simple program to test the module.

Listing 7.3 *test_ave.pl*

```
use strict;
use warning s;
use average;
use vars qw(@raw_data);

my $flag = read_data("num.txt");
if (not $flag) {
    die("Could not read file");
}

my $element_count = $#raw_data + 1;
print "Read $element_count items\n";

my @average = moving_average(3);
print "Moving average\n";
foreach my $item (@average)
{
    print "$item\n";
}
```

More on *use*

When Perl sees a use statement such as

```
use average;
```

the interpreter searches for the module file named average.pm. It searches through a series of directories specified by the system variable @INC. Normally, this array contains the locations of all the Perl standard module libraries as well as the current directory.

A typical Linux @INC array might look like

```
/usr/lib/perl5/5.00503/i386-linux
/usr/lib/perl5/5.00503
/usr/lib/perl5/site_perl/5.005/i386-linux
/usr/lib/perl5/site_perl/5.005
.
```

This can be modified by the -I switch on the command line. For example, if you have a local module library in the directory /usr/local/lib/perl, then you can use modules within it if you run your program with a -I flag that points to it:

```
perl -I/usr/local/lib/perl average.pl
```

Another way of adding to @INC is through the environment variable PERL5LIB. This variable contains a list of additional module directories to be searched, separated by colons. For example to add two directories to your library path, use the commands from the following operating systems/shells:

- UNIX/Linux (csh):

```
setenv PERL5LIB /usr/local/perl/lib:/home/sdo/perl/lib
```

- UNIX/Linux (sh, bash):

```
PERL5LIB=/usr/local/perl/lib:/home/sdo/perl/lib;export PERL5LIB
```

- Microsoft Windows:

```
set PERL5LIB=/usr/local/perl/lib:/home/sdo/perl/lib
```

Structuring Your Modules

You can structure your module library into modules, submodules, sub-sub-modules, and so on. Suppose that you have a top-level module directory called /usr/local/perl/lib. You tell Perl about this directory by putting the -I/usr/local/perl/lib switch on the command line.

Create a module called call. The name of the module file is call.pm. If you put the module in the top-level directory, you can then use the module with the statement

```
use call;
```

You can make this a submodule by putting it in a subdirectory of your module library. In this call, you want to make this a part of the "phone" system, so put it in a subdirectory called phone. The use statement is now

```
use phone::call;
```

Table 7.2 summarizes some of the various module constructions.

Table 7.2 **Paths and *use* Statements**

Module Path	use Statement
$LIB/call.pm	use call;
$LIB/phone/call.pm	use phone::call;
$LIB/phone/basic/call.pm	use phone::basic::call;
	$LIB is the location of the module library.

Special Blocks (*BEGIN, END*)

The code in the special block labeled BEGIN will be executed as soon possible in the program. This gives a module writer a place to put his initialization code. For example:

```
BEGIN {
    $vowels = "aeiou";    # Initialize the vowel table
}
```

Note that BEGIN blocks are executed at compile time, so if you check your syntax using the perl -c command, all your BEGIN blocks will be executed.

An END block is executed as late as possible. This is usually after an exit call or other normal terminations. (Special terminations, such as an interrupt signal or other exceptions, cause the END blocks to be skipped.)

For example:

```
END {
    unlink("tmp.$$");
}
```

For those who have not browsed the online documentation yet, unlink is a standard function to delete a file (perldoc -t -f unlink), and $$ is a built-in variable containing the process number of the current program (perldoc perlvar).

Finally, there is the code in the module itself, which is not in any subroutine. This code is executed after the BEGIN blocks when the module is loaded. This code must end in a statement that returns true to let Perl know that the module loaded correctly.

Consider the module in Listing 7.4.

Listing 7.4 *begin.pm*

```
use strict;
package begin_mod;
```

continues

Listing 7.4   **Continued**

```
END {
    print "END\n";
}

print "Module\n";

BEGIN {
    print "BEGIN\n";
}
1;
```

When you load this module with a `use begin_mod` statement, the program prints the following:

```
BEGIN
Module
```

After the program finishes, the program prints this:

```
END
```

Note that because you loaded this module with a `use` statement, these three print statements will be executed even if you only compile the program.

use Versus *require*

Perl has two ways of bringing in a module: the `use` statement and the `require` statement.

There are many technical differences between the two statements, but basically you should use a `use` statement for all the modules you write.

The `require` statement is much more suited to special-purpose applications, such as bringing in converted C header files (check out the online documentation for the command `h2ph` for more information on this) and other special files. One of these special files is the module `Exporter`. But in general, unless the module's documentation specifies the `require` statement, use `use`.

Summary

In this chapter, you learned how Perl lets you organize your programs into subroutines, packages, and modules. Good organization is key to producing good software. One of Perl's strengths is its extensive module library, and the module system in Perl makes all that possible.

Exercises

1. Write a subroutine that swaps two arrays.
2. Write a subroutine that verifies that the argument is a correctly formed integer. For extra credit, give it a flag that lets it check for integers; floating-point numbers (with and without exponents); complex, hexadecimal, and octal numbers; or any combination of these.
3. Write a module to count the words, lines, and characters in a string.
4. Write a module to print a hash nicely. Handle the case when the values contain new lines. (For extra credit, handle the case when the value contains unprintable characters.)
5. Write a function to encode a string so that it may be enclosed in double quotes safely. For example:

```
This "string" contains a backslash (\)
```

becomes

```
"This \"string\" contains a backslash (\\)"
```

Write a function that decodes strings as well.

Resources

Online Documentation

- `perldoc perlsub`—How to create a subroutine.
- `perldoc perlmod`—Module creation information.
- `perldoc perltoot`—Object-oriented tutorial.

Modules

- `Exporter`—Perl module to handle all the details of creating a public interface for a module.
- `vars`—Module that helps you define global variables.

Object-Oriented Programming

IN CHAPTER 7, "SUBROUTINES AND MODULES," you learned how to organize your code into subroutines, packages, and modules. In this chapter, you'll find out how to create objects and use the object-oriented features of Perl.

Using a Hash as an Object

Suppose that you want to create a module that handles time. The time module should let you

- Create a time from two integers—say 8:30 out of 8 and 30.
- Add and subtract times (8:30–1:20=7:10).
- Turn the time into a string for printing.

This chapter starts with a function to take two integers and return a time hash. Actually, the function returns a reference to the hash. The function to create a new time looks like this:

```
sub new($$)
{
    my $hours = shift; # Initial hours
    my $minutes = shift; # Initial minutes
    my $self = {};    # The hash we are creating
```

```
        $self->{hours} = $hours;
        $self->{minutes} = $minutes;
        return ($self);
    }
```

All this example really does is take the hours and minutes that you get as parameters and stuffs them in a hash. This function returns a reference to the hash you created.

Note that this function does not do any limit or error checking.

Now define a function to add one hash to another:

```
sub add($$)
{
    my $self = shift;     # The hash we wish to add to
    my $other = shift;    # The other hash

    $self->{hours} += $other->{hours};
    $self->{minutes} += $other->{minutes};
    $self->{hours} += int($self->{minutes} / 60);
    $self->{minutes} %= 60;
}
```

Like all functions that manipulate the object (the hash), the first argument to this function is the hash you are manipulating.

This code is straightforward. It simply adds together the two elements of the time and then handles any minutes that might have overflowed.

Again, note that you don't do any range or error checking. You assume that the result is < 24:00.

The subtract function works pretty much the same. You can see it in Listing 8.1.

Finally, you need something to turn a time into a string. For that you have the to_string function:

```
sub to_string($)
{
    my $self = shift;     # The hash to turn into a string

    return(sprintf("%d:%02d",
        $self->{hours}, $self->{minutes}));
}
```

Listing 8.1 contains the full time_hash package.

Listing 8.1   *time_hash.pm*

```
use strict;
use warnings;
#
# A package to handle time data (implement using a hash)
```

```perl
#
package time_hash;

sub new($$)
{
    my $hours = shift; # Initial hours
    my $minutes = shift; # Initial minutes
    my $self = {};    # The hash we are creating

    $self->{hours} = $hours;
    $self->{minutes} = $minutes;
    return ($self);
}

sub add($$)
{
    my $self = shift;    # The hash we wish to add to
    my $other = shift;    # The other hash

    $self->{hours} += $other->{hours};
    $self->{minutes} += $other->{minutes};
    $self->{hours} += int($self->{minutes} / 60);
    $self->{minutes} %= 60;
}

sub subtract($$)
{
    my $self = shift;    # The hash we wish to subtract from
    my $other = shift;    # The other hash

    $self->{hours} -= $other->{hours};
    $self->{minutes} -= $other->{minutes};
    while ($self->{minutes} < 0) {
        $self->{minutes} += 60;
        $self->{hours}--;
    }
}

sub to_string($)
{
    my $self = shift;    # The hash to turn into a string

    return(sprintf("%d:%02d",
    $self->{hours}, $self->{minutes}));
}

1;
```

The next step is figuring out how to use the `time hash` package. You can create a new time variable using the function `time_hash::new`. For example:

```
my $time1 = time_hash::new(1,30);
my $time2 = time_hash::new(8,40);
```

You then can add and subtract time, using the functions `add` and `subtract`. For example to add $time2 to $time1, use the statement

```
time_hash::add($time1, $time2);
```

You can print the results with the statement

```
print "Time1 is ", time_hash::to_string($time1), "\n";
```

Listing 8.2 shows a simple test routine.

Listing 8.2   *test_hash.pl*

```
use strict;
use warnings;

use time_hash;

my $time1 = time_hash::new(1,30);
my $time2 = time_hash::new(8,40);

print "Time1 is ", time_hash::to_string($time1), "\n";
print "Time2 is ", time_hash::to_string($time2), "\n";
time_hash::add($time1, $time2);
print "Time1 is ", time_hash::to_string($time1), "\n";
```

Design Notes

You should note a few things about the design of the package. First, the first parameter for every function, except `new`, is a reference to the object being acted on. This technique is commonly used to do object-oriented programming when you don't have an object-oriented language.

Second, the name `new` was chosen to be the constructor for the object. There's nothing magical about the name `new`, except that every C++ programmer associates `new` with construction of an object.

Finally, in all the functions, the variable `$self` is used to refer to the object. Again, you could have used any name; by convention, most Perl programmers use `$self` to refer to the current object. (C++ uses the built-in keyword `this` to do the same thing.)

Basic Perl Objects

The `time_hash` package has all the ingredients that make up an object. Data and functions act on that data. In Perl, these are called *methods*; in C++, they are called *member functions*.

The only problem is that you must manually specify the class variable every time you call a method. It would be nice if you could do that automatically.

The hash knows all about the data contained in it. The only thing it doesn't know is what methods can be used on that data, and you need that information if you are about to write object-oriented code. Perl solves this problem through the use of the `bless` function.

This function tells Perl to associate the subroutines (methods) in the current package or, in other words, the package where this function was called with the current hash. Modify your `new` function and put the following statement at the end of it:

```
    return (bless $self);
```

Now object `$self` (a hash created by the new function in the `time_hash` package) is associated with this package.

Now to create a new `time_hash` variable, use the following statement:

```
    my $time1 = time_hash::new(1, 30);
```

Perl looks for the method `new` in the package `time_hash` and calls it. The `new` method returns an object, also known as a *blessed hash*.

Here's how to call the `add` function:

```
    $time1->add($time2);
```

This adds `$time2` to `$time1`. Notice that you didn't have to specify the package name. Because `$time1` is a blessed hash, Perl knows that it comes from the `time_hash` package and therefore knows how to find the `time_hash::add` function.

Perl does one other thing in this case; it adds the hash reference (`$time1`) to the beginning of the parameter list. So, although you call `add` with one parameter (`$time2`), the `add` function receives two parameters (`$time1`, `$time2`).

The `add` function begins with

```
sub add($$)
{
    my $self = shift;    # The hash we wish to add to
    my $other = shift;   # The other hash
```

The first thing that the function `add` does is take the reference to the hash off the parameter list and assign it to `$self`. The variable `$self` is the equivalent of the C++ keyword `this`. It is a pointer to data in the class.

However, in C++ you can omit references to this when you access member functions. You can't do this in Perl; the $self is required. For example:

```
$self->{minutes}
```

Although there's nothing magical about using the variable name $self, it has become the standard name used by most Perl programmers.

Because of the way Perl does object-oriented programming, all the member functions, except new, look the same as in Listing 8.3.

However, your use of this package is much simpler. You can see the new test program in Listing 8.3.

Listing 8.3   *test_obj.pl*

```
use strict;
use warnings;

use time_hash;

my $time1 = time_hash::new(1,30);
my $time2 = time_hash::new(8,40);

print "Time1 is ", $time1->to_string(), "\n";
print "Time2 is ", $time2->to_string(), "\n";
$time1->add($time2);
print "Time1 is ", $time1->to_string(), "\n";
```

Polymorphism

One nice thing about C++ classes is the capability to create a derived class. For example, you can define a base class animal and then create derived classes for pigs, horses, and dogs.

In C++, a derived class might look like this:

```
class dog: public animal {
    // ....
```

You can do the same thing in Perl through the use of the @ISA array. In a derived class, or package, the derived class contains a list of base packages. For example:

```
package dog;
@ISA = qw(animal);
```

When Perl looks for a method (C++ member function), it first looks in the package being called. It then searches through the packages specified by the @ISA array.

The search is done depth first, so if you have the following packages:

```
package computer;
@ISA = qw(motherboard case);

package motherboard;
@ISA = qw(cpu memory);

package case;
@ISA = qw(power_supply disks);
```

the search order for the methods in the package computer is

> computer
>> motherboard
>>> cpu
>>> memory
>> case
>>> power_supply
>>> disks

Note that the searching occurs only if you have a variable of the type `computer`. For example, suppose that `start_disk` is a method in the package `disks`. Then you can use the following code:

```
my $server = computer->new();
$server->start_disk();
```

It will not work if you call a method directly:

```
computer::start_disk($server);   # Fails
```

Information Hiding

In C++, the protection keywords `public`, `private`, and `protected` tell the user who may access the member functions and member variables. In Perl, everything is public. No access protection exists at all.

Common Mistake: Exporting the Methods

When you design an ordinary package, you must put all the public functions and variables in the `@EXPORT` array. Otherwise, they will not be readily accessible to the caller when strict syntax checking is turned on.

continues

However, when you are doing object-oriented programming, the methods (functions) are addressed through the object. For example:

```
$time->to_string();
```

Because $time has been blessed, Perl knows what methods are associated with this object. In this case, the methods do not need to be exported.

If they are, it pollutes the namespace unnecessarily, so don't export methods.

Operator Overloading

Perl enables you to perform operator overloading. This enables you to define a function that's called when two time objects are added such as the following:

```
my $time3 = $time1 + $time2;
```

This section defines a new package called time_over that uses operator overloading to allow you to add, subtract, and print times.

To define a function for adding two time classes, you need to use the overload package:

```
use overload (
    '+' => \&add,
    '-' => \&subtract,
    '""' => \&to_string
);
```

Now when Perl sees you add two time objects, it calls this function to perform the addition. Listing 8.4 shows the subroutine to add two time objects.

Listing 8.4   *add* **Function**

```
# Incomplete function, see below for the full version
sub add($$)
{
    my $time1 = shift;  # The first time for adding
    my $time2 = shift;  # The second time for adding
    my $result = {};    # Result of the addition

    $result->{hours} = $time1->{hours} + $time2->{hours};
    $result->{minutes} = $time1->{minutes} + $time2->{minutes};
    $result->{hours} += int($result->{minutes} / 60);
    $result->{minutes} %= 60;
    return (bless $result);
}
```

But what happens when you add a `time` object to a number? For example:

```
my $time1 = $time1 + 10;
```

The answer is that Perl calls your `add` function. Unfortunately, your function can't handle this situation.

In C++, you would solve this problem by overloading the `add` function. Thus, you would create two functions:

```
time &add(const time &t1, const time &t2);
time &add(const time &t1, const int t2);
```

Perl doesn't let you overload functions. Instead, all `add` calls, no matter what the type of the variable, are funneled through this one function.

So the function needs to be smart enough to detect when the second parameter is an object and when it's a scalar. To do this, use the `ref` function. If `$var` is a reference, the `ref` function returns the name of the object being referenced. If `$var` is not a reference, the `ref` function returns `undef`.

So to check whether you have a number, use the following statement:

```
if (not ref($time2))
```

If you find that you have a number, change it to an object:

```
if (not ref($time2)) {
    $time2 = new time_over($time2);
}
```

Listing 8.5 shows the full `add` function.

Listing 8.5 **Full *add* Function**

```
sub add($$)
{
    my $time1 = shift;    # The first time for adding
    my $time2 = shift;    # The second time for adding
    my $result = {};    # Result of the addition

    if (not ref($time2)) {
    $time2 = new time_over($time2);
    }

    $result->{hours} = $time1->{hours} + $time2->{hours};
    $result->{minutes} = $time1->{minutes} + $time2->{minutes};
    $result->{hours} += int($result->{minutes} / 60);
    $result->{minutes} %= 60;
    return (bless $result);
}
```

So you've taken care of the following case:

```
$time1 = $time2 + 10;
```

but what happens when you have

```
$time1 = 10 + $time2;
```

The answer is that Perl switches the operators so that `$time2` is first and then calls the add function.

Perl also does a number of other little things behind your back. If you use the `+=` operator and don't explicitly specify a function for it, Perl turns the `+=` into an add. It also does the same for the `++` operator. So by defining the code for one operator, you can perform all sorts of explicit and implied additions:

```
$time1 = $time2 + $time3;
$time1 += 5;
$time1 += $time2;
$time1++;
```

The `subtract` function looks pretty much like `add`, but there's a problem. When the first argument is a number and the second argument is an object, Perl switches the argument. This is not a problem with addition, but in subtraction, it causes strange answers.

Fortunately, Perl supplies an extra argument that tells you when the operands have to be switched. This flag is true if Perl has flipped the arguments for you.

To use this in the `subtract` function, you must first grab the argument:

```
sub subtract($$$)
{
    my $time1 = shift;    # The hash we wish to subtract from
    my $time2 = shift;    # The other hash
    my $flag = shift;     # The manipulation flag
```

Then after all the reference stuff is handled, check to see whether the arguments need to be flipped:

```
    if ($flag) {
        ($time1, $time2) = ($time2, $time1);
    }
```

Finally, overload the operator double quote ("). This operator is used to turn the object into a string. This is useful for printing. For example:

```
print "The time $time\n";
```

Listing 8.6 shows the full overloaded time package. Listing 8.7 presents the code used to test it.

Listing 8.6   ***time_over.pm***

```perl
use strict;
use warnings;
package time_over;

sub add($$);
sub subtract($$$);
sub to_string($$);

use overload (
    '+' => \&add,
    '-' => \&subtract,
    '""' => \&to_string
);

sub new($;$)
{
    my $class = shift;    # The class name
    my $hours = shift;    # Initial hours
    my $minutes = shift; # Initial minutes
    my $self = {};        # The hash we are creating

    if (not defined($minutes)) {
    $minutes = 0;
    }

    $self->{hours} = $hours;
    $self->{minutes} = $minutes;
    return (bless $self, $class);
}

sub add($$)
{
    my $time1 = shift;    # The first time for adding
    my $time2 = shift;    # The second time for adding
    my $result = {};      # Result of the addition

    if (not ref($time2)) {
        $time2 = new time_over($time2);
    }

    $result->{hours} = $time1->{hours} + $time2->{hours};
    $result->{minutes} = $time1->{minutes} + $time2->{minutes};
    $result->{hours} += int($result->{minutes} / 60);
    $result->{minutes} %= 60;
    return (bless $result);
}

sub subtract($$$)
{
```

continues

Listing 8.6   **Continued**

```perl
        my $time1 = shift;    # The hash we wish to subtract from
        my $time2 = shift;    # The other hash
        my $flag = shift;     # The manipulation flag
        my $result = {};      # The result we are computing

        if (not ref($time2)) {
            $time2 = new time_over($time2);
        }
        if ($flag) {
            ($time1, $time2) = ($time2, $time1);
        }
        $result->{hours} = $time1->{hours} - $time2->{hours};
        $result->{minutes} = $time1->{minutes} - $time2->{minutes};
        while ($result->{minutes} < 0) {
            $result->{minutes} += 60;
            $result->{hours}--;
        }
        return (bless ($result));
    }

sub to_string($$)
{
    my $time = shift;     # The hash to turn into a string

    return(sprintf("%d:%02d",
    $time->{hours}, $time->{minutes}));
}

    1;
```

Listing 8.7   *test_over.pl*

```perl
use strict;
use warnings;

use time_over;

my $time1 = time_over->new(1,30);
my $time2 = time_over->new(8,40);

my $time3 = $time1 + $time2;
print "$time1 + $time2 = $time3\n";

my $time4 = $time1 + 10;
print "$time1 + 10 = $time4\n";

my $time5 = 10 - $time2;
print "10 - $time2 = $time5\n";
```

```
$time5 = $time2 - 1;
print "$time2 - 1 = $time5\n";

my $time6 = time_over->new(8,40);
my $time7 = $time6;
$time6 += 2;
print "8:40 += 2 => $time6\n";

$time6++;
print "10:40++ => $time6\n";
```

Summary

With Perl's object-oriented features and operator overloading, it's easy to create simple-to-use, reusable code. Proper organization and a good design are key to making an efficient and effective program.

In the next few chapters, you'll see how to apply the techniques provided here to use Perl to solve some real-world problems. These include CGI programming to handle web forms, using the Tk package to build a GUI, and even mixing C and Perl programs together through the use of inline C functions.

Exercises

1. Write a persistent list object. This object acts just like an array except that it stores its values in a file and reloads when the program is run again. In other words, the values of the array persist even after the program is terminated.

2. Write a package to handle Roman numerals.

3. Write classes to support a workflow tool. The base class should provide
   - A title for this step in the workflow
   - A flag indicating whether the work has been done
   - A virtual method called do_it, which actually does the work

   There are two different types of steps: manual, which is done by an operator, and automatic, which is done by a system command. Devise derived classes to handle both these cases.

4. Write a complex number class.

5. Devise a base class called person and derived classes for men and women with different methods. Try to avoid triggering your organization policy on sexual harassment in the process.

Resources

Online Documentation

- **`perldoc perlobj`**—Basic information on creating Perl objects.
- **`perldoc perlboot, perldoc perltoot, perltootc`**—A three-part tutorial on the object-oriented features of Perl.
- **`perldoc perlbot`**—Object-oriented tricks and tips.

Modules

- **`overload`**—Module to handle operator overloading.

9

Advanced I/O

IN CHAPTER 2, "PERL BASICS," YOU LEARNED how to do basic I/O. This chapter takes a look at the rich set of features Perl has for doing I/O. These features include pipes as well as files. You'll also learn about reading and writing binary files as well as other special operations.

Opening a File (Revisited)

As you already know, to open a file for reading, you use the following statement:

```
open FILE_VAR, "<file_in.txt";
```

And to open a file for writing, you use this statement:

```
open FILE_VAR, ">file_out.txt";
```

Perl uses the special character > to indicate that it should open a file for writing and < for a read indicator.

Other special characters are recognized as well. For example, if you want to append to a file, use the >> indicator:

```
open LOG_FILE, ">>command.log";
```

Opening a Pipe

Suppose that you are going to write a report to the screen. If you just write the report, the data scrolls off the top of the screen. So to be nice, you want to write out a page of data and wait for the user to press a key. Then you would write out a new page and so on. This behavior is similar to what the more command does. A cheap way of doing this is to require the user to pipe the output of the program to more:

```
$ perl report.pl ¦ more
```

Or you could use Perl's write-to-pipe feature to do the work yourself.
For example:

```
open REPORT_FILE, "¦ more";
```

When Perl sees the special character ¦, it opens a pipe to the command (in this case more) and sends all data written to <REPORT_FILE> to that pipe.

Pipes can be used for input as well. For example, the UNIX/Linux find command finds a list of files and prints the results to screen if needed. Suppose that you want a list of all the files in /release/software that end in .c.

You can locate them with the find command:

```
find /release/software -name '*.c' -print
```

Now if you want to get that list into a program, all you have to do is use the open statement with the pipe symbol on the right side of the file specification:

```
open LIST_FILE, "find /release/software -name '*.c' -print ¦" or
    die("Could not execute the find command");
my @file_list = <LIST_FILE>;
chomp(@file_list);
close (LIST_FILE);
```

Note that if you are running on Microsoft Windows, you need to use the DIR command in the open statement:

```
open LIST_FILE, "DIR C:\\*.c /s/b ¦" or
    die("Could not execute the DIR command");
```

Open Summary

As you can see in Table 9.1, you can pass many different flags to the open function.

Table 9.1 *open* **Flags**

Flag	Description
`<file.txt`	Open for reading
`>file.txt`	Open for writing
`>>file.txt`	Append to file
`+<file.txt`	Open file for reading and writing
`+>file.txt`	Create a new file for reading and writing
`¦ command`	Open a pipe from the Perl program to `command` (for writing)
`command ¦`	Open a pipe from the `command` to the Perl program (for reading)

Using the Backtick (`) Operator

The `find` example goes to a lot of trouble just to read the output of a command and put it in an array. The backtick (`) operator does this in one operation. For example, you could write `find` code as

```
my @file_list = `find /release/software -name '*.c' -print`;
chomp(@file_list);
```

The backtick operator (`) executes the command enclosed in the backticks and whatever the command prints. In the array context, it returns an array containing each line of the output. In the scalar context, it returns a string containing the entire output of the program. Lines are separated by newlines.

sysopen (Advanced open)

The `sysopen` function call gives you greater control over the opening of a file handle. The format of this function call is similar to that of the C `open` function:

```
sysopen FILEHANDLE,FILENAME,MODE [, PERMS];
```

In this case, `FILEHANDLE` is the file to be opened. The `FILENAME` is the name of the file to be opened. `MODE` is open mode. It can be 0 for read, 1 for write, and 2 for read write; however, these values may not work on some operating systems such as Macintosh.

Or you can use the package `Fcntl` to bring in the symbols `O_RDONLY`, `O_WRONLY`, and `O_RDWR`. This module provides all the flags available on your system. Other flags such as `O_APPEND` and `O_NONBLOCK` are available as well.

Finally, if you are creating a file, the *PERMS* parameter specifies the permissions to be used. (Permissions correspond to the UNIX permission bits if you're on UNIX. If you're on Microsoft Windows, these bits are ignored.)

For example, suppose that you want to open a file for reading and writing with permissions that allow everyone to read and write the file. You would use the sysopen call:

```
use Fcntl;
sysopen DATA_FILE, "data.txt", O_RDWR, 0666;
```

Reading a Binary File

Perl is designed to handle string data. If you are reading or writing binary data in Perl, you've probably got the wrong language. Notwithstanding this fact, it is possible to do binary I/O with Perl.

In this section, you see how to write a program that reads a binary file and dumps it out as a series of hex numbers and characters. A typical run looks like

```
53 65 61 72 63 68 43 61: S e a r c h C a
74 3d 62 65 72 65 69 63: t = b e r e i c
68 25 33 64 70 6b 77 25: h % 3 d p k w %
32 36 74 69 74 65 6c 25: 2 6 t i t e l %
33 64 32 26 62 65 72 65: 3 d 2 & b e r e
69 63 68 3d 70 6b 77 26: i c h = p k w &
73 70 72 61 63 68 65 3d: s p r a c h e =
32 26 44 6f 53 65 61 72: 2 & D o S e a r
63 68 3d 31 26 46 6f 72: c h = 1 & F o r
6d 4d 61 6b 65 3d 32 39: m M a k e = 2 9
26 46 6f 72 6d 50 72 69: & F o r m P r I
63 65 3d 2d 37 36 36 39: c e = - 7 6 6 9
31 32 32 35 26 46 6f 72: 1 2 2 5 & F o r
6d 43 61 74 65 67 6f 72: m C a t e g o r
79 3d 37 26 46 6f 72 6d: y = 7 & F o r m
45 5a 3d 31 39 39 37 2d: E Z = 1 9 9 7 -
```

Start by opening the file:

```
use strict;
use warnings;

open IN_FILE, "<$ARGV[0]" or
    die("Could not find file $ARGV[0]");
```

Perl assumes that all files are text files. This means that on Microsoft Windows and other systems that do not use the UNIX/Linux text format, Perl edits the input stream to change the native operating system newline characters to a single newline (\n).

This is not what you want if you are dealing with binary files, so you need to tell Perl that your file is binary using the `binmode` function call:

```
binmode(IN_FILE);
```

Next loop through and read the file. This is done with the Perl `read` function call. The Perl `read` function works pretty much like the C `read` function, only it reads the file using the buffered I/O mechanism. (For an unbuffered read, use the `sysread` function.)

Like C's `read`, the Perl `read` function takes three arguments: a file variable, a buffer in which to store the data, and a number of bytes to read. The return value is the number of bytes read.

In the dump program, you want to read in the first 8 bytes:

```
while (1) {
    my $buffer;
    my $read_size = read(IN_FILE, $buffer, 8);
```

Note that Perl strings are different from C strings. C strings use the null character (\0) as an end-of-string delimiter. Perl's strings have no delimiter. They can contain anything, including a null character. This makes it possible to store binary data in a Perl string, something that can't be done with a C string.

The `read` call returns 8 bytes of binary data. Now check to see that you actually got 8 bytes and exit the loop if there is a problem or if you run out of bytes:

```
if ($read_size < 8) {
    last;
}
```

Now you have the buffer as a scalar. Because almost all of Perl's operators deal with strings, there's not much you can do with it at this point. You need to transform it into something you can use.

You do this through the `unpack` function call. This function's job is to unpack binary data and turn it into an array of values.

The question is, how do you turn a set of bits into a string? After all, there are many different ways of expressing a bit pattern. For example, ASCII character "L" can be presented as

01001100	(Binary)
L	(ASCII)
76	(Decimal)
4C	(Hexadecimal)
0114	(Octal)

All represent the same bit pattern. So how's unpack going to know which representation you want to use? The answer is that unpack uses a *TEMPLATE* parameter to decide how to unpack the value.

The general form of the function is

```
@result = unpack TEMPLATE, $buffer;
```

A b in the template indicates a binary number, an H indicates a hex one, and so on. (See perldoc -f pack for a list of template characters. Yes, that's pack, not unpack, for a list of the unpack template characters.)

You want to deal with the buffer as a series of two-digit hex numbers, so use the template "H2". Because you want eight values out of the buffer, you need to repeat this specification eight times. The unpack function call looks like

```
my @hex = unpack("H2" x 8, $buffer);
```

You also want to print a character representation of the data. For that, you need to split the buffer into characters. Again, use the unpack function and the template "a1" (a—ASCII character; 1—one at a time).

```
my @char = unpack("a1" x 8 ,$buffer);
```

The rest of the program is devoted to changing any special characters in the @char array to "." and printing the results. Listing 9.1 shows the full program.

Listing 9.1 *dump.pl*

```
use strict;
use warnings;

open IN_FILE, "<$ARGV[0]" or
    die("Could not $ARGV[0]");

binmode(IN_FILE);
while (1) {
    my $buffer;
    my $read_size = read(IN_FILE, $buffer, 8);

    if ($read_size < 8) {
        last;
    }

    my @hex = unpack("H2" x 8, $buffer);
    my @char = unpack("a1" x 8 ,$buffer);

    foreach my $ch (@char)
    {
        if (($ch lt ' ') || ($ch gt "~")) {
            $ch = ".";
```

```
        }
    }
    print "@hex: @char\n";
}
```

One final note: This program does not properly handle the case where a file does not end on an 8-byte boundary. In other words, if your file has 15 bytes in it, the program will dump the first 8 and quit.

File Handling Package

If you are doing more than just simple I/O, then you'll probably want to use the `IO::Handle` package. This package provides several useful functions that allow you to manipulate a file.

These functions allow you to do things such as seek to a given location in a file, truncate a file, get file status information (similar to the C `stat(2)` function), and other tasks.

For example, one problem with `STDOUT` is that it is buffered if you are writing to something other than the console. This normally is not a problem, but in some circumstances (such as writing to a pipe), this can be a problem.

The solution is to tell Perl to flush `STDOUT` after each output call. This is done using the `autoflush` method:

```
STDOUT->autoflush(1);
```

For more information, see `perldoc -m IO::Handle`.

Passing a File Handle to a Subroutine

To pass a file handle to a subroutine, use `*` in the subroutine prototype type to indicate a file handle parameter. But getting the file handle into something you can use is a little tricky. For that, you need a module called `Symbol`:

```
use Symbol;

sub print_it(*)
{
    my $file_handle = qualify_to_ref(shift, caller);
```

You can now use this file handle in a `print` statement just like a normal Perl file handle:

```
print $file_handle "Hello World\n";
```

Remember that there is no comma after the file handle.

To call this function, just put the file handle in the parameter list:

```
    print_it(STDOUT);
```

You must use a module because Perl treats file handles differently from other variables. When you specify STDOUT in the parameter, Perl treats this parameter as a *bare word* and passes the string STDOUT to the subroutine.

The qualify_to_ref function takes this string and converts it into a reference to the file handle.

Actually, you don't get a reference to a file handle; rather, you get a type-glob to the file handle. This is discussed in more detail in the next section.

References to a File Handle

You can't take a reference to a file handle—at least not directly. However, you can use a trick called a typeglob to do virtually the same thing. The syntax is

```
    my $ref = \*FILE_HANDLE;
```

You can now use $ref as a file handle, for example:

```
    my $ref = \*STDOUT;
    print $ref "Hello World\n";
```

So how is a typeglob different from a normal reference? The answer is the statement

```
    my $ref = \*FOO;
```

makes $ref a sort of reference for all variables, no matter what type, whose name is FOO. Thus this statement also assigns %$ref the value of %FOO, $$ref is the same as $FOO, @$ref gets @FOO, and finally the subroutine FOO() is &$ref.

The typeglob was an early method for creating references before real references were put in the language. Although it has been made obsolete by better references, in most cases, it still is useful when it comes to file handle references.

Summary

As you can see, Perl has a rich set of I/O functions. These give you a tremendous amount of flexibility in dealing with all the different data that you can process in your Perl scripts.

Exercises

1. Write a program to check whether two files are equal. Make sure that it works on binary files.

2. Write a conversion program that converts text files between the various end-of-line style formats. The three formats available are

- **UNIX/Linux**—End of line is linefeed (`\012`).
- **Microsoft Windows**—End of line is carriage-return/linefeed (`\015\012`).
- **Apple**—End of line is carriage-return (`\015`).

3. Write two programs that communicate to each other through a shared file.

4. Write a replacement for the command `more` that pages through text. Include a capability to go back.

5. Write a program that goes through a log file and checks to see whether any lines match a particular pattern. The program should not exit; rather, it should wait for the file to grow, and when it does, it should examine any new lines added to the file.

Resources

Online Documentation

- `perldoc perlref`—Information on references including references to file handles.

Modules

- `Fcntl`—Provides named open flags, such as `O_RDONLY` and `O_RDWR`.
- `IO::Handle`—An object-oriented interface to the I/O system.
- `IO::File`—A superclass of `IO::Handle` for files.
- `Symbol`—Symbol table manipulation functions.

Functions

- `perldoc -f open`—Information on opening a file.
- `perldoc -f sysopen`—An interface to the systems `open` call.
- `perldoc -f binmode`—Set the binary mode of a file.

- **perldoc -f read**—Read a series of bytes from a file.
- **perldoc -f write**—Write a series of bytes to a file.
- **perldoc -f pack**—Turn a list of strings into binary data.
- **perldoc -f unpack**—Turn binary data into strings that Perl can use.

10

POD

PERL COMES WITH ITS OWN BUILT-IN DOCUMENTATION system. In Chapter 1, "Exploring Perl," you learned how to use that system to access the huge repository of online documentation that comes with Perl.

In this chapter, you'll learn how to create such documents.

POD (Plain Old Documentation)

Perl uses a documentation format called *POD* (*Plain Old Documentation*). POD enables you to put the documentation for a program in the program itself. The system was designed to be simple and easy to use so that writing documentation would be easy.

The simplicity also makes it possible for people to create a wide variety of POD converters (pod2html, pod2man, pod2tex), which convert POD format documents into something more readable.

Documenting a Program

Suppose that you have written a program that converts US dollars to Hong Kong (HK) dollars, and you want to document it. You can do so by embedding POD documentation in the Perl script itself.

POD documentation begins with a line =pod and ends with =cut. Anything between the =pod or other POD directive and =cut lines is considered a comment by Perl but is considered documentation by the POD tools.

Start the script with the usual stuff, put in the POD documentation, and then follow this with the rest of the program. An abbreviated version of the program looks like this:

```
use strict;
use warnings;

=pod
The pod documentation (to be done)
=cut
# The rest of the script
print "This program solves all the worlds problems.\n";
```

Now all you have to do is put something between these two directives.

A semistandard style has developed over the years when it comes to documenting programs. This style was started by the UNIX man pages and copied into the Perl documentation system. You don't have to follow this standard, but it is the one that everyone has come to expect, and the one that's documented here.

NAME

The first section of the documentation is the NAME section. In it, you give the name of your program and a short one-line description of what it does.

In the case of the money conversion program, this looks like

```
=head1 NAME
```

```
us2hk - Convert US$ to HK$ (or vice versa)
```

The =head1 directive tells POD that this is a level 1 heading. The text NAME will be printed in big bold letters in the typeset of the documentation. Other levels of heading from (=head2) to (=head6) are available for your needs.

A blank line occurs after the =head1 directive. POD uses blank lines to separate things. In this case, you are separating the heading from the paragraph that follows.

This paragraph is actually a single line listing the name of the program (us2hk) and a single line description. (It's a very short paragraph.)

POD considers text that begins in column 1 to be a part of a paragraph that can be typeset. Paragraphs are separated by blank lines.

SYNOPSIS

The SYNOPSIS section lists the program name and all the options and other arguments that can be passed to it. The SYNOPSIS section looks like

```
=head1 SYNOPSIS

    us2hk [-u] [-r=<rate>] <amount>
```

Again, this is a level 1 head (=head1). If the next line is indented with one or more spaces, POD considers it to be a code example or command, and it will be typeset in monospace courier type. Also no typesetting conversions are made on the text.

In this example, the command is us2hk. It can take a -u flag. Because this flag is in square brackets ([ ]), it is optional.

The second flag also is optional. It takes an argument indicated by *<rate>*.

Finally, the *<amount>* argument is not in square brackets ([ ]), so it is not optional.

DESCRIPTION

The DESCRIPTION section contains a description of what the program does. This can run for several paragraphs:

```
=head1 DESCRIPTION

The I<us2hk> converts United States
dollars to Hong Kong dollars.   It can optionally
convert form HK to US as well.

It is an extremely useful program if
you ever go to Hong Kong and find out
that a copy of Microsoft Windows 2000
that you need to purchase is selling
for $1600.00 (HK).
```

This section has two paragraphs. They are separated by a blank line. The paragraphs are not indented because POD considers indented text a code example, not a paragraph.

The first paragraph uses the I<...> escape. This tells POD to turn the enclosed text into italics. The other font controls include B<...> for bold and C<...> for code. The online document perlpod contains a complete list of escapes.

OPTIONS

Next you need to document the list of options. A list in POD starts with the following directive:

```
=over 4
```

The number 4 is the number of spaces to be used for indenting the list. Each item in the list is identified by an item directive:

```
=item <text>
```

Finally, the list is ended with the following directive:

```
=back
```

The option list looks like this:

```
=head1 OPTIONS

The I<us2hk> command takes the following arguments:

=over 4

=item B<-u>

Convert from US$ to HK$.  The default is HK$-E<gt>US$.
=item B<-r=>I<rate>

Specify the conversion rate for US$ to HK$ instead of the default: 0.128.  (1:8)


=back
```

This example has a problem with the explanation of the -u option. You want to say "The default is HK$->US$." But the greater than (>) is a special character, and you can't put it in the text. So you must use the escape code: E<character>, which enables you to put special characters in the text.

Table 10.1 lists the escape characters.

Table 10.1 **POD Escape Characters**

Escape Character	Character Escaped
E<lt>	<
E<gt>	>
E<sol>	/
E<verbar>	¦
E<*nnn*>	Character whose decimal number is nnn

SEE ALSO

Finally, you have the SEE ALSO section, which provides a recommended reading list to users:

```
=head1 SEE ALSO

L<units>
```

The L<...> escape tells POD that the enclosed text is a link. This is the proper way of representing the name of another documentation. The POD translators (see "Turning POD into Something Readable") translate a link into the appropriate value of the resulting document format.

Checking the Results

To make sure that you have done a good job on your POD documentation, you can use the command podchecker to check the POD documentation for errors:

```
podchecker us2hk.pl
```

Finally, you can view the results with the perldoc command:

```
perldoc us2hk
```

Putting It All Together

Listing 10.1 contains the complete POD documentation for the function.

Listing 10.1   *us2hk.pl*

```
=head1 NAME

us2hk - Convert US$ to HK$ (or vice versa)

=head1 SYNOPSIS

    us2hk [-u] [-r=<rate>] <amount>

=head1 DESCRIPTION

The I<us2hk> command converts United States dollars to
Hong Kong dollars.   It
can optionally convert from HK to US as well.

It is an extremely useful program if you ever
go to Hong Kong and find
that a copy of Microsoft Windows 2000 that
you need to purchase is selling
for $1600.00 (HK).
```

continues

Listing 10.1 Continued

```
=head1 OPTIONS

The I<us2hk> command takes the following arguments:

=over 4

=item B<-u>

Convert from US$ to HK$.  The default is HK$-E<gt>US$.

=item B<-r=>I<rate>

Specify the conversion rate for US$ to HK$ instead of the default: 0.128 (1:8).

=back

=head1 SEE ALSO

L<units>
```

Figure 10.1 shows the printed copy of this documentation.

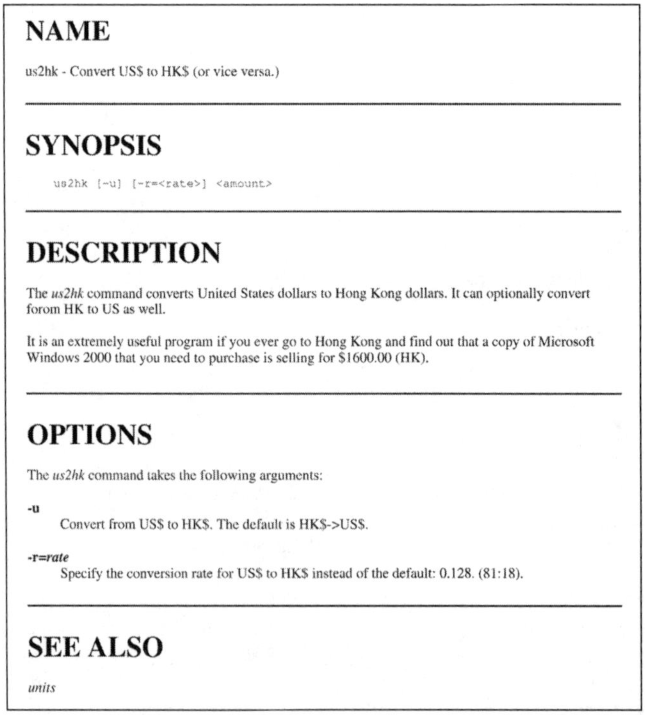

NAME

us2hk - Convert US$ to HK$ (or vice versa.)

SYNOPSIS

        us2hk [-u] [-r=<rate>] <amount>

DESCRIPTION

The *us2hk* command converts United States dollars to Hong Kong dollars. It can optionally convert forom HK to US as well.

It is an extremely useful program if you ever go to Hong Kong and find out that a copy of Microsoft Windows 2000 that you need to purchase is selling for $1600.00 (HK).

OPTIONS

The *us2hk* command takes the following arguments:

-u
        Convert from US$ to HK$. The default is HK$->US$.

-r=*rate*
        Specify the conversion rate for US$ to HK$ instead of the default: 0.128. (81:18).

SEE ALSO

units

Figure 10.1 POD documentation for us2hk.pl typeset.

Turning POD into Something Readable

The POD file format is used as input by several translators, which turn it into something you can read. One command you're already familiar with is perldoc. It reads the POD documentation from the command specified, formats it, and prints it on the screen.

A number of other POD-related commands format the text in a variety of ways. For example, the pod2html program turns POD into HTML, which can be viewed by Netscape or Internet Explorer. (Or imported into Microsoft Word so that it can be converted to Quark Express to become a typeset in a book.)

Table 10.2 lists the standard POD converters.

Table 10.2 **POD Converters**

Converter	Description
pod2html	Converts to standard HTML
pod2latex	Output is for the LaTeX text processor
pod2man	Format for the old UNIX nroff, troff, groff processors.
pod2text	Text output
pod2usage	Prints out the usage section of a POD document

Putting a *--help* Option in Your Files

One nice thing you can do with your program is to list the full documentation when the users give you a -h or --help option. One way of doing this is to put the following subroutine in your code:

```
# If --help is on the command line display the documentation
# and exit.
sub display_help()
{
    if (not defined ($ARGV[0])) {
        return;    # No options at all
    }
    if ( ($ARGV[0] eq "-h") or ($ARGV[0] eq "--help")) {
        exec("perldoc $0");
        exit (8);
    }
}
```

This subroutine checks to see whether the option -h or --help is present on the command line. It then performs an exec call to execute the command `perldoc $0.`When Perl runs, it puts the name of the program in `$0`, so the exec function executes the following command:

```
perldoc <program-name>
```

This causes `perldoc` to print the POD documentation contained in the source. The `exec` call does not return, but if something goes wrong and it does, the program aborts with an `exit(8)`.

(If you want to execute a command and return to the script, use the `system` function.)

The POD Template

A POD document has many sections, and remembering them all can be difficult. The technique I use is to start with a template, fill in the sections I need, delete the sections I don't, and thus get good documentation: (This template is rather long. Cut it down and only use the sections which are relevant to your situation.)

```
=pod

=head1 NAME

program - a program that does something useful

=head1 SYNOPSIS

    program [-x] [-x=<value>] <file> [<file> ...]

=head1 DESCRIPTION

The I<program> does something very useful.

=head1 OPTIONS

The I<program> takes the following arguments:

=over 4

=item B<-x>

An option that's just a single letter.

=item B<-x=>I<value>

An option that takes a I<value> as an argument.

=back

=head1 RETURN VALUE
```

Exit values are:

```
=over 4

=item 0
```

Success.

```
=item 1
```

Failure

```
=item 8
```

Bad failure.

```
=back

=head1 EXAMPLES
```

An example of how to use the program to do something is:

```
        program -x -x=foo in_file.txt
```

```
=head1 WARNINGS
```

Just because you're paranoid it doesn't mean that they aren't out
to get you.

```
=head1 DIAGNOSTICS
```

Most of the error messages are self explanatory.

```
=head1 ENVIRONMENT

=over 4

=item I<ENV>
```

An environment variable that affects the program.

```
=back

=head1 FILES

=over 4

=item /tmp/foo.lock
```

A lock file used to make sure that we don't try and update
the database from two programs at the same time.

```
=back

=head1 AUTHOR

A. Writer, E<lt>a.writer@localhostE<gt>.

=head1 BUGS

The command I<program> does not exist.

=head1 SEE ALSO

L<another_program>, L<yanp>

=head1 COPYRIGHT

Copyright 2001, by Someone at Some Company.

=cut
```

This template is not an official standard. Rather, it is a result of scanning existing documentation and finding common elements. You may want to adapt it for your environment.

(For example, one of my earliest jobs was to edit all the documentation that came with a UNIX system and turning "BUGS" into "NOTES".)

Summary

According to Oualline's law of documentation, 90 percent of the time, the documentation is lost. Out of the remaining 10 percent, 9 percent of the time it will be a version or two out of date and therefore completely useless. The 1 percent of the time that you have the documentation and the correct version of the documentation, it will be written in Japanese (my Japanese readers might want to substitute the term "English" here).

Perl has beaten the odds and created a standard way of documenting your programs. By keeping the documentation inside the program, things do not get lost.

One strength of the Perl CPAN archive is that almost all the modules are documented. That means that not only are they useful, but also you have the documentation so that you can use them.

One final note: Far too many programmers skip the documentation step or put it off until tomorrow. The results are undocumented Perl programs. Perl is not the most readable language in the world, so an undocumented program quickly becomes obsolete.

Always document your programs. Even if you are writing the program only for yourself, document it for practice. The more you write, the easier it is, and the better you'll become at it. Remember, your program is not finished until you tell people how to use it.

Exercise

1. Add POD documentation to all the scripts you've done so far.

Resources

Online Documentation

- **perldoc perlpod**—Description of the POD documentation formation.

Commands

- **pod2html**—Turns POD into HTML.
- **pod2latex**—Turns POD into LaTeX (a documentation formatting system found on most Linux systems and a few UNIX ones).
- **pod2man**—Turns POD into man format. (Man format can by read by the UNIX/Linux man command and turned into printed documentation by the nroff, groff, troff, and ditroff commands.)
- **pod2text**—Prints POD documentation as text.
- **podchecker**—Checks POD documentation for errors.

11

Under the Hood

P ERL IS A COMPLEX LANGUAGE THAT DOES many wonderful things behind your back. This chapter looks at how some of these features are implemented so that you can truly understand how Perl works and can exploit this language to maximum benefit.

What Really Goes on When You Use Perl

Because Perl is an interpreted language, you can do things that you can't do with compiled languages. For example, you can create code that changes the symbol table (adding or removing variables). You also can define new subroutines or replace old ones. In other words, self-modifying code is back.

Perl not only lets you write self-modifying code, in some cases Perl makes you depend on it. Fortunately, almost all these cases happen behind your back, but still it's important to know what's going on.

Perl executes some statements at compile time and others at runtime. The use statement is executed at compile time. You should remember that this statement is used to bring other modules.

Take a look at what happens when you issue a use statement such as

```
use my_module qw(start_it process_it end_it);
```

First, the module my_module.pm is read in and compiled. If no error occurs, the code in any BEGIN blocks in my_module is executed, followed by any code in the module that's not in any subroutine. If the code returns a good (nonzero, usually 1) result, the module loaded successfully.

Next, Perl calls the module's import function (if there is one). The argument list is the name of the module followed by the list of items in the use list. In this case, Perl would execute the statement

```
my_module::import("my_module", "start_it", "process_it", "end_it");
```

The import function normally does some symbol table manipulation and creates the names "start_it", "process_it", and "end_it" in the calling program. Normally, you don't have to do this yourself; the Exporter module does it for you (more on this later in this chapter). In fact, the module name is supplied so that subclasses such as Exporter know whose symbols they are exporting to the outside world.

How *use strict* Works

The strict module uses the import method a little differently. Before going into the details, you need to learn a little more about strict. Consider the following statement:

```
use strict;
```

This turns on all strict syntax checking. But you don't have to turn on everything. You can turn on just variable checking with the statement

```
use strict "vars";
```

The other more restricted forms of strict are

- **strict "refs"**—Do not allow symbolic references.
- **strict "subs"**—Prevents the automatic conversion of barewords to subroutines.

Now getting back to the statement

```
use strict "vars";
```

This does not cause the function strict::vars to be made available to the calling program. Rather, it turns on strict variable checking.

The strict module does this by changing the state of the Perl compiler inside its import function (actually, the variable $^H if you must know). A pseudocode version of strict::import is

```
package strict;
sub import($module, @list)
{
    # $module is ignored

    # if the list is empty, turn on everything;
    # Turn on the bits represented by the keywords in @list;
}
```

You also can say the following statement:

```
no strict "vars";
```

In this case, the `unimport` function is called rather than the `import` function. The job of the `unimport` function is to turn off Perl's internal syntax checking flags.

Remember that the `use` command executes the `import` function at compile time. Because of that, the `import` function can, at compile time, change the internal state of the compiler to make the syntax checking more strict.

The *use vars* Statement

The vars module, which is used to declare global variables, is another example of the use of a nonstandard `import` function. For example, suppose that you put the statement

```
use vars qw($alpha @beta %gamma);
```

in your code. When Perl sees this, it executes the statement

```
vars::import(qw(vars $alpha @beta %gamma));
```

The vars module then does some magic that results in the global symbols `$main::alpha`, `@main::beta`, and `%main::gamma` being created. (This assumes that you call the module from the top-level file. If you call it from inside a package, the package name will be used rather than `main`.)

The pseudocode for this function is

```
package vars;
sub import($module, @list)
{
    foreach $variable (@list) {
        # define the variable in the caller's namespace;
    }
}
```

Again the `import` function does something a little different.

The *Exporter* Package

The Exporter package defines a function called import. Unlike the other packages discussed, the import function does what it's supposed to do, namely import a function from the package into the caller's namespace. It does this through some magic involving typeglobs and references, but it doesn't matter how it does it; the thing works.

This is another case of a Perl module using some of the hidden syntax features of the language to modify the program—in this case, the symbol table—on-the-fly.

How *import* and *AUTOLOAD* Work

Perl follows the following algorithm when you call the function:

```
package->method()
```

First, it looks in the package for the given method. Then it searches through all the methods in all the packages specified by the @ISA array.

Next, it searches for an AUTOLOAD method using the same search algorithm. If it finds one, it calls it using the statement

```
package->AUTOLOAD(package, method, arguments);
```

Remember that Perl is an interpreted language. It is entirely possible to define a new subroutine during the middle of a program's execution. The AUTOLOAD method facilitates this process. The idea is that if you don't have a method defined, you can use the AUTOLOAD method to define it and then execute it.

The reason Perl lets you defer the loading of the function is speed. It takes time to compile things. If you don't compile them, you save that time. However, there is a cost to be paid in complexity.

Using AUTOLOAD is not easy, and it's just one more thing you have to worry about. Besides, if you are really concerned about speed, you wouldn't be using Perl in the first place.

Summary

Hopefully this look under the hood helps you understand how Perl works a little better. As a language, Perl is a little different, and understanding what goes on behind your back can be useful.

Resources

Online Documentation

- **perldoc -f use**—Documentation of the details of the use statement.
- **perldoc perlbot**—Perl's bag of tricks document, which describes how to use AUTOLOAD.

Modules

- **Exporter**—Handles the exporting of symbols from the package to the main program.
- **AutoSplit**— Helps prepare your program for autoloading.
- **AutoLoader**—Helps you autoload the functions created by AutoSplit.
- **strict**—Turns on strict syntax checking.
- **vars**—Declares global variables.

12

CGI Programming

PERL IS THE LANGUAGE BEHIND MANY OF THE interactive web pages you see today. Whenever you enter data into a form or get information from an interactive report, you are probably dealing with Perl.

Interactive web pages use a programming API called CGI (Common Gateway Interface) to handle the interaction between the user and the application. Because of its excellent string handling capabilities, Perl is an ideal language for writing web applications.

This chapter shows you how the CGI system works and how to write simple CGI programs to power your web site.

This chapter is oriented toward a UNIX or Linux system because that's what most web servers run on.

Simple CGI

You need to understand what happens when a CGI program is executed. It all starts when a user requests a URL either by clicking on a link or by typing it into his browser.

The browser sends a request to the web server telling it, "I want to get a resource with the URL named `http://www.webserver.com/cgi-bin/hello.pl`."

The web server looks at the URL and breaks it down into its components. The key parts are the directory `cgi-bin` and the filename `hello.pl`. Normally, the server would merely return the file `hello.pl`, but because it's in the directory `cgi-bin` and because the server's configuration tells it that `cgi-bin` contains CGI programs, it executes the program, capturing the output and sending it to the web server.

The user's web browser then sees a resource coming from the web server and displays it or offers to save it on a hard drive. As far as it's concerned, the web browser sent in a request and got back a web page.

Now that you have an idea of what's going on, you'll see how to write the first program.

CGI Hello World

Start with the CGI version of "Hello World". Although simple, the program may be more of a challenge to get running than your usual Perl program.

The program itself is simple enough, as shown in Listing 12.1.

Listing 12.1   *hello.pl*

```
#!/home/sdo/local/bin/perl -T
# Replace the above line with the path
# to your Perl program

use strict;
use warnings;

print <<EOF
Content: text/html

<HEAD><TITLE>Hello</TITLE></HEAD>
<BODY>
<P>
Hello World!
</BODY>

EOF
```

The first thing to notice is that the program begins with the line

```
#!/home/sdo/local/bin/perl -T
```

This is a special "magic line" used on UNIX/Linux systems to turn the script into a program. (See Appendix B, "Turning Perl Scripts into Commands," for details.) You'll have to replace that line with one that contains the full path to your installation of Perl, so this script will require a little customization.

You are passing the Perl interpreter the -T switch to turn on something called "taint" checking. This is a security feature discussed in detail later.

Next, the program prints out the following:

```
Content: text/html
blank line
```

That is, it prints Content: text/html followed by a blank line. These two lines tell the browser that a web page follows.

Then the web page itself is printed.

Running the Program

The next step is to get the program to run. First, you set the execute permission using the command

```
chmod a+rx hello.pl
```

Next, you must put the program in a place where the web server can execute it. The exact directory is going to be configuration dependent. If you are running the Apache web server, the default location of the CGI scripts is in the directory www/cgi-bin and its subdirectories. (The directory varies from system to system. Even different distributions of Linux put the CGI directory in different places. Some common installation directories are ~www/var/cgi-bin and ~apache/cgi-bin.)

For this example, assume that you are running Linux with Apache and have a default configuration. Move the script into that directory:

```
mv hello.pl www/cgi-bin
```

The next step is to see whether you can run the script from the browser. You do that by specifying the URL of the script. Again, this is system and configuration dependent. If you are running Apache in the default configuration (as in this example), the URL would be

```
http://www.webserver.com/cgi-bin/hello.pl
```

Replace *webserver* with the name of your system.

Figure 12.1 shows the result of loading this URL into an Internet Explorer window.

Figure 12.1   Hello World (CGI version).

Common Problem: Wrong Directory or Misconfigured Server?

Sometimes when you type in your URL, the script appears rather than the output of the script (see Figure 12.2).

The problem probably is caused by putting the script in the wrong directory. Scripts are executed only if they are put in a CGI-enabled directory. If a script is put in an ordinary web page directory, it's treated as an ordinary web page and is displayed.

The solution is to put the script in the correct directory. Your web site administrator can help you.

On the other hand, if you're sure that you've got the right directory, it's possible that your web server could be misconfigured.

In either case, work with your web server administrator to solve the problem or read the section "Debugging a CGI Script" later in the chapter.

continues

Figure 12.2   Error: Script is displayed, not executed.

Basic Forms

This example creates a web form that allows the user to fill in a survey and send it in electronically.

Figure 12.3 shows the full server page.

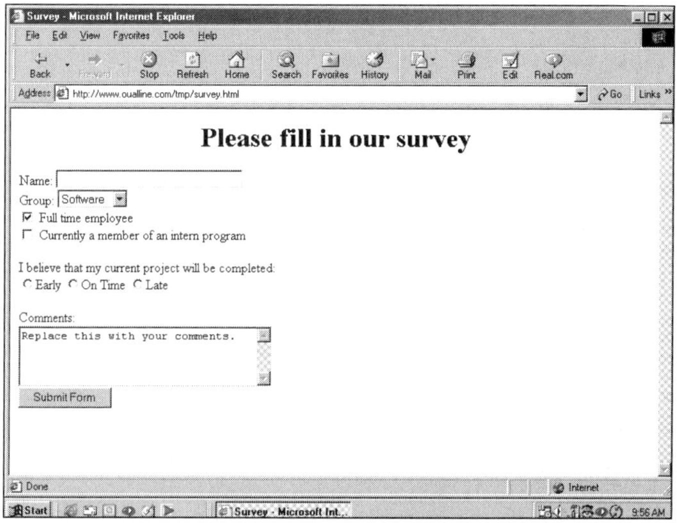

Figure 12.3   Survey form.

The survey page is actually a CGI form. This example assumes that you are familiar with basic HTML, but you may not be familiar with CGI forms.

The page starts with the usual items:

```
<HEAD><TITLE>Survey</TITLE></HEAD>
<BODY>
<CENTER><H1>Please fill in our survey</H1></CENTER>
```

Next, you deal with the special form-related tags.

FORM Statement

Now that you've taken care of the bookkeeping, you need to specify what you want from the server. This is done through the use of a form.

The form starts with the line

```
<FORM ACTION="http://www.webserver.com/cgi-bin/record.pl" METHOD="POST">
```

This line uses an absolute web address (one starting with http) for the ACTION field. You could have used a relative address as well:

```
<FORM ACTION="/cgi-bin/record.pl" METHOD="POST">
```

Relative URLs are system independent. Using them means that you can move your FORM from system to system and the URL still refers to the local system. This means that you need to keep the CGI script as well.

The FORM tag indicates that this is the beginning of a form. The ACTION button tells the web browser the URL to use when the form is submitted.

Finally the METHOD tells the browser how to encode the data in the form. Two possible methods are "GET" and "POST". In the "GET" method, the form's information is encoded as part of the URL. For example, if you've ever seen a URL that looked something like

```
http://www.webserver.com/cgi-bin/record.pl?name=sam
```

you've seen what happens when you use the GET method.

The other method, POST, sends the form data in the HTTP header that's sent to the browser to run the program and get the next page.

The advantage of the GET method is that because the form's data is contained in the URL, you can bookmark the submitted URL. This makes it useful for things such as web search engines or stock quotes where you might want to bookmark the page you see after submitting the form.

For example, the page http://quote.yahoo.com/q?s=rhat&d=v1 contains the current Redhat stock quote as generated by one of Yahoo's CGI programs.

However, if you don't want your information exposed at the top of the screen, use POST. Also there is a 1024 character limit on the data that can be sent by a GET method, so for large forms, you must use a POST.

Because the data sent by the GET method is part of the URL, it's visible to the user. (It's also recorded in the web server's logs.) Having visible data is useful for debugging, but you don't want to use it for secure data such as passwords or credit card numbers.

Also because the GET is really an enhanced URL, you can bookmark a GET form. You can't do this with a POST because the data disappears when you leave the page.

Text Blanks

You now need to tell the browser what data you want to get from the user. The first thing is the user's name. The code for this is

```
<P>
Name:
<INPUT TYPE="text" NAME="name" SIZE="30">
```

The <INPUT> directive tells the browser to ask the user for information. The TYPE attribute tells the browser what type of information is wanted. In this case, it's a single line of text (TYPE="text").

The NAME attribute is used to give this blank a name, and the SIZE specifies how big a blank to make.

Option List

You want to know what group the user belongs to. He can be in Software, Marketing, or Support. To get this information, put an option list in the web page:

```
<SELECT NAME="group" SIZE=1>
   <OPTION>Software</OPTION>
   <OPTION>Marketing</OPTION>
   <OPTION>Support</OPTION>
</SELECT>
```

The <SELECT> tag encloses a list of options. Each option in the list is put inside an <OPTION> tag.

Check Boxes

The next two items in the form are a couple of check boxes. In this case, you need to return to the <INPUT> tag to specify these:

```
<INPUT TYPE="checkbox" NAME="work" VALUE="1" CHECKED>
Full time employee</INPUT>
<BR>
<INPUT TYPE="checkbox" NAME="intern" VALUE="1">
Currently a member of an intern program</INPUT>
```

The first check box is named "work", and a value of 1 is returned if it's set. The CHECKED attributed tells the browser that this check box is initially checked.

The second box has no such attributes, so by default it will be unchecked.

Radio Buttons

Just below the two check boxes is a series of three radio buttons.

The code for this is

```
<P>
I believe that my current project will be completed:
<BR>
<INPUT TYPE="radio" NAME="schedule" VALUE="early">Early</INPUT>
<INPUT TYPE="radio" NAME="schedule" VALUE="ontime">On Time</INPUT>
<INPUT TYPE="radio" NAME="schedule" VALUE="late">Late</INPUT>
```

The TYPE attribute is "radio" to create radio buttons. All the radio buttons in a set have the same name. In this case, it's "schedule".

The VALUE is used by the system to tell the CGI program which button is selected.

Because no radio button has the attribute CHECKED, no button will be selected by default.

Text Areas

This form starts with the "Name" blank. This blank allowed you to type in a single line. Now you want to let the user type in comments. This is a multiple line blank.

The code for this is

```
<TEXTAREA NAME="comments" COLS="35" ROWS="4">
Replace this with your comments.
</TEXTAREA>
```

The <TEXTAREA> directive begins a text box. The NAME attribute tells the system what identifier to use for the blank. The attributes COLS and ROWS specify the width and height of the box.

The initial text for the box appears between the <TEXTAREA> and the </TEXTAREA> directives.

Hidden Input

Now you come to a section that doesn't appear on the form. That's for the hidden input. This type of INPUT directive lets you embed information in the form that the user doesn't see. This example uses it to embed a version number into the form.

The directive is

```
<INPUT TYPE="hidden" NAME="version" VALUE="1.0">
```

The Submit Button

Finally, you need to add a button that lets the user send the data in the form to the program:

```
<INPUT TYPE="submit" VALUE="Submit Form">
```

When the user clicks on this button, the form is submitted to the web server.

Putting It All Together

Listing 12.2 shows the full version of the web form.

Listing 12.2   *survey.html*

```
<HEAD><TITLE>Survey</TITLE></HEAD>
<BODY>
<CENTER><H1>Please fill in our survey</H1></CENTER>

<!-- Replace the ACTION below with the path to your script --!>
<FORM ACTION="/cgi-bin/record.pl" METHOD="POST">

<P>
Name:
<INPUT TYPE="text" NAME="name" SIZE="30">
<BR>
Group:
<SELECT NAME="group" SIZE=1>
    <OPTION>Software</OPTION>
    <OPTION>Marketing</OPTION>
    <OPTION>Support</OPTION>
</SELECT>
<BR>
<INPUT TYPE="checkbox" NAME="work" VALUE="1" CHECKED>
Full time employee</INPUT>
<BR>
<INPUT TYPE="checkbox" NAME="intern" VALUE="1">
Currently a member of an intern program</INPUT>
<BR>
<P>
I believe that my current project will be completed:
<BR>
<INPUT TYPE="radio" NAME="schedule" VALUE="early">Early</INPUT>
<INPUT TYPE="radio" NAME="schedule" VALUE="ontime">On Time</INPUT>
<INPUT TYPE="radio" NAME="schedule" VALUE="late">Late</INPUT>
<P>
```

continues

Listing 12.2   **Continued**

```
Comments:
<BR>
<TEXTAREA NAME="comments" COLS="35" ROWS="4">
Replace this with your comments.
</TEXTAREA>
<INPUT TYPE="hidden" NAME="version" VALUE="1.0">
<BR>
<INPUT TYPE="submit" VALUE="Submit Form">
</FORM>
</BODY>
</HTML>
```

Creating the CGI Program

Now that the web form is created, you need a program to handle it. This section describes how to make a simple CGI program to read the form data.

When the user clicks on the Submit button, the browser encodes the data in the form and sends it to web server. The web server then runs the CGI program and sends the data to it.

A lot of details are involved in the encoding and decoding of form data. Fortunately, you don't have to worry about them because there are Perl modules to do the work for you.

CGI Versus CGI::Thin

Most books on CGI programming describe how to use the CGI module rather than of the `CGI::Thin` module. The `CGI::Thin` module is a short, simple module that does everything you want it to.

The CGI module also does everything you want. The problem is that CGI module also contains hundreds of functions that you don't want. As a result, it's large and bloated. Finding the correct function in this mess is difficult.

So for both speed and simplicity, this chapter uses the `CGI::Thin` module.

Before getting started, you'll need to install two modules:

- **CGI::Thin**—Decodes CGI data.
- **HTML::Entities**—Text-to-HTML encoder.

The CGI program begins with

```
#!/usr/local/bin/perl -T
use strict;
use warnings;
```

```
use CGI::Thin;
use CGI::Carp qw(fatalsToBrowser);
use HTML::Entities;
```

Again, the first line is the magic line that tells Linux where to find Perl and to start it with the "Taint" flag set.

Next, specify the modules you are using.

When the CGI program runs, the first thing it does is print the special string that tells the web server that a HTML page follows:

```
print "Content-type: text/html\n";
print "\n";
```

CGI programs are notoriously difficult to debug (more on this in the "Debugging a CGI Script" section). First you must call a debug routine that prints out all the data in the form. This will be a big help if anything goes wrong.

The debug routine begins by getting the data out of the form by calling the Parse_CGI function. This function knows all about communicating with the web server and how to decode form data:

```
    my %form_info = Parse_CGI();
```

The function returns the form data in the form of a hash where the key comes from the NAME attribute of the input directive, and the value comes from what the user entered (in the case of text entry) or the VALUE attribute in the case of check boxes or options.

For example, if the user checked the blank specified by

```
<INPUT TYPE="checkbox" NAME="intern" VALUE="1">
Currently a member of an intern program</INPUT>
```

the CGI program would see

```
    $form_info{"intern"} = "1";
```

For debugging, you want to print the hash. You can do so in a small loop:

```
foreach my $cur_key (sort keys %form_info) {
    # WARNING: SEE BELOW
    print "$cur_key = $form_info{$cur_key}\n";
}
```

But there is a problem with this. What if the user entered data containing HTML code? For example:

```
This is a <B>Good</B> job.
```

In this case, when this string is printed it will be intercepted as an HTML string resulting in

```
This is a Good job.
```

If you wanted to see exactly what the user typed this would be wrong. In this case, things are not too bad because the user was nice enough to type legal HTML code. But the user could have typed

```
Will be finished in "< two weeks".
```

Because of the "<" in this text, the browser will think that this is an HTML directive and try to execute it.

You need to encode the output so that special characters don't cause funny things to happen. For example, if you want to print the previous comment, it needs to be printed as

```
Will be finished in "&lt; two weeks".
```

That's where the `HTML::Entities` module comes in. It provides the function `encode_entities` that turns text into HTML so that it can be printed. So the actual print loop is

```
foreach my $cur_key (sort keys %form_info) {
    print encode_entities($cur_key), " = ",
      encode_entities($form_info{$cur_key}), "\n";
}
```

Actually, you're not quite there. Sometimes the system will have multiple values for the same key—for example, when you have a form with a multiple selection list in it. In this case, the `Parse_CGI` function sets the hash's value to an array reference.

You need to check for this and handle it properly:

```
if (ref $form_info{$cur_key}) {
    #.... print array @{$form_info{$cur_key}}
} else {
    #.... print scalar $form_info{$cur_key}
}
```

Note that the `ref` function returns `true` if the scalar is a reference and `undefined` if it's not.

The server communicates with the application through not only the CGI protocol but also the environment. So after you print all the CGI parameters, you print the environment as well.

Recording the Data

After the `debug` function comes the body of the program, which records the data. This is simple, straightforward Perl, so the details are not discussed here.

About the only significant thing to notice is that all the output files are named form.*<time>*, where *<time>* is the system time in seconds. This guarantees that you have unique names for your output files (assuming that two people don't submit reports at exactly the same time).

The other thing to notice about the filename is that no user input goes into creating it. In other words, nothing from the form is used in selecting the filename. This is a security measure. Security is discussed in more detail in the section "Security."

Writing a Response

The last part of the program writes a response to the user to let him know that his data has been submitted:

```
print <<EOF;
<H1>Thanks</H1>
<P>
Thank you for your time.  Your information has been
recorded.
EOF
```

Putting It All Together

Listing 12.3 shows the full version of the CGI script.

Listing 12.3   *record.pl*

```
#!/home/sdo/local/bin/perl -T
use strict;
use warnings;

use CGI::Thin;
use CGI::Carp qw(fatalsToBrowser);
use HTML::Entities;

my $out_dir = "/tmp";

######################################################
# debug -- Output debugging information for the web form
#
#  All form data and the environment is printed.
######################################################
sub debug()
{
    print "<H1>DEBUG INFORMATION</H1>\n";
    print "<H2>Form Information</H2>\n";
```

continues

Listing 12.3   **Continued**

```perl
    # -------- print form information -----
    my %form_info = Parse_CGI();
    foreach my $cur_key (sort keys %form_info) {
        print "<BR>";
        if (ref $form_info{$cur_key}) {
            foreach my $value (@{$form_info{$cur_key}}) {
                print encode_entities($cur_key), " = ",
                        encode_entities($value), "\n";
            }
        } else {
            print encode_entities($cur_key), " = ",
                    encode_entities($form_info{$cur_key}), "\n";
        }
    }

    # -------- print environment ------
    print "<H2>Environment</H2>\n";
    foreach my $cur_key (sort keys %ENV) {
        print "<BR>";
        print encode_entities($cur_key), " = ",
            encode_entities($ENV{$cur_key}), "\n";
    }
}
sub write_report()
{
    # The information from the form
    my %form_info = Parse_CGI();

    # The current time in seconds
    my $time = time();

    open OUT_FILE, ">$out_dir/form.$time" or
        die("Could not open $out_dir/form.$time");

    print OUT_FILE "Name: $form_info{name}    Group: $form_info{group}\n";
    if ($form_info{work}) {
        print OUT_FILE "Full Time Employee\n";
    }
    if ($form_info{intern}) {
        print OUT_FILE "Part of the Intern program\n";
    }
    if (not defined($form_info{schedule})) {
        print OUT_FILE "*** Did not select a schedule\n";
    } else {
        print OUT_FILE "Schedule: $form_info{schedule}\n";
    }
    print OUT_FILE "Comments:\n";
    print OUT_FILE "$form_info{comments}\n";
    close (OUT_FILE);
}
```

```
print "Content-type: text/html\n";
print "\n";
debug();
write_report();
print <<EOF;
<H1>Thanks</H1>
<P>
Thank you for your time.  Your information has been
recorded.
EOF
```

Debugging a CGI Script

CGI programs are debug resistant. Frequently, you'll get only the message "Internal Server Error" on the screen with no clue as to what happened. Also, the old trick of putting print statements through your code won't work. You don't have a screen to print to. This section looks at the various bugs that can occur and how to deal with them.

Getting Past *"Internal Server Error"*

Suppose that you are trying to execute a CGI script and the server returns a screen titled "Internal Server Error" or "Forbidden". This indicates that your CGI script could not be run or that it returned something that confused the server.

To take care of this problem, you should check the following:

1. Try checking the syntax of your program with the command:

```
perl -wcT script.pl
```

2. Make sure that your program is executable and readable by everyone. Remember that the server will be executing the script, not you. That means that the Linux/UNIX user who executes the account is not you.

3. If possible, check the server's error log to see what just happened. If you are using the most common web server, Apache, then the default location of the log file is /var/log/httpd/error_log. (Again, this is system/installation dependent.)

If this fails, you can try running the program manually or get additional help from your server administrator. This will help you to get past most "software errors" that your script can generate.

Interactive Debugging

There are two ways of debugging interactively. The first is to simulate the web server environment, and the second is to get the web server to start the debugger for you.

To simulate the server environment, this section creates a short Perl script that reads in the form information, encodes it, and then calls the program.

To do this, you need the module `CGI::Enurl`, which provides the function `enurl`. This function does the reverse of `Parse_CGI`; it takes a hash and returns an encode string representing the hash.

The simulation function starts by asking the user for the name of the script and then gets the form data in the form of key/value pairs. Next, it encodes the string with the `enurl` function:

```
my $url_info = enurl \%cgi_info;
```

One of the simplest ways of passing data to a CGI program is through the environment. You simulate that by setting some key environment variables and then executing the program itself:

```
# Set a minimal set of environment variables
$ENV{QUERY_STRING} = $url_info;
$ENV{REQUEST_URI} = "$prog?$url_info";
$ENV{REQUEST_METHOD} = "GET";
exec("perl -d $prog");
```

A typical run looks like

```
perl debug.pl
Script name: /home/httpd/cgi-bin/record.pl
Enter key=value
(End with a blank line)
> name=oualline
> group=Software
> schedule=early
> version=1.0
> work=1
>

Loading DB routines from perl5db.pl version 1.0402
Emacs support available.

Enter h or `h h' for help.

main::(/home/httpd/cgi-bin/record.pl:33):
33:     print "Content-type: text/html\n";
DB<1>
```

You can now debug the CGI program normally. Listing 12.4 shows the full version of the debug program.

Listing 12.4   *debug.pl*

```perl
use strict;
use warnings;

use CGI::Enurl;

my %cgi_info = ();      # CGI Information we are creating

print "Script name: ";
my $prog = <STDIN>;
chomp($prog);

print "Enter key=value\n";
print "(End with a blank line)\n";

# Get pairs that look like    name=value
while (1) {
    print "> ";
    my $line = <STDIN>;
    chomp($line);

    if ($line eq "") {
        last;
    }

    if ($line !~ /^([^=]*)\s*=\s*(.*)$/) {
        print "ERROR: Could not understand $line\n";
        next;
    }
    $cgi_info{$1} = $2;
}

# Encode the CGI information for simulation
my $url_info = enurl \%cgi_info;

# Set a minimal set of environment variables
$ENV{QUERY_STRING} = $url_info;
$ENV{REQUEST_URI} = "$prog?$url_info";
$ENV{REQUEST_METHOD} = "GET";
exec("perl -Td $prog");
```

Server-Started Debuggers

Another way to debug a CGI program is to have the server start the debugger.
This may be a little difficult because the program starts with no terminal
connected to it.

If you are using the X Windows system, you can perform some tricks to connect the debugger to your display. The first step is to find out what the name of your display is. This is done through the command

```
echo $DISPLAY
:0.0
```

This example uses the display :0.0. The next step is to create a shell script that starts the debug on the specified window.

If you are starting the ptkdb debugger, the script is shown in Listing 12.5.

Listing 12.5   *record.ptkdb*

```
#!/bin/sh
DISPLAY=:0.0
export DISPLAY
exec perl -wTd record.pl "$*"
```

The first line is a magic line that tells the system that this is a shell (sh) script. The next two lines tell the system which display to use. Finally, the real program is executed using the debugger.

The script must be placed in the CGI directory and made executable.

Next, create a web form that calls the debug wrapper (record.ptkdb) rather than the real script (record.pl).

Finally, you need to tell the X Windows system that you are going to connect to it from a CGI program and that it's okay to accept connections from the web server. This is done with the command

```
xhost +
```

Now when you submit the debugging form, the script record.ptkd runs. It redirects the output to your display (:0.0 in this example) and then starts the debugger on your script.

To summarize, the steps in doing a server debug are

1. Find out what display you are running (echo $DISPLAY).
2. Create a wrapper that sets the display and starts the debugger.
3. Put the wrapper in the CGI directory.
4. Create a form that calls the wrapper.
5. Enable connections to your display from another system (xhost +).
6. Run your debugging form.

You can use almost the same technique to debug the program using the command-line debugger. In this case, you use the xterm program to create a new window for debugging. Listing 12.6 shows how this is done.

Listing 12.6   *record.debug*

```
#!/bin/sh
exec /usr/bin/X11/xterm –display :0.0 –e perl –wTd record.pl "$*"
```

Noted that when you use this debugging technique, all the output of CGI program is sent to the terminal, not the web server. The result is that you see everything, and the web browser gets a "Internal Server Error" message.

Security

Web forms have their own set of security problems. Fortunately, the operating system, the web browser, and Perl all provide some security against hackers. But that doesn't mean that you should ignore it.

The first line of defense comes from the operating system and web browser. The web browser runs under a special user account, typically named www or something similar. This means that all CGI scripts can access only the data available to this user and can destroy only the files writable by this user.

However, sometimes this can be a problem. Suppose that you want the data created by your CGI program to be owned by you rather than the user www. Linux and UNIX solve this problem through use of something called a setuid bit. If a script has this bit set, the script runs as the user who owns it, not the user who invoked it.

To create a setuid script, all you have to do is issue the correct chmod command:

```
chmod u+s script.pl
```

This command tells the system that when script.pl is run, that it is to be run as if you ran it.

Taint Mode

The next defense against hackers is Perl's Taint mode. This is enabled by the –T switch on the first line of the program. In Taint mode, anything supplied from the outside is considered tainted and generates an error if used in an insecure manner.

Say that you have a form that lets a user submit a name and password, and you want to validate it using an external program. Here's an insecure code fragment that does the job:

```
my $user = $form_data{USER};
my $password = $form_data{PASSWORD};

my $status = system("validate_user $user $password");
if ($status == 0) {
```

```
        print "User is good\n";
    } else {
        print "User is bad\n";
    }
```

So what's wrong with this program? The problem is that the user can supply anything he wants for his username. This can be something reasonable such as `sam`, or it can be something that allows him to hack the system such as `sam ; rm -rf /`.

The second answer causes the system command to execute the command

```
validate_user sam ; rm -rf /
```

Because a semicolon is the command separator for the shell, this is actually two commands: the `validate_user` and an `rm -rf`. This is not what was intended.

In general, Perl's Taint mode prevents you from using any unchecked user input in a system or open function.

For example, when Taint mode is turned on, using tainted user input in a system call results in an error like the following:

```
Insecure dependency in system while running with -T switch
➥at passwd.pl line 7, <> line 1.
```

Direct assignment will not remove the taint from the data. However, if you extract a string from tainted data, the result is untainted. For example:

```
$tainted_data =~ /^(\s+)$/;
my $untainted_data = $1;
```

Also anything coming in from the environment is considered tainted. In particular, Perl will not do a system command if the path is tainted. To remove this taint, you'll need to set the path yourself as well as remove from your environment any variables that might affect the shell:

```
$ENV{PATH} = "/bin:/usr/bin:/usr/X11R6/bin";
delete @ENV{'IFS', 'CDPATH', 'ENV', 'BASH_ENV'};
```

How Perl Programs Break

Experience is the best teacher; unfortunately, experience in a security disaster is not something you really want to have. So take a few minutes to learn about what not to do.

First, remember that usernames, filenames, and other user input can contain special characters. You've already seen how a username of `sam ; rm -rf /` can create havoc.

Don't assume that filenames contain only legal characters. For example, suppose that your script is designed to fetch any file in the tree /home/status/ data, and you write this as

```
chdir("/home/status/data");
open IN_FILE, "<$user_supplied_file_name";
```

The filename supplied by the user can look like something simple (status.txt) or something designed to get data it shouldn't (../../../etc/passwd). In the second case, file specification gives the user access to the system password file. This file is useful to a hacker.

The Code Red worm uses a variation of this trick to break into Microsoft IIS servers. The server checked for something so simple as ../.., but there are ways of hiding this path using Unicode, which the worm exploited.

Another mistake is to assume that a hidden input field has not been altered by the user. Remember that users can write their own web pages and point them to your CGI program. A couple of online stores found out about this problem the hard way. The stores put the price of an item in a hidden field called PRICE in their generated web pages. The hackers came along and saw the line

```
<INPUT TYPE="hidden" NAME="price" VALUE="298.99">
```

and did a minor edit before submitting the form to the store:

```
<INPUT TYPE="hidden" NAME="price" VALUE="2.99">
```

Needless to say, they were getting the digital cameras very cheap.

Cookies

One problem with writing CGI programs is that each run is done in isolation. It's difficult to carry information from one run to the next.

One solution to this is to use hidden INPUT tags. Another solution is the use of cookies. A *cookie* is a named string that the server sends the browser. The browser can then send it back upon request.

Say that you want to send a cookie to the browser. You first need the CGI::Thin::Cookies module. (This was installed when you installed CGI::Thin.) You then use it to send a cookie using the Set_Cookie function:

```
use CGI::Thin::Cookies;
#.....
Set_Cookie(
    NAME => "Username",
    VALUE => $user,
    EXPIRES => "+14d"
);
```

This example sends a cookie called "Username" whose value is the name of the user. The cookie expires in 14 days.

The call to Set_Cookie must be done before you output the HTML heading line (the "Content: text/html" line).

To get the cookie back, you call the Parse_Cookies function. This function returns a hash containing all the cookies sent by the browser to the server. (Note: This includes only the cookies in place at the start of the script. It does not include any cookies sent during the script.)

So in the example, where you sent the NAME cookie, you could expect to get it back on the next run with the code

```
use CGI::Thin::Cookies;

my %cookies = Parse_Cookies();

if (defined($cookies{NAME})) {
    print "<P> Hello $cookies{NAME}\n";
}
```

Cookies are discussed more in Chapter 15, "Putting It All Together" when a real CGI program is created that allows the user to access a disk inventory system.

Summary

CGI programming is a mix of the fairly easy and the extremely tricky. Writing the CGI programs is fairly easy. Getting them to work, however, can be tricky. Hopefully, the techniques and tools presented here will make the chore of creating CGI scripts a little easier.

Exercises

1. Create a script that prints out the current status of the system. What's in the report is left to your imagination, but some items it could include are the current date, the amount of disk space free on each file system, how long the system has been up, and so on.

2. Write a CGI script for debugging. This script prints out the values of all the form data and environment variables supplied to the script.

3. Write a form that allows a user to register his product. It should take as input the name, address, and phone number of the user and store it so that it can be used later by the marketing department for a mailing list.

4. One problem that plagues system administrators is the number of users who ask to have a file restored. Create a CGI system to automate this. Include a form that allows the user to submit a request (please restore this file) and a report form for the system administrator (here's the files you've got to restore). You can embellish this with additional reports and forms as needed.

5. Create an online testing system. This system would ask the user a series of questions, score the results (letting the user know where he went wrong), and record how well the user did.

Resources

Online Documentation

- `perldoc perlsec`—Perl security information page. This page provides extensive information on Taint mode.

Modules

- `CGI::Thin`—Handles the decoding of the information that comes into a CGI program (a small, version of CGI).

- `CGI::Thin::Cookies`—Handles the sending and receiving of cookies (part of the `CGI::Thin` module).

- `CGI::Carp`—Intercepts `die` and other bad things that can happen to a CGI program and displays an error for the user.

- `CGI`—Does everything a CGI program might want and many things you don't want. The much smaller and simpler `CGI::Thin` module is recommended for almost all applications.

- `CGI::Enurl`—Encodes a URL in the same way as the browser does when it sends a form to the user.

- `Taint`—Provides the tainted function, which tests to see whether a variable is tainted.

Web Sites

- `http://www.securityfocus.org`—Good general system security site.

13

Creating GUIs with Tk

IF YOU WANT TO WRITE A GUI for a Perl program, then the Tk module is the way to go. It lets you easily create powerful and functional GUIs. The other nice thing about the Tk package is that it's portable, so you can use your programs both on Microsoft Windows and UNIX/Linux systems.

Tk Basics

To use the Tk module, you need to know some basics first. This chapter starts with an impractical example, the Tk version of "Hello World" (see Listing 13.1).

Listing 13.1   *hello.pl*

```
use strict;
use warnings;

use Tk;

sub byebye()
{
```

continues

Listing 13.1 **Continued**

```
     exit (0);
}

my $tk_mw = MainWindow->new();
my $tk_button = $tk_mw->Button(
    -text => "Hello World",
    -command => \&byebye
);

$tk_button->pack(
    -side => 'top'
);

MainLoop();
```

When run, this program displays a window containing a single button labeled "Hello" as seen in Figure 13.1. When this button is clicked, the program exits.

Figure 13.1 Hello World program.

Three important graphical elements are involved in this program.

At the top level is the window. In this case, because it's the first (and only) window, it's called the Main Window. You put all the GUI elements in this window.

Next are the GUI elements, also called *widgets*. This example has only one widget, the Hello button.

The final element is the geometry manager. It is responsible for telling Tk where to put the widgets in the window. This example uses the `pack` geometry manager. It tells Tk to stuff the widgets as close together as possible.

You learn about these elements in more detail as you study the Tk module.

Tk Widgets

The Tk module provides many widgets. These include

- **Button**—A button you can click on.
- **Label**—A text or graphic label.
- **Checkbox**—A box that can be checked.
- **Radiobutton**—Lets you select from a set of options.

- **Listbox**—Displays a list of items and lets you select one or more of them.

- **Menus**—Lets you build command menus.

- **Dialogs**—Pop-up windows for messages and other common selections.

- **Text**—Contains multiple lines of text. This is a flexible widget in which you can embed widgets and have all sorts of fun. (More on this in the upcoming "*text*" section.)

- **Canvas**—A widget in which you can draw shapes, text, and widgets.

- **MainWindow**—The top-level menu for your application.

- **TopLevel**—A pop-up window.

The Tk system comes with a number of demonstration programs that let you see what widgets are available. The first demonstration program is called widget, and it's installed when you first install Tk.

To run the program, just type **widget**. Note that if you are using ActiveState's Perl, you'll find the widget.bat command in the \PERL\EG\TK directory.)

The program gives you an overview of almost all the various types of widgets as well as several demonstrations of their use (see Figure 13.2). For example, if you click on item 7, Two Labels Displaying Images, you see a demonstration of two image labels. Click on the See Code button and code for the demonstration appears.

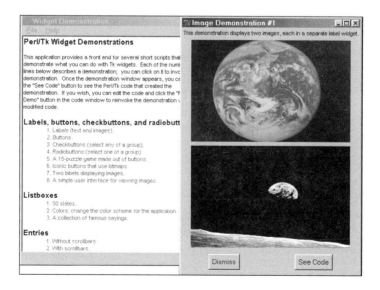

Figure 13.2 Widget demonstration program.

Widget Documentation

To get documentation on each widget, use the `perldoc` command. For example, to get information on the `Button` widget, use the command:

```
perldoc Tk::Button
```

This documentation lists all the information specific to the `Button` widget. But because the `Button` widget is derived from the basic widget, it inherits many options from this base object. To find out about the generic options, use the command:

```
perldoc Tk::options
```

Using Widgets

All Tk programs start by creating a main window. All other widgets are children of this window and inherit the attributes of this widget. To create a main window, call the `MainWindow->new()` function:

```
my $tk_mw = MainWindow->new(
    -title => "This is the main window",
    -background => "cyan"
);
```

The option `-title` sets the title of the window. The `-background` sets the background of the window and all its child widgets. (See `perldoc Tk::CmdLine` for a list of main window options.)

Now create a button under the main window:

```
my $tk_exit_button = $tk_mw->Button(
    -text => "Exit",
    -command => \&exit,
    -background => "red",
    -foreground => "white"
);
```

In this case, you are creating a push button labeled Exit (white letters on a red background). When you click on it, the function `exit` is called.

The button is created as a child of the main window, thus use the `$tk_mw->Button` call to create it.

One thing is missing from the button specification: the system doesn't know where to put it. It goes in the main window, but where?

To answer this question, you need to use a geometry manager. This is a set of functions that handle the placement of widgets. This example uses the most popular geometry manager, `pack`.

This function tells Tk that the button is to be packed up at the top of the window and attached to the upper-right (ne) corner of the window:

```
$tk_exit_button->pack(
    -side => "top",
    -anchor => "ne"
);
```

You can join these two function calls and create and manage the widget at the same time:

```
my $tk_exit_button = $tk_mw->Button(
    -text => "Exit",
    -command => \&exit,
    -background => "red",
    -foreground => "white"
)->pack(
    -side => "top",
    -anchor => "ne"
);
```

The Main Event Loop

The last thing you need in the Tk program is a call to the event loop handler. This is a short loop that waits for an event and then handles it. It's a simple function call:

```
MainLoop();
```

As you can see, this covers all the main elements of a Tk program that are present in the "Hello World" program. There's no difference between "Hello World" and a real-world program except for some added complexity.

Geometry Managers

The geometry manager is responsible for determining where the widgets get placed inside the window. This section discusses the four basic geometry managers: pack, grid, place, and form.

pack

The basic algorithm of the pack geometry manager is to "shove the widgets together as closely as possible in the indicated direction." There are four pack regions: top, bottom, left, and right.

The geometry manager must not only support the initial placement of the widgets, but also must redo the layout if the size of the window changes. The pack algorithm lets you anchor a widget to a point within the packing region.

This is done through the -anchor option. Figure 13.3 shows the values for this option.

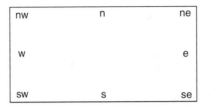

Figure 13.3 Anchors.

In addition, the geometry manager manages the size of the widget. The -expand option controls whether the widget expands to fill the available space. In addition, the -fill option tells the geometry manager whether the widget is to fill the available space. The value of -fill can be "x", "y", "both", or "none".

You'll see how these things work in a real example. Figure 13.4 shows the main window of the tk_grep.pl program. (Listing 13.2 shows the full program.)

Figure 13.4 tk_grep.pl.

You'll see how to assemble this window. At the top is a "Pattern" blank. This is actually two widgets, a label (the Pattern text) and a blank (an Entry widget). You want this pair at the top of the window.

So you need a grouping widget. This widget is called a Frame. A Frame is a widget in which you put other widgets. In this case, you create a Frame and pack the Label and Entry widgets into it.

The Label is packed on the left side, the Entry on the right.

Now you need to consider expansion options. You don't want the label to grow even if you resize the window, so it will not expand. The text entry can grow, however, but only in the x direction. (You don't want it going any higher.)

The code for creating the top frame looks like the following:

```
my $pattern = "Text";
my $tk_frame = $tk_mw->Frame(
    );
```

```
$tk_frame->Label(
    -text => "Pattern"
    )->pack(
    -side => "left"
    );
$tk_frame->Entry(
    -textvariable => \$pattern
    )->pack(
    -side => "right",
    -fill => "x",
    -expand => 1
    );
```

Now you need to pack the frame as well. It will be packed against the top of the window, and it can expand in the x direction. So the pack command is

```
$tk_frame->pack(
    -side => "top",
    -fill => "x"
);
```

This process is repeated for the Files blank.

For the two action buttons (Search, Cancel), simply pack them on the left and right sides.

Figure 13.5 shows the various widgets and their packing options.

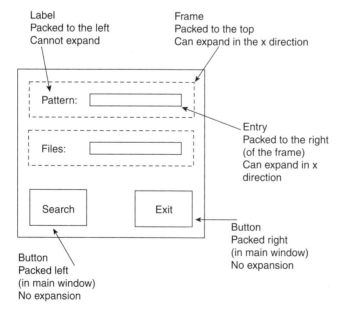

Figure 13.5 Window packing options.

As you can see, with the `pack` geometry manager and a few frames you can make complex GUIs with a few simple commands.

grid

The `grid` geometry manager allows you to lay out your widgets in a set of rows and columns. It is not as flexible as the `pack` geometry manager, but it is useful in some cases.

The manager comes with a number of options and even lets you create grids with widgets that span rows and columns.

place

The `place` geometry manager lets you do all the work of deciding where you want your widgets yourself. In other words, you must explicitly place the widgets inside the window.

form

A newer geometry manager is the `form`. It gives you the capability to describe the location of a widget in a variety of ways. One way is to specify a location in terms of a percentage of the window. In other words, you can say "I want this widget to be put 30 percent below and 10 percent to the right of the upper-left corner."

The `form` also lets you specify a widget's location through attachments and springs, which gives you a way of placing your widget relative to other widgets.

Note that the `form` geometry manager is new and, as of this writing, not completely documented or implemented yet.

Special Widgets

Most widgets, such as buttons, labels, and entries, are simple and straightforward. However, some are more complex and deserve more attention.

Scrollbars

Say that you want to create a list of options. You can do this using the `ListBox` widget. But you may have more items than can be displayed at one time.

No problem, just create a `Scrollbar` widget. Now all you need to do is connect the movement callbacks from the scrollbar to your `ListBox` widget.

Coding this operation is both time consuming and tricky, so the makers of Tk created a way of automatically adding scrollbars to a widget through the `Scrolled` method.

For example, if you wanted to create a `ListBox` 10 lines high and 30 characters wide, you would use the command

```
$tk_mw->Listbox(
    -height => 10,
    -width => 30
);
```

If you wanted to create one with a vertical scrollbar, you would use the command

```
$tk_mw->Scrolled(
    'Listbox',
    -scrollbars => "eo",
    -height => 10,
    -width => 30
)->pack(
    -side => "top",
    -expand => "yes",
    -fill => "both"
);
```

The first argument to the `Scrolled` method is the widget to be created. The option `-scrollbars` tells the method where the scrollbars are to be created. It contains one or more directions (n, s, e, w).

Each direction can be followed by the letter o. This tells Tk that the scrollbar is to be displayed only if needed. Without the o, the scrollbar will always be displayed. So for example, the option

```
    -scrollbar => "eos"
```

causes a scrollbar to be displayed on the east (right side) of the widget if needed, and another scrollbar is placed on the south (bottom) of the widget. The bottom scrollbar will always be present.

Text

The `Text` widget contains multiline text—no surprise there. It also lets you place things other than text, such as images and widgets.

Text tags are used to specify a portion of the text. For example, suppose that you want to highlight some text. One way of doing this is to change the background to yellow. The first thing you need to do is create a tag that defines how highlighted text is supposed to look. Naturally, this tag is called `'highlight'`, and it is created with the code

```
$text_box->tagConfigure('highlight', background => 'yellow');
```

In this example, `$text_box` is a text widget. The `tagConfigure` function is used to create or change a tag. The name of the tag is `'highlight'`. We could have chosen any name for this tag, but `'highlight'` seemed to be the easiest to remember. This is followed by the list of attributes for this tag. In this case, there's only one attribute, background, and you want it to be yellow.

Now that you have defined the tag, apply it to the first two lines of the text. This is done by adding the tag to the text:

```
$text_box->tagAdd('highlight',
    "0.0",
    "1.0 lineend");
```

This example changes the first line (numbered 0 and 1) and adds the tag 'highlight'. This turns the background yellow (in addition to any other tags that apply to this text).

You start at the beginning of the first line—that's line 0, character 0, or "0.0". You end at the end of the second line. This is specified as "1.0 lineend", or in Tk terms, line 1, character 0, and then go to the end of line (lineend).

Tags give you great flexibility in displaying text. You also can bind events (see the following section, "Events") to tags, which allows them to respond to events such as mouse clicks, function keys, focus changes, and other events.

Events

The widgets in the Tk collection do a pretty good job of handling their own events. For example, the Button widget handles a mouse click by calling the function specified by -command. The Text Entry widget handles keypress events by putting the characters typed in the entry.

But sometimes you may want to handle additional events. The bind method is used to connect an event, widget, and subroutine together. For example, suppose that you want to implement a status line in which context help is displayed when the mouse is placed over a widget.

The two events you are interested are <Enter> (mouse enters the widget's window) and <Leave> (mouse leaves the widget). The bind calls look like the following:

```
$tk_exit_button->bind('<Enter>',
    sub {display_help("Exits the program");});

$tk_exit_button->bind('<Leave>',
    sub {display_help("");});
```

In this case, the widget is an Exit button called $tk_exit_button. When the mouse enters the button, a help message "Exits the program" is displayed. When the mouse leaves, the message is erased.

A wide variety of events can be bound. The online documentation Tk::Bind contains a complete list.

General Design Hints

This section discusses some common-sense techniques that you can use to make designing your GUI a little easier.

Widget Layout

In almost all cases, `pack` is the only geometry manager you'll need. Start by deciding what widgets you want at the top of your window. Put them in a frame, packing them from left to right. Then pack the frame against the top of the main window.

Repeat this process until all your widgets have been created.

This method works for about 95 percent of the GUIs I've designed. (The other 5 percent required the `grid` geometry manager.)

Handle Placement Then Expansion

Don't worry about the `-expand` and `-fill` options until you have your widgets where you want them. Then go back and add in these options.

The next step is to test your program and resize the main window. If you did your `-expand` and `-fill` options right, things should look nice. If not, try again.

Use *ptkdb*

The `ptkdb` debugger is great for Tk applications. If you use the normal debugger, you won't see your widgets until you enter the `MainLoop`. Because of the way the `ptkdb` debugger works, when you create a widget and manage it, the widget appears instantly.

This means that if you are using `pack` to manage your widgets, you can see exactly how `pack` is placing your widgets on the screen.

Putting It All Together

This section goes through the design and implementation of a real-world program. The assignment is to come up with a pattern-searching program called `tk_grep.pl`.

The GUI for this program was shown earlier (refer to Figure 13.4).

The user specifies a regular expression in the Pattern box and a set of files in the Files box and then clicks on Search to search all the files for the given pattern. The results are shown in a pop-up window.

First, you need a main window:

```
my $tk_mw = MainWindow->new();
```

Next, you construct the main GUI. The top two widgets are a label for the Pattern string and an Entry for the pattern itself. You also need a frame in which to put them.

So create the frame and the two widgets. First the frame:

```
my $tk_top_frame = $tk_mw->Frame(
)->pack(
    -side => "top",
    -fill => "x"
);
```

The frame goes against the top of the window. It is allowed to expand to fill any extra space, but in the x direction only. Next add in the label:

```
$tk_top_frame->Label(
    -text => "Pattern:"
)->pack(
    -side => "left"
);
```

The label goes on the left side of the frame. It does not expand in any way.

The text entry follows:

```
my $tk_entry = $tk_top_frame->Entry(
    -textvariable => \$pattern
)->pack(
    -side => "right",
    -fill => "x",
    -expand => 1
);
```

The text entry is on the right side of the frame. It is allowed to expand in the x direction.

So the frame and entry can expand in the x direction. This means that if you make the window larger, the geometry manager will make the frame larger in the x direction. Because the frame is larger, the entry widget will grow to fill the available space (see Figure 13.6).

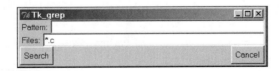

Figure 13.6 tk_grep after stretching.

The next line contains the Files blank. Because this requires essentially the same code as the first line, a subroutine called `lab_box` was created to do the work for both lines. You just call it twice.

Finally, you have two action buttons at the bottom of the window:

```
$button_frame->Button(
        -text => "Search",
        -command => sub {search($tk_mw);}
    )->pack(
        -side => "left",
        -anchor => "e"
    );

$button_frame->Button(
        -text => "Cancel",
        -command => sub {print "Cancel Pushed\n"; exit(); }
    )->pack(
        -side => "right",
        -anchor => "w"
    );
```

Searching

When the Search button is clicked, the program needs to search a list of files and display the results in a pop-up window.

The first step is to check the input to make sure that it's valid:

```
sub search($)
{
    my $parent = shift; # The parent window for our popup
#...
    if ($pattern eq "") {
        error_box($parent, "No search pattern");
        return;
    }
    if ($file_list eq "") {
        error_box($parent, "No file specification");
        return;
    }
```

Next, you need to get a list of files to check. This is done using the `glob` function, which takes a file specification with wildcards (`*`, `?`, and so on) in it and returns a list of the matching files:

```
    my @file_list = glob($file_list);
```

At this point, you know that all the input fields are valid, so the results appear in the pop-up window:

```
my $tk_top = $parent->Toplevel();

my $tk_text = $tk_top->Scrolled(
        'Text',
        -scrollbars => "osoe",
        -width => 80,
        -height => 10,
        -wrap => 'none'
    )->pack(
        -side => "top",
        -expand => 1,
        -fill => "both"
    );
```

The results are placed in a Text widget. Because the widget may have scrollbars, the Scrolled method is used to create it. The scrollbars will be at the
bottom (s) and right (e). They will appear only if needed (o).

The other element of this window is a Close button, which destroys the
window:

```
$tk_top->Button(
        -text => "Close",
        -command => sub {$tk_top->destroy();}
    )->pack(
        -side => "top",
        -anchor => "w"
    );
```

The code then goes through each line of each file and checks to see whether
it matches the pattern. If it does, a line number is added, and the result is
inserted onto the end of the text in the Text widget:

```
if ($line =~ $pattern) {
    my $display_line = sprintf("%3d %s",
            $line_number, $line);
    $tk_text->insert('end', $display_line);
}
```

The only other significant GUI element is the error box, which is displayed
when there's a problem. For this, you use a special method called messageBox.

The messageBox function displays a message and then waits until the user
responds to it. This is different from most other Tk widgets, which use a call-
back function to handle events.

In this case, you want an error type message box to be displayed, so use the
following code:

```
sub error_box($$)
{
    my $parent = shift;
    my $message = shift;
```

```
        $parent->messageBox(
            -icon => "error",
            -title => "Error",
            -message => $message,
            -type => "ok");
    }
```

Listing 13.2 contains the full tk_grep.pl program.

Listing 13.2   *tk_grep.pl*

```
use strict;
use warnings;

use Tk;
use Tk::LabEntry;

my $pattern = "";        # The pattern to search for
my $file_list = "*.c";   # The files to search

######################################################
# error_box($parent, $message)
#
# Display an error message and wait until the user
# presses OK to continue.
######################################################
sub error_box($$)
{
    my $parent = shift; # The parent window
    my $message = shift;# The message to display

    $parent->messageBox(
        -icon => "error",
        -title => "Error",
        -message => $message,
        -type => "ok");
}
######################################################
# search($main_window)
#
# Perform a search through all the files
######################################################
sub search($)
{
    my $parent = shift; # The parent window for our popup

    if ($pattern eq "") {
        error_box($parent, "No search pattern");
        return;
    }
    if ($file_list eq "") {
```

continues

Listing 13.2   **Continued**

```perl
        error_box($parent, "No file specification");
        return;
    }

    # The list of files to search
    my @file_list = glob($file_list);
    if ($#file_list == -1) {
        error_box($parent, "No files match the specification");
        return;
    }

    # The top level window for our results
    my $tk_top = $parent->Toplevel();

    # The window to contains the actual text of the
    # results
    my $tk_text = $tk_top->Scrolled(
            'Text',
            -scrollbars => "osoe",
            -width => 80,
            -height => 10,
            -wrap => 'none'
        )->pack(
            -side => "top",
            -expand => 1,
            -fill => "both"
        );

    $tk_top->Button(
            -text => "Close",
            -command => sub {$tk_top->destroy();}
        )->pack(
            -side => "top",
            -anchor => "w"
        );

    # Loop through each file
    foreach my $cur_file (@file_list)
    {
        if (not open(IN_FILE, "<$cur_file"))
        {
            error_box($parent, "Could not open $cur_file");
            next;
        }

        # Loop through each line
        my $line_number = 1;
        while (1) {
            my $line = <IN_FILE>;
```

```perl
            if (not defined($line)) {
                last;
            }

            if ($line =~ $pattern) {
                my $display_line = sprintf("%3d %s",
                        $line_number, $line);
                $tk_text->insert('end', $display_line);
            }
            $line_number++;
        }
        close (IN_FILE);
    }
}


####################################################
# lab_box($window, $label, $var)
#
# Create a box consisting of a label and a entry.
####################################################
sub lab_box($$$)
{
    my $window = shift; # the parent of the widgets
    my $label = shift;  # The text for the label
    my $var = shift;    # The variable for the entry

    # The frame we use to hold our two widgets
    my $frame = $window->Frame(
        )->pack(
            -side => "top",
            -fill => "x"
        );
    $frame->Label(
            -text => $label
        )->pack(
            -side => "left"
        );
    # The entry widget
    my $tk_entry = $frame->Entry(
            -textvariable => $var
        )->pack(
            -side => "right",
            -fill => "x",
            -expand => 1
        );
    $tk_entry->bind('<Return>', sub {search($window);});
}

# The main window
my $tk_mw = MainWindow->new();
```

continues

Listing 13.2   **Continued**

```
lab_box($tk_mw, "Pattern: ", \$pattern);
lab_box($tk_mw, "Files: ", \$file_list);

# The frame we use for the buttons
my $button_frame = $tk_mw->Frame(
    )->pack(
        -side => "top",
        -fill => "both"
    );

$button_frame->Button(
        -text => "Search",
        -command => sub {search($tk_mw);}
    )->pack(
        -side => "left",
        -anchor => "e"
    );

$button_frame->Button(
        -text => "Cancel",
        -command => sub {print "Cancel Pushed\n"; exit(); }
    )->pack(
        -side => "right",
        -anchor => "w"
    );

MainLoop();
```

Summary

The Tk module gives you a quick and simple way to create GUIs for your Perl programs. Though simple, its powerful and flexible framework enables it to easily handle complex interfaces.

GUIs are a great way to simplify command input; and adding a GUI to a Perl tool transforms it from a tool used by command-line power users into a tool used by everybody.

Exercises

1. Write a program that displays a single button labeled "Don't push me." When the user clicks it, change the label to read "Don't push me again." (In memory of Douglas Adams and *The Hitchhiker's Guide to the Galaxy*.)

2. Write a command that takes as its single argument a message and displays a pop-up window containing the message. This sort of command is useful for scripts that want to display a warning or error message but that have no GUI.

3. Write a front end to the UNIX `find` command. (If you're on Microsoft Windows, you can use the `find2perl` command to generate your own version of `find` and write a front end to it.)

4. Write a program that checks the amount of free space on each of your drives and displays the result graphically.

5. As part of an inspection system you need to record the following information for each inspection:

   - Number of inspectors
   - Time spent inspecting
   - Number of lines inspected
   - Number of defects found

   Write a GUI that records this information for each inspection.

Resources

Online Documentation

The Tk system contains extensive documentation. This section does not list all the documents but includes only the most useful ones.

- `Tk`—Index of all the Tk documents.
- `Tk::overview`—Overview of the Tk system.
- `Tk::UserGuide`—More extensive introduction to the Tk system.
- `Tk::Button`—Typical widget.
- `Tk::pack`—Geometry manager that packs widgets as closely together as possible.
- `Tk::grid`—Grid-oriented geometry manager.
- `Tk::options`—A list of options common to all widgets as well as functions you can call to manipulate them.

Demonstrations

- **widget**—The Tk widget demo, which shows you what almost all the Tk widgets look like.
- **Other demos**—Distributed with the Tk source are a number of other demonstrations. Unfortunately, these are not installed when you install the Tk module, so if you want to a look at them, you'll need to unpack the sources to the Tk module and look for things with the word "demo" in them.

Web Sites

- **http://tcl.activestate.com/**—The official Tcl/Tk web site.
- **http://spectcl.sourceforge.net/**—GUI builder for Perl/Tk. Unfortunately, this GUI builder limits you to the grid geometry manager.

Combining C and Perl with Inline::C

As YOU MIGHT HAVE GUESSED, C IS better than Perl for some things, and Perl is better than C for other things. The `Inline` module enables you to combine both languages. That way, you can use C to do what C does well and use Perl for what Perl does well.

This chapter shows you how to use the `Inline` module to actually put C code into your Perl program as well as gives you an introduction to Perl's internals so that you can make maximum use of this module.

What Is the *Inline* Module?

You can combine C and Perl in several different ways. One of the most common is to use C to create a Perl module. This is useful and flexible, but it is complex and difficult to get right. Also you have to know a bit about Perl's internals to create a really good module.

Another way of marrying C and Perl is to use the embedded Perl interpreter. But again, the process is not as easy as it looks, and you have to know a lot about the internals of Perl.

Finally, you can use the `Inline` module. This module lets you put your C code in your Perl program. When the code is needed, the module compiles and loads it for you. This method avoids many of the hassles of dealing with both languages. In fact, the `Inline` module goes to a lot of trouble to make it almost unnecessary to be concerned with the internals of the Perl interpreter. (You still have to get your hands dirty, but this is the cleanest interface possible.) Note that if you haven't done so already, you need to download and install the `Inline::C` module.

Hello World

This section starts with yet another version of "Hello World". Listing 14.1 uses Perl to call a function named `say_hello`, which is written in C.

Listing 14.1 *hello.pl*

```
use strict;
use warnings;

use Inline "C";

sub say_hello();

say_hello();


__END__
__C__
void say_hello() {
    printf("Hello World\n");
}
```

> **Note**
>
> To use `Inline::C` on Microsoft Windows, you must have installed a C compiler. By default, the `Inline::C` module assumes that you have installed the Microsoft C++ compiler.
>
> You must be able to compile a C program from the command line before you can use `Inline::C`.

The program starts by telling Perl that you want to include some inline C code with the statement

```
use Inline "C";
```

This is followed by a Perl prototype for the function `say_hello`:

```
sub say_hello();
```

The keyword __END__ is used to tell Perl that it has reached the end of the program. (At least as far as the Perl code is concerned.)

This is followed by the __C__ keyword that tells the Inline module that the C code follows.

Finally there is the C function itself:

```
void say_hello() {
    printf("Hello World\n");
}
```

When the Inline function does its work, it examines the function headers of the C code and parses the argument list. The parser is not a full C parser and is somewhat limited. In particular, if you tried to declare the function as

```
void say_hello(void) {
```

the operation would fail. (More on arguments in section, "Simple Arguments and Return Values.")

Also you did not have to include the <stdio.h> header file. That header file along with the "perl.h" header file is automatically included.

When this program is first run, it takes a long time because the Inline module is working. It strips out your C code, adds some glue, and then compiles it. The result is a loadable Perl module, which it then loads.

The next time you run the program, the Inline module checks to see whether it needs to recompile or whether it can use the existing module. If the old module works, the compilation step is skipped, and the program runs much faster.

All this work is done in the _Inline directory. You can safely delete this directory; the next time the program is run, it will be re-created.

Simple Arguments and Return Values

One thing that C is good at is bit handling. In this section, you create a set of functions to handle a bit array. For simplicity, make it a fixed size (16×16).

You'll need two C functions, one to set a bit to a given value and the other to return the value of the bit. Listing 14.2 contains the functions along with a little Perl code to test it.

Listing 14.2 *bits1.pl*

```
use strict;
use warnings;

use Inline "C";
```

continues

Listing 14.2   **Continued**

```
sub set_bit($$$);
sub test_bit($$);

set_bit(1,1,1);
set_bit(1,2,1);
if ((test_bit(1,1) != 1) ||
    (test_bit(1,2) != 1) ||
    (test_bit(1,3) != 0)) {
    die("Test #1 Failed");
}

set_bit(1,1,0);

if (test_bit(1,1) != 0) {
    die("Test #2 Failed");
}
print "Successed!\n";
__END__
__C__

#define X_SIZE 16
#define Y_SIZE 16
static int array[X_SIZE/8][Y_SIZE];

void set_bit(int x, int y, int value) {
    if (value != 0)
        array[x/8][y] |= (0x80 >> (x % 8));
    else
        array[x/8][y] &= ~(0x80 >> (x % 8));
}

int test_bit(int x, int y)
{
    return ((array[x/8][y] & (0x80 >> (x % 8))) != 0);
}
```

At this point, the most important part of the code is what you didn't write. You didn't have to take care of all the data conversions between Perl's internal scalar types and the function parameters. All that work was done behind the scenes by Inline.

Dealing with Trouble

Unfortunately, no one is perfect. From time to time, you'll make a mistake and your program won't compile. When that happens you'll get an error message such as this:

```
A problem was encountered while attempting to compile and install your Inline
C code. The command that failed was:
  make > out.make 2>&1

The build directory was:
/home/oualline/bits/_Inline/build/bits1_pl_51cd

To debug the problem, cd to the build directory,
and inspect the output files.

  at bits1.pl line 0
INIT failed--call queue aborted.
```

The directory, _Inline/build/..... (UNIX systems), contains the intermediate files that Inline created behind the scenes. Because your program wouldn't compile, the module decided to save its work so that you can use it to figure out what happened.

Table 14.1 provides the typical elements of a build directory and a brief description of each.

Table 14.1 **Contents of a Typical *build* Directory**

File	Description
INLINE.h	Functions defined by the Inline module for use by inline programs
Makefile	The file used to "make" the inline C code you wrote
Makefile.PL	The Perl program used to make the file Makefile
bits1_pl_51cd.c	The C program generated by the utility xsubpp from the .xs file
bits1_pl_51cd.xs	Your C code—sort of (see below)
out.Makefile_PL	Output of the Makefile.PL command
out.make	Output of the make and link commands
pm_to_blib	Intermediate file

The out.make file contains the output of the compilation. Any error messages will be stored here. The other significant file is the .xs file. It contains a version of your inline code, which is compiled by the Perl utility xsubpp into C code, which is then compiled into a local module. If there is a problem with your C code, the errors will refer to a line in this file.

The xs format combines C code with information about it so that Perl can use the C functions provided. The format of this file is documented in the online document perldoc perlxs. You don't have to worry about the format of this file because the Inline module takes care of creating it for you.

How Perl Handles Variables

Suppose that instead of using a static variable for your bit array, you want to pass it a Perl scalar and let the program store its data there. To do so, you need to know a little about how Perl stores its data internally.

All Perl scalar variables are represented by the type sv defined in the perl.h file. The definition of this type is

```
struct sv {
    void*       sv_any;      /* pointer to something */
    U32         sv_refcnt;   /* how many references to us */
    U32         sv_flags;    /* what we are */
};
typedef struct sv SV;
```

The sv_any field points to the data held in the scalar. This can be a Perl string (called a *byte array* by C programmers) or a reference to a hash, array, code, scalar, or typeglob.

The sv_refcnt is a reference count used by Perl to determine when to free the variable. Finally, the sv_flags are flags used by Perl to handle variable type information and booking information.

Accessing Perl's *SV* Variables

You don't normally access the contents of an sv directly. Instead, Perl provides a rich set of functions that let you create and access sv variables.

For example, the SvIV macro turns a scalar into an integer. (If the scalar doesn't contain an integer value, the conversion does the best it can.) For example:

```
void do_square(SV *value) {
            int number = SvIV(value);
```

If you want to set a scalar value to an integer, you can use the sv_setiv macro:

```
sv_setiv(value, 56);
```

Finally, if for some reason you need to create a scalar, there is a set of newSV... macros. For example:

```
unsigned char array[5] = {1, 2, 3, 4, 5};
new_value = newSVpv(array, 5);
```

The online document perldoc perlguts gives you a good introduction to the sv variable type and the functions that manipulate it. Table 14.2 contains a short list of some of the more important functions that can be used with svs. For a complete list of all the functions you can use (all variable types), see the online document perlapi.

Table 14.2 **Some Important Functions that Can Be Used with *SV*s.**

Function	Meaning
SV *result = NEWSV(*count*, *length*)	Create a new SV. Set the reference count to *count* and allocate *length* bytes. (Nothing is put in the SV, but *length* bytes are reserved.)
SV *result* = newSViv(*integer*)	Create a new SV and assign it the integer value *integer*.
SV *result = newSVnv(*float_value*)	Create a new SV and assign it the floating-point value float_value.
SV *result = newSVpv(*string*, *length*)	Create a new SV and assign it the string value *string*. The number of bytes copied is specified by the *length* variable. If this variable is zero, then the length of the string is computed using the strlen function.
flag = SvIOK(*SV_ptr*)	Return true if the *SV_ptr* points to an SV that contains an integer.
integer = SvIV(*SV_ptr*)	Turn an SV into an integer.
double_value = SvNV(*SV_ptr*)	Turn an SV into a double.
string = SvPV(*SV_ptr*)	Turn an SV into a string (char *).

Using *SV*

Now rewrite the bits program to let the user pass in an array. First change the function header so that it accepts a Perl scalar:

```
void set_bit(SV *bits, int x, int y, int value) {
```

The next step is to turn the SV into something you can use, namely an array and a length. This is done through the SvPV macro:

```
int len;    /* Length of the bit array */
/* The bit array */
unsigned char *array = SvPV(bits, len);
```

Now that you have the array, check to see whether it has the correct number of bytes in it. If it's the wrong size, write out an error message and call the Perl internal function croak. (This is the equivalent of the Perl language function dic.) For example:

```
if (len != SIZE_BYTES) {
    fprintf(stderr, "Bit array must be %d bytes long\n", SIZE_BYTES);
    croak("Can not continue");
}
```

Since SvPV is a macro, it is able to modify len and stores the length of the scalar there.

Except for a little bit of glue and some math, that is all you have to do. Listing 14.3 shows the full program.

Listing 14.3 *bits2.pl*

```perl
use strict;
use warnings;

use Inline "C";

sub set_bit($$$$);
sub test_bit($$$);

# The bit array we are using
my $bits = pack("C*", (0) x 32);

set_bit($bits, 1,1,1);
set_bit($bits, 1,2,1);
if ((test_bit($bits, 1,1) != 1) ||
    (test_bit($bits, 1,2) != 1) ||
    (test_bit($bits, 1,3) != 0)) {
    die("Test #1 Failed");
}

set_bit($bits, 1,1,0);

if (test_bit($bits, 1,1) != 0) {
    die("Test #2 Failed");
}
print "Tests passed\n";

__END__
__C__

#define X_SIZE 16
#define Y_SIZE 16

/* Size (in bytes) of the bit array */
#define SIZE_BYTES ((X_SIZE * Y_SIZE) / 8)

/* Index into an array which is actually a string */
static unsigned char *element(unsigned char *data, int x, int y)
{
    return (&data[y * (X_SIZE/8) + x]);
}

void set_bit(SV *bits, int x, int y, int value) {

    int len;    /* Length of the bit array */
    /* The bit array */
```

```
    unsigned char *array = SvPV(bits, len);

    if (len != SIZE_BYTES) {
        fprintf(stderr, "Bit array must be %d bytes long\n", SIZE_BYTES);
        croak("Can not continue");
    }

    if (value != 0)
        *element(array, x/8, y) |= (0x80 >> (x % 8));
    else
        *element(array, x/8, y) &= ~(0x80 >> (x % 8));
}

int test_bit(SV *bits, int x, int y)
{
    int len;     /* Length of the bit array */
    /* The bit array */
    unsigned char *array = SvPV(bits, len);

    if (len != SIZE_BYTES) {
        fprintf(stderr, "Bit array must be %d bytes long\n", SIZE_BYTES);
        croak("Can not continue");
    }

    return (
        ((*element(array, x/8, y)) & (0x80 >> (x % 8)))
        != 0);
}
```

Returning Multiple Values

Perl lets you return things, such as arrays and hashes, to the calling function. To
do this from C, you must directly manipulate the Perl argument stack.
Specifically, you have to push a lot of stuff onto it.

Suppose that you want to return an array containing the coordinates of
each location containing a set bit.

You have the usual function call heading and local variable declaration:

```
void get_values() {
    int x, y;
    Inline_Stack_Vars;
```

But something new has been added. The Inline system uses a number of variables to keep track of what it's doing with the stack. These are declared by the
macro Inline_Stack_Vars. (The variables are sp, items, ax, and mark, so don't
use any of these names in your program.)

The next step is to clear out the old stack information. (The stack contains
the parameters passed to you, and you want to start with a clean stack.) This is

accomplished with the statement

```
Inline_Stack_Reset;
```

Now all you need to do is go through and test each bit to see whether it's set. When you find one that is, push two scalars (x and y) on the stack using the macro `Inline_Stack_Push`.

Now x and y are C integers, and you need Perl scalars. For that conversion, call the function `newSViv`, which, if you decode it, reads "new scalar value (SV) from integer value (iv)."

The code looks like this:

```
for (x = 0; x < X_SIZE; ++x) {
    for (y = 0; y < Y_SIZE; ++y) {
        if (test_bit(x, y)) {
            Inline_Stack_Push(newSViv(x));
            Inline_Stack_Push(newSViv(y));
        }
    }
}
```

Finally, you need to tell the system that you're finished playing with the stack:

```
Inline_Stack_Done;
```

So the four steps in dealing with the Perl stack are

1. Declare the variables (`Inline_Stack_Vars`).
2. Clear the old junk out (`Inline_Stack_Reset`).
3. Put the new data on (`Inline_Stack_Push`).
4. Tell Perl that you are finished (`Inline_Stack_Done`).

Listing 14.4 shows the complete program.

Listing 14.4   *bits3.pl*

```
use strict;
use warnings;

use Inline "C";

sub set_bit($$$);
sub test_bit($$);
sub get_values();

set_bit(1,1,1);
set_bit(1,2,1);
if ((test_bit(1,1) != 1) ||
    (test_bit(1,2) != 1) ||
    (test_bit(1,3) != 0)) {
    die("Test #1 Failed");
}
```

```perl
set_bit(1,1,0);

if (test_bit(1,1) != 0) {
    die("Test #2 Failed");
}
set_bit(2,3,1);
my @expected = (
        1,2,
        2,3
);
my @results = get_values();
if (@results ne @expected) {
    die("Test #3 failed");
}

print "Test passed\n";

__END__
__C__

#define X_SIZE 16
#define Y_SIZE 16
static unsigned char array[X_SIZE/8][Y_SIZE];

void set_bit(int x, int y, int value) {
    if (value != 0)
        array[x/8][y] |= (0x80 >> (x % 8));
    else
        array[x/8][y] &= ~(0x80 >> (x % 8));
}

int test_bit(int x, int y) {
    return ((array[x/8][y] & (0x80 >> (x % 8))) != 0);
}

void get_values() {
    int x, y;
    Inline_Stack_Vars;

    Inline_Stack_Reset;

    for (x = 0; x < X_SIZE; ++x) {
        for (y = 0; y < Y_SIZE; ++y) {
            if (test_bit(x, y)) {
                Inline_Stack_Push(newSViv(x));
                Inline_Stack_Push(newSViv(y));
            }
        }
    }
    Inline_Stack_Done;
}
```

Calling Perl from C

Sometimes you'll need to call a Perl function from your C code. For example, in the Tk graphical environment, Perl functions are called when a window event occurs, such as when a button is clicked.

In this example we're going to update our code to call the Perl function handler error. Up to now all your C functions have called croak when they encountered an error. Aborting the program for any little problem is a drastic way of handling a problem.

So for a change, you'll call the Perl function handle_error instead. In C, you can execute any Perl command using the eval_pv function. For example:

```
eval_pv("main::handle_error('message')", 0);
```

The arguments to this function are a string, which contains executable Perl code, and a flag. If the flag is set, the function aborts the program if there is a syntax error in the string.

The result of executing the string (a SV*) is returned by the function. Listing 14.5 shows the complete function and a short test routine.

Listing 14.5   *error.pl*

```
use strict;
use warnings;

use Inline "C";

sub handle_error($)
{
    my $msg = shift;

    print "ERROR: $msg\n";
    print "Continuing anyway\n";
}

cause_trouble();

__END__
__C__
void cause_trouble() {
    eval_pv("main::handle_error('Trouble caused');", 0);
    return;
}
```

Configuring *Inline*

You can supply a number of configuration parameters to the `Inline` package. The first is the `DIRECTORY` option. This tells `Inline` which directory (the default is _Inline) to put the code in that it generates. For example, if you wanted to use the directory `c_stuff`, you would use the Perl statement

```
use Inline (C => 'DATA',
    DIRECTORY => "./c_stuff");
```

Other common options include those shown in Table 14.3.

Table 14.3 *Inline* **Options**

Option	Description
INCLUDE	A set of -I options used to specify where the include files reside
LIBS	The library options for the C compiler
CC	The name of the C compiler
CCFLAGS	Compiler flags
MAKE	The name of the make command

With these options, you should be able to compile almost any C program with ease. Additional options can be found in the online documentation.

Making a Distributable Module

Currently, there is no simple way of creating a portable module using the `Inline` package. However, if you really want to create one, you can follow the procedures outlined in the `Inline-FAQ` document.

The developer of the `Inline` package, Brian Ingerson, has promised that it will be possible to turn `Inline` code into a module with a single command "real soon now."

Summary

The `Inline` function is the easiest way to join C and Perl code together. That's because it hides most of the Perl details from the C programming.

But it's not possible to cover up everything, so sometimes you do have to dive into the internals of Perl to unlock the full power of this interface between languages.

Exercises

1. Write a C subroutine that computes the parity of an integer value.

2. Create a function that computes the 16-bit CRC for a string.

3. Many different C libraries are available. Pick one and write a set of Inline::C functions for it. (For example, try the zlib compression library; you can find it at http://www.zlib.org.)

4. Write a high-speed version of unpack. This function takes a single scalar string as its argument, assumes that it's an array of integers (int[]), and returns a Perl version of the integer array.

Resources

Online Documentation

- **perldoc ExtUtils::MakeMaker**—Used by module makers to create a Makefile.PL (which creates a Makefile, which creates your module).

- **perldoc Inline-FAQ**—Frequently Asked Questions (and answers) for the Inline module.

- **perldoc Inline-Support**—How to get support for the Inline module.

- **perldoc Inline::C-Cookbook**—A set of small examples on how to use various features of Inline.

- **perldoc perlapi**—The set of internal Perl functions that a C programmer can call.

- **perldoc perlcall**—How to call Perl functions from C.

- **perldoc perlguts**—A tutorial on the guts of Perl; describes the SV structure and the functions that operate on it.

- **perldoc perlxs**—The format of the file used to describe C functions to Perl.

- **perldoc perlxstut**—A tutorial on writing XS files.

- **perldoc ExtUtils::xsubpp**—Documentation for the xsubpp utility.

Modules

- **Inline**—The master module for using other languages inside Perl.
- **Inline::C**—The interface between C and Perl.
- **Inline::CPP**—An interface between C++ and Perl.
- **Inline::***—Inline is available for many other languages as well from Assembler and Basic to Java. Check out the CPAN repository for your favorite language.

Utilities

- **h2xs**—A program that converts h files (which are used by C) to xs files (which are used by the Perl module compiler).
- **xsubpp**—Converts xs files into C code.

15

Putting It All Together

Y OU'VE LEARNED A GREAT DEAL ABOUT PERL in the previous chapters, and now it's time to put your knowledge to use. This chapter covers how to design a small, real-world system and how to use Perl to implement it.

If you're like me you have a few floppies and CD-ROMs lying about. Organizing these disks can be a chore. This chapter shows you how to create a database to support the cataloging of program disks.

To make things convenient for all users, the example program implements three front ends to the system: a command-line interface, a GUI version, and a set of CGI programs.

But before you get to the various interfaces, you need to design the core functions.

Perl and Databases

You need to learn a little bit about how Perl handles databases. Perl contains a tie function that connects a variable with a package. For example, let's tie the Perl variable %db to the DB_File package as follows:

```
use DB_File;
tie(my %db, 'DB_File', 'my_info.db');
```

This tells Perl that all accesses to the hash `%db` are to be turned into method calls to the package `DB_File`. This means that now the following statement is actually a function call:

```
$db{password} = "Surfs Up";
```

The function is provided by the `DB_File` package. This package is one of the many small databases available for Perl. In fact, this one comes with the core Perl distribution. When this package sees this statement, it stores a new key/value pair in the database.

One nice thing about this is that your data is preserved between program runs. Thus, if one item is stored in the database one day, it will still be there when the program runs another day.

The `tie` statement consists of three parts. The first is a variable to be tied. This can be an array, scalar, or hash. The next parameter is the package to be used. In the example, this is `DB_File`.

Finally, there are the arguments to the package. In this case, you're using only one, the name of the database: `my_info.db`.

The `tie` function connects the hash to the database. If you want to break this connection, use the `untie` function:

```
untie(%db);
```

MLDBM Package

There is a problem with the `DB_File` packages. You can put only scalars in the database. It won't work with references.

For example, attempting to store a reference fails:

```
$db{users} = [qw(tom dick harry)];
```

However, another database interface, `MLDBM`, does allow you to store and retrieve complex data. Actually, this is not a database but a wrapper that sits between the tied variable and the actual database. Its job is to encode and decode the data so that you think you are dealing with complex data structures, and the database thinks it's dealing with scalars.

When you bring in the `MLDBM` package, you need to give it two parameters: the name of the package to use for the underlying database and the name of a package that is to be used for encoding and decoding the data.

For the disk database (in the file `disk.pm`), ask for the `MLDBM` package using the following statement:

```
141  use MLDBM qw(DB_File Storable);
```

(Line numbers refer to the full program which can be seen in Listing 15.1.)

Later when you want to use the database, you use the `tie` function to connect the database and a Perl hash variable:

```
167          $database = tie (%disk_db,
168                  'MLDBM', $db_file,
169                  O_RDWR|O_CREAT, 0640);
```

In this example, `%disk_db` is the Perl hash, and the name of the database file is contained in the variable `$db_file`. The other parameters tell the `DB_File` package that you want to open the database for both reading and writing, to create it if necessary, and to use the UNIX permissions `0640` for the new file (if any).

Now look at what happens when you do a complex assignment such as this:

```
$db{users} = [qw(tom dick harry)];
```

Perl sees that `%db` is a tied hash, so it calls the method `MLDBM::STORE`. This function sees that you are trying to store any array of elements, so it calls `Storable::Freeze` to turn the array into an encoded scalar. `MLDBM::STORE` then uses the `DB_File` database to store the key (users) and the encoded data.

This works well and almost transparently. There is just one thing that can get you into trouble—a statement like this:

```
$db{users}[0] = "sam";
```

In this case, Perl takes a look at `$db{users}`. It's a reference to an array. You want to change the first element of this array. Because you are not changing anything in the hash proper, Perl does not call `MLDBM::STORE`.

Again, the reference (`$db{users}`) is not being changed but rather the array being referenced (`@{$db{users}}`), and that doesn't trigger the `tie` logic. As a result, stores such as this will not make it into the database.

So what do you do? You have to split up the operation into stages. For example:

```
my $ref = $db{users};
${@{$ref}}[0] = "sam";
$db{users} = $ref;
```

That last statement does modify `%db` and triggers the `MLDBM::STORE` call.

Now that you know how to access a database, take a look at what goes into it.

Dealing with Simultaneous Database Accesses

It's possible that many people will use the database system at the same time. That means that you have to deal with the problem of simultaneous access to the database.

The DB_File package deals with this in a limited way. The database can be opened read-only or read-write. An unlimited number of people can open the database read-only. Only one program at a time can open the database read-write. If a second person attempts to open the database read-write, he will be blocked until the first program finishes changing the database and closes it.

If you open the database read-only and then another program changes it, these changes are not reflected in your copy. In other words, the data is "frozen" when you open the database read-only. (At least as far as you're concerned.)

This means that if you want to use the database, you should get in quickly, do your work, and get out. Keeping the database open for a long time is not a good idea.

Other databases do not have these limitations, and there are Perl interfaces to them. The DB_File database was chosen because the amount of data you are dealing with is small and because it comes with the Perl core distribution. In other words, it was the simplest thing to use.

The DB_File database limits you to one write at a time, which is okay for short, simple applications. But this won't do for more complex jobs. For them, you'll need a better database. Two of the most popular ones are MySQL and PostgreSQL. (See Appendix C, "Beyond Perl," for more information.)

Database Design

Now take a look at the database design. The first thing to look at is the data you are organizing. In this case, it's disks. I organize my disk into several broad categories, including the following:

- Floppies
- Zip disks
- Bare CD-ROMs (These are CD-ROMs that I store without their cases.)
- CD-ROMs with cases (These are CD-ROMs stored with their cases. The cases are kept because they contain valuable information such as instruction sheets, licenses, or other information.)

Each disk is identified by its category and an index number. For example, the first floppy disk is assigned the identifier F1 (F for floppy disk, 1 for first disk). This identifier makes it easy to find the disk. All I have to do is go to my floppy cabinet and select the first disk.

Similarly, if I want to find my "Redhat 5.1 Disk," I look up the identifier in the database and find that it's disk B37. I then go to the CD organizer containing disks B33–B64 and grab the CD-ROM. Because everything is in order, everything is easy to find after I find the identifier.

The database is designed to make it easy to find a given disk. Because each identifier is unique, you will use the identifier as the key to the hash. The data is another hash containing the following fields:

DESCRIPTION—The description of the CD-ROM.

CATEGORY—The category the disk is assigned to.

Database Implementation

The example implementation uses a Perl object to hold the database. The first method defined is called new, and it creates the object.

The new function takes two parameters: the name of the database and the variable $flag is set if you want to open the database read-only. After getting the parameters, create the database using the following statement:

```
159     if ($flag) {
160         # The database information
161         $database = tie (%disk_db,
162                 'MLDBM', $db_file,
163                 O_RDONLY, 0640);
164         $self->{READ_ONLY} = 1;
165     } else {
166         # The database information
167         $database = tie (%disk_db,
168                 'MLDBM', $db_file,
169                 O_RDWR|O_CREAT, 0640);
170         $self->{READ_ONLY} = 0;
171     }
```

In this case, %disk_db contains the database data. The $database variable is used if you want to control the database.

Storing and Retrieving Records

After you have the database object, you can put data in it using the modify_disk method. Stripped to its bare essentials, this is done by simply assigning the database hash a new value:

```
192     $self->{DISK_DATA}->{$id} = {%data};
```

After the data is recorded, you can get it using the get_disk method. Again this method is simple; just return the hash data:

```
229     return ($self->{DISK_DATA}->{$id});
```

Creating a new entry is accomplished by the `new_disk` method. This is a little more complicated than the `modify_disk` method because it must find an unused disk ID:

```
210        for ($index = 0; ; $index++) {
211            $id = $category.$index;
212            if (not defined($self->{DISK_DATA}->{$id})) {
213                last;
214            }
215        }
```

But after a free ID is found, the disk is created using a simple assignment:

```
216        $self->{DISK_DATA}->{$id} = {%data};
```

Finally, there is a function to return a list of all the keys in the database. Normally, this is a simple `return` statement:

```
268        return (sort key_sort keys %{$self->{DISK_DATA}});
```

Actually, things are not that simple if you decide to sort the result. Sorting involves a lot of regular expressions and other fun, but aside from the bookkeeping, the logic of the function is simple:

```
246  sub key_sort {
247        $a =~ /(.)(.*)/;
248        my $letter1 = $1;    # Letters in the first key
249        my $digits1 = $2;    # Digits in the first key
250
251        $b =~ /(.)(.*)/;
252        my $letter2 = $1;    # Letters in the second key
253        my $digits2 = $2;    # Digits in the second key
254
255        if ($letter1 ne $letter2) {
256            return ($letter1 cmp $letter2);
257        }
258        return ($digits1 <=> $digits2);
259  }
```

The *disk.pm* Module

Listing 15.1 contains the full `disk.pm` module. It includes the object constructor, `new`, as well as the accessory methods and `get_disk`.

Listing 15.1 also includes the function `DESTROY`, which is called when the `disk.pm` database object is destroyed. It closes the database by using the following statement to `untie` the hash:

```
277        untie $self->{DISK_DATA};
```

The `disk.pm` module provides the following functions:

- `disks->new` — Creates a new database object
- `$db->new_disk` — Creates a disk

- $db->update_disk — Updates an entry
- $db->get_keys — Gets the IDs for all the disks
- $db->delete_disk — Deletes a disk

Listing 15.1 *disk.pm*

```
1   use strict;
2   use warnings;
3
4   package disks;
5   =pod
6
7   =head1 NAME
8
9   disks.pm - Data database manipulation class
10
11  =head1 SYNOPSIS
12
13      $db = disks->new($file, $read_only)
14
15      $db->update_disk($id, %data);
16
17      $id = $db->new_disk($category, %data);
18
19      $disk_ref = $db->get_disk($id);
20
21      @keys = $db->get_keys();
22
23      delete_disk($id)
24
25  =head1 DESCRIPTION
26
27  The I<disks> package provides functions that allow the user to
28  store and retrieve information about a set of disks.  The disks
29  can be floppy, zip, cd-rom, or whatever.  The database makes no
30  distinction between them.
31
32  =head1 Functions
33
34  =over 4
35
36  =item $db = disk->new($file, $read_only)
37
38  Open a database.
39
40  =head2 Parameters
41
42  =item I<$file>
43
44  The file name for the database.
```

continues

Listing 15.1 **Continued**

```
45
46  =item I<$read_only>
47
48  If set, the database is opened read only.  If not set, the database
49  is opened for reading and writing.
50
51  =back
52
53  The database will be created if does not exist (and you are opening
54  it read/write.)
55
56  =head2 Return
57
58  The database object or undef it the database could not
59  be opened.
60
61  =item $db->update_disk($id, %data);
62
63  Update the information about a given disk in the database.
64
65  =head2 Parameters
66
67  =over 4
68
69  =item Id
70
71  Id of the disk.
72
73  =item I<%data>
74
75  Hash containing the information about the disk.
76
77  =back
78
79  =head2 Return Value
80
81  None.
82
83  =item $id = $db->new_disk($category, %data);
84
85  Returns the entire set of data store in the database.  This is a
86  hash reference whose keys are the days and whose values are a
87  hash containing the key items listed above.
88
89  =head2 Parameters
90
91  =over 4
92
93  =item $category
94
95  The category letter for the new data.  The system will use this
```

```
 96  to find a slot in the database for this disk.
 97
 98  =item %data
 99
100  The data describing the disk.
101
102  =back
103
104  =head2 Returns
105
106  The generated ID number of the disk.
107
108  =item $disk_ref = $db->get_disk($id);
109
110  Get the disk information for a given disk.
111
112  =head2 Parameters
113
114  =over 4
115
116  =item $id
117
118  The id of the disk we want.
119
120  =back
121
122  =head2 Returns
123
124  A reference to the hash containing the disks data or
125  undef if the id does not match any disk.
126
127  =item @keys = $db->get_keys();
128
129  Returns a lit of all the keys in the database.
130
131  =item delete_disk($id)
132
133  Deletes the disk from the database
134
135  =back
136
137  =cut
138
139  use Fcntl;
140  use DB_File;
141  use MLDBM qw(DB_File Storable);
142  use Carp;
143  use POSIX;
144
145  #######################################################
146  # new($db_file, $flag) -- Open a disk database
147  #
```

continues

Listing 15.1 **Continued**

```
148  #  If $flag is set, enable writing.
149  #####################################################
150  sub new($$) {
151      my $class = shift;  # The class name
152      my $db_file = shift;# The name of the database file
153      my $flag = shift;   # Read only flag
154      my $self = {};      # Hash that represents me
155
156      my $database;       # The database object
157      my %disk_db;        # The disk data in the database
158
159      if ($flag) {
160          # The database information
161          $database = tie (%disk_db,
162                  'MLDBM', $db_file,
163                  O_RDONLY, 0640);
164          $self->{READ_ONLY} = 1;
165      } else {
166          # The database information
167          $database = tie (%disk_db,
168                  'MLDBM', $db_file,
169                  O_RDWR|O_CREAT, 0640);
170          $self->{READ_ONLY} = 0;
171      }
172      if (not defined($database)) {
173          return (undef);
174      }
175      $self->{DATABASE} = $database;
176      $self->{DISK_DATA} = \%disk_db;
177      return (bless($self, $class));
178  }
179  #####################################################
180  # update_disk($id, %data)
181  #
182  # Update the data for a disk
183  #####################################################
184  sub update_disk($$%) {
185      my $self = shift;           # The class
186      my $id = shift;             # The disk id number
187      my %data = @_;              # The data to record
188
189      if ($self->{READ_ONLY}) {
190          die("Database is read only");
191      }
192      $self->{DISK_DATA}->{$id} = {%data};
193  }
194  #####################################################
195  # new_disk($category, %data)
196  #
197  # Create a new disk
198  #####################################################
199  sub new_disk($$%) {
```

```
200     my $self = shift;           # The class
201     my $category = shift;       # The disk category
202     my %data = @_;              # The data to record
203
204     if ($self->{READ_ONLY}) {
205         die("Database is read only");
206     }
207     my $index;  # Index used for computing the id
208     my $id;     # The new id number we just generated
209
210     for ($index = 0; ; $index++) {
211         $id = $category.$index;
212         if (not defined($self->{DISK_DATA}->{$id})) {
213             last;
214         }
215     }
216     $self->{DISK_DATA}->{$id} = {%data};
217     return ($id);
218 }
219 #####################################################
220 # get_disk -- Returns a hash containing disk information
221 #       on a given disk
222 #
223 # Returns a reference to the data hash
224 #####################################################
225 sub get_disk($) {
226     my $self = shift;   # The class
227     my $id = shift;     # The id for the disk
228
229     return ($self->{DISK_DATA}->{$id});
230 }
231 #####################################################
232 # delete_disk -- Delete a given disk
233 #####################################################
234 sub delete_disk($$) {
235     my $self = shift;   # The class
236     my $id = shift;     # The id for the disk
237
238     delete ($self->{DISK_DATA}->{$id});
239 }
240 #####################################################
241 # key_sort -- Sort by the disk key (<letter><number>)
242 #
243 # Keys are in $a and $b, returns number as required by
244 # sort.
245 #####################################################
246 sub key_sort {
247     $a =~ /(.)(.*)/;
248     my $letter1 = $1;   # Letters in the first key
249     my $digits1 = $2;   # Digits in the first key
250
```

continues

Listing 15.1 **Continued**

```
251        $b =~ /(.)(.*)/;
252        my $letter2 = $1;    # Letters in the second key
253        my $digits2 = $2;    # Digits in the second key
254
255        if ($letter1 ne $letter2) {
256            return ($letter1 cmp $letter2);
257        }
258        return ($digits1 <=> $digits2);
259    }
260    #####################################################
261    # get_keys -- Return a list of all the keys in the
262    #        database
263    #####################################################
264    sub get_keys($)
265    {
266        my $self = shift;    # The class
267
268        return (sort key_sort keys %{$self->{DISK_DATA}});
269    }
270
271    #####################################################
272    # destroy the variable (called automatically by perl)
273    #####################################################
274    sub DESTROY($)
275    {
276        my $self = shift;    # The class
277        untie $self->{DISK_DATA};
278    }
279
280    1;
```

The database requires a little configuration. This will be different on each system, so all the configuration information is placed in one module's disks_config.pm (see Listing 15.2). This is the only module you can expect the user to play with. It contains the filename of the database and a list of categories.

Listing 15.2 *disks_config.pm*

```
 1    =pod
 2
 3    =head1 NAME
 4
 5    disks_config.pm -- Configuration data for the disks programs
 6
 7    =head1 SYNOPSIS
 8
 9        require disks_config;
10
```

```
11      print "The database is at $db_file";
12
13
14  =head1 DESCRIPTION
15
16  This file contains the location of the disks database.
17
18  =head1 FILES
19
20  =over 4
21
22  =item disks.db
23
24  The name of the database file.  The actual path to this file is
25  controlled by the I<disks_config.pm> package.
26
27  =back
28
29  =head1 AUTHOR
30
31  Steve Oualline, E<lt>oualline@www.oualline.comE<gt>.
32
33  =head1 SEE ALSO
34
35  L<disks_config.pl>
36
37  =head1 COPYRIGHT
38
39  This program is distributed under the GPL.
40
41  =cut
42  package disks_config;
43
44  use Exporter;
45  use vars (qw($db_file @ISA @EXPORT %category_to_name));
46
47  @ISA = 'Exporter';
48  @EXPORT = (qw($db_file %category_to_name));
49
50  $db_file = 'disks.db';
51
52  #
53  # Category to name mapping
54  #
55  %category_to_name = (
56          'F' => "Floppy",
57          'B' => "Bare CDROM",
58          'P' => "Packaged CDROM",
59          'Z' => "Zip disk"
60  );
61
62  1;
```

Command-Line Utilities

Now that the core of the system is ready, you need a couple of front-end functions. The first, `new_disk.pl`, adds a disk to the database. The logic for this function is fairly trivial. All it does is grab the category and disk description from the command line and call `new_disk`.

Similarly, the `update_disk.pl` command takes a disk ID and description from the command line and then uses `update_disk` to modify an existing disk.

Finally, the `report.pl` command reads all the data from the database and prints a report.

All these scripts are simple with minimal logic. But they do serve a purpose because they are useful when it comes to testing the `disks.pm` module. Besides, they also provide the user a command-line interface to the database. The code for each is presented in Listings 15.3 through 15.5.

Listing 15.3   *new_disk.pl*

```
 1  use strict;
 2  use warnings;
 3
 4  =pod
 5
 6  =head1 NAME
 7
 8  new_disk.pl - Add a new disk to the collection
 9
10  =head1 SYNOPSIS
11
12      perl new_disk.pl <category> <description>
13
14  =head1 DESCRIPTION
15
16  The I<new_disk.pl> records disk information in the database.  It then
17  displays the id number of the disk.
18
19  =head1 ARGUMENTS
20
21  =over 4
22
23  =item I<category>
24
25  A single letter representing the category of the disk.  Currently we
26  have defined the following categories:
27
28  =over 4
29
30  =item F
31
```

```
32  Floppy
33
34  =item C
35
36  CD-ROM
37
38  =item Z
39
40  Zip disk.
41
42  =back
43
44  =item I<description>
45
46  A description of the disk.
47
48  =head1 FILES
49
50  =over 4
51
52  =item disks.db
53
54  The name of the database file.  The actual path to this file is
55  controlled by the I<disks_config.pm> package.
56
57  =back
58
59  =head1 AUTHOR
60
61  Steve Oualline, E<lt>oualline@www.oualline.comE<gt>.
62
63  =head1 SEE ALSO
64
65  L<disk_report.pl> L<update_disk.pl>
66
67  =head1 COPYRIGHT
68
69  This program is distributed under the GPL.
70
71  =cut
72
73  use disks;
74  use disks_config;
75
76  if ($#ARGV != 1) {
77      print STDERR "Usage is $0 <category> <description>\n";
78      exit (8);
79  }
80  # Category name to key translation
81  %reverse_category = reverse %category_to_name;
82  my $db = disks->new("disks.db", 0);
```

continues

Listing 15.3   **Continued**

```
83  if (not defined($db)) {
84      die("Could not open disks.db");
85  }
86  # Make category upper case
87  $ARGV[0] = uc($ARGV[0]);
88
89  if (not defined($category_to_name{$ARGV[0]})) {
90      print STDERR "$ARGV[0] is not a legal category\n";
91      print STDERR "Legal categories are:\n";
92      foreach my $key (sort keys %category_to_name) {
93          print STDERR "\t$key:$category_to_name{$key}\n";
94      }
95      exit (8);
96  }
97  my $id = $db->new_disk($ARGV[0],
98          CATEGORY => $reverse_category{$ARGV[0]}),
99          DESCRIPTION => $ARGV[1]);
100 if (not defined($id)) {
101     print STDERR "ERROR: Could not create disk\n";
102 } else {
103     print "Disk created.  ID=$id\n";
104 }
```

Listing 15.4   *update_disk.pl*

```
1  =pod
2
3  =head1 NAME
4
5  update_disk.pl - Update an existing disk
6
7  =head1 SYNOPSIS
8
9      perl update_disk.pl I<id> I<description>
10
11 =head1 DESCRIPTION
12
13 The I<update_disk.pl> updates the disk information for a given disk.
14
15 =head1 ARGUMENTS
16
17 =over 4
18
19 =item I<id>
20
21 The disk's identification.
22
23
```

```
24  =item I<description>
25
26  A description of the disk.
27
28  =head1 FILES
29
30  =over 4
31
32  =item disks.db
33
34  The name of the database file.  The actual path to this file is
35  controlled by the I<disks_config.pm> package.
36
37  =back
38
39  =head1 AUTHOR
40
41  Steve Oualline, E<lt>oualline@www.oualline.comE<gt>.
42
43  =head1 SEE ALSO
44
45  L<disk_report.pl> L<new_disk.pl>
46
47  =head1 COPYRIGHT
48
49  This program is distributed under the GPL.
50
51  =cut
52  use strict;
53  use warnings;
54
55  use disks;
56  use disks_config;
57
58  if ($#ARGV != 1) {
59      print STDERR "Usage is $0 <id> <description>\n";
60      exit (8);
61  }
62
63  my $db = disks->new("disks.db", 0);
64
65  if (not defined($db)) {
66      die("Could not open disks.db");
67  }
68
69  if (not defined ($db->update_disk($ARGV[0], DESCRIPTION => $ARGV[1]))) {
70      print STDERR "Error: Could not find the disk $ARGV[0]\n";
71  } else {
72      print "Disk updated\n";
73  }
```

Listing 15.5 *report.pl*

```
 1  use strict;
 2  use warnings;
 3
 4  =pod
 5
 6  =head1 NAME
 7
 8  report.pl - Print a report about our disk library
 9
10  =head1 SYNOPSIS
11
12      perl report.pl
13
14  =head1 DESCRIPTION
15
16  The I<report.pl> prints a report containing all the disk information
17
18  =head1 FILES
19
20  =over 4
21
22  =item disks.db
23
24  The name of the database file.  The actual path to this file is
25  controlled by the I<disks_config.pm> package.
26
27  =back
28
29  =head1 AUTHOR
30
31  Steve Oualline, E<lt>oualline@www.oualline.comE<gt>.
32
33  =head1 COPYRIGHT
34
35  This program is distributed under the GPL.
36
37  =cut
38
39  use disks;
40  use disks_config;
41
42  # The database to use
43  my $db = disks->new($db_file, 1);
44  if (not defined($db)) {
45      die("Could not open $db_file");
46  }
47  # The data in the database
48  my @key_list = $db->get_keys();
49
```

```
50  # Print each as we find it
51  foreach my $cur_id (@key_list) {
52      my $data = $db->get_disk($cur_id);
53      printf "%3s: %-s\n", $cur_id, $data->{DESCRIPTION};
54  }
```

GUI Interface

In addition to the command-line interface, a GUI interface is created using
the Tk toolkit (see Figure 15.1).

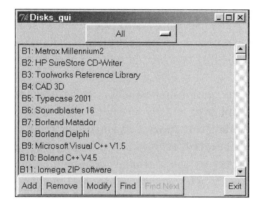

Figure 15.1   GUI interface to the disk database.

To build this GUI, we start by constructing the main window. At the top of
this window is a category selector. This selector (set to All in Figure 15.1) lets
the user decide which type of disk is displayed. The selector is constructed
using a `Tk::Optionmenu` widget.

Below the category selector is the list of disks. A `Tk::Listbox` widget is used
for the display.

At the bottom of the window is the action frame that contains all the
action buttons.

The Add Pop-Up Window

When the user clicks the Add button, a pop-up window appears that allows
him to add the text (see Figure 15.2).

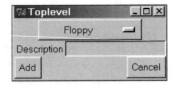

Figure 15.2   The pop-up window that appears when you click Add.

The code for this can be seen in the function add_modify in Listing 15.6. (It's called add_modify because it also displays the modify pop-up as well.)

This function uses a widget called the LabEntry to display the description of the disk. This widget is a little unusual in that it's not documented in the Tk documentation. But there are still ways to figure out what it does. The first is to see whether any demonstration programs use it. You can do this by looking through the files installed in Tk/demos. You'll find the Tk directory under the Perl library directory.

Looking through the demonstration tells you that the notebook.pl demonstration contains a number of examples telling you how to use the widget.

Another way of finding out about the widget is to take a look at the source code to the module (LabEntry.pm) itself.

Or if you want a shortcut, the module is documented here. The widget consists of a Tk::Frame, which contains a Tk::Label and Tk::Entry object. You can use any options for the widget that are allowed for a normal Label or Entry. One additional option -labelPack specifies the arguments sent to pack when the Label subwidget is packed. In other words, if you want the label to be packed on the left-hand side, then you need -labelPack =>[-side => "left". If you want it to stick to the left, you also need -anchor => "w".

To create a LabEntry to enter your weight, use the code

```
244        $tk_popup->LabEntry(
245                -label => "Description",
246                -textvariable => \$description,
247                -labelPack => [ -side => 'left']
248        )->pack(
249                -side => 'top',
250                -expand => 1,
251                -fill => 'x'
252        );
```

The rest of the logic is straightforward. Most of the code is bogged down with the details of creating the GUI and responding to buttons.

Find and Find Again

Some code introduces new elements. The GUI contains two buttons: Find and Find Next. Because you cannot repeat a previous find until you've performed a Find, the Find Next button starts out disabled:

```
449  $tk_find_next = $tk_action_frame->Button(
450          -text => "Find Next",
451          -command => \&find_next,
452          -state => 'disabled'
453      )->pack(
454          -side => 'left'
455      );
```

When the user does his first search, the `configure` method calls for this widget to change its state from `'disabled'` to `'normal'`:

```
311      if ($find_str ne "") {
312          $tk_find_next->configure(-state => 'normal');
313      }
```

Listing 15.6 presents the code for the disk database GUI.

Listing 15.6 *disk_gui.pl*

```
1   =pod
2
3   =head1 NAME
4
5   disks_gui.pl - Display and modify the disk database
6
7   =head1 SYNOPSIS
8
9       perl disks_gui.pl
10
11  =head1 DESCRIPTION
12
13  The I<disks_gui.pl> displays a GUI which lets you view and update
14  the disk database.
15
16  =head1 FILES
17
18  =over 4
19
20  =item disks.db
21
22  The name of the database file.  The actual path to this file is
23  controlled by the I<disks_config.pm> package.
24
25  =back
26
27  =head1 AUTHOR
28
```

continues

Listing 15.6   **Continued**

```
29  Steve Oualline, E<lt>oualline@www.oualline.comE<gt>.
30
31  =head1 COPYRIGHT
32
33  This program is distributed under the GPL.
34
35  =cut
36
37  use strict;
38  use warnings;
39  use Tk;
40  use Tk::LabEntry;
41
42  use disks;
43  use disks_config;
44
45  my $cur_category = "All";# Current category
46  my $tk_mw;                 # Main window
47  my $tk_list;               # The list of disks
48  my $tk_find_next;          # Button to find then next item
49
50  my @id_list = ();          # A list of ID's displayed in the
51                             # GUI list
52
53  my %reverse_category;         # Reverse category list
54  #################################################
55  # error($message)
56  #
57  # Display a popup error message window
58  #################################################
59  sub error($)
60  {
61      my $message = shift;       # Error message
62
63      $tk_mw->messageBox(
64          -icon => "error",
65          -title => "Error",
66          -message => $message,
67          -type => "ok");
68  }
69  #################################################
70  # info($message)
71  #
72  # Display a popup information message window
73  #################################################
74  sub info($)
75  {
76      my $message = shift;       # Error message
77
78      $tk_mw->messageBox(
79          -icon => "info",
80          -title => "Information",
```

```perl
81              -message => $message,
82              -type => "ok");
83  }
84  ########################################################
85  # Populate list -- Put the disks in the list
86  ########################################################
87  sub populate_list()
88  {
89      # The database containing the disk information
90      my $db = disks->new($db_file, 1);
91
92      $tk_list->delete(0, 'end');
93
94      if (not defined($db)) {
95          return;
96      }
97      # The data in the database
98      my @key_list = $db->get_keys();
99
100     my $cat_letter;    # Category as letter
101
102     if ($cur_category ne "All") {
103         $cat_letter = $reverse_category{$cur_category};
104     } else {
105         $cat_letter = "";
106     }
107     @id_list = ();
108
109     # Print each as we find it
110     foreach my $cur_id (@key_list) {
111         # The data from the database
112         my $data = $db->get_disk($cur_id);
113
114         # Filter on category
115         if (($cat_letter ne "") and
116             ($cat_letter ne $data->{CATEGORY})) {
117             next;
118         }
119
120         # The data as a line
121         my $line = sprintf "%3s: %-s", $cur_id, $data->{DESCRIPTION};
122         $tk_list->insert('end', $line);
123         push(@id_list, $cur_id);
124     }
125 }
126 ########################################################
127 # change_option -- Called when we change the category
128 ########################################################
129 sub change_option {
130     if (defined ($tk_list)) {
131         populate_list();
132     }
```

continues

Listing 15.6 **Continued**

```
133  }
134  ########################################################
135  # remove_disk -- Remove a disk from the list
136  ########################################################
137  sub remove_disk {
138      my $selection = $tk_list->curselection();
139      if (not defined($selection)) {
140          error("No disk selected.");
141          return;
142      }
143      my $db = disks->new($db_file, 0);
144      $db->delete_disk($id_list[$selection]);
145      $db = undef;
146      populate_list();
147  }
148
149  my $description = "";   # Description for add/modify
150  my $add_category = "";  # Category for the current add/modify
151  my $tk_popup;  # Popup menu for add/modify
152  ########################################################
153  # do_add -- Actually add the disk to the system
154  ########################################################
155  sub do_add()
156  {
157      my $db = disks->new($db_file, 0);
158      if ($description =~ /^\s*$/) {
159          error("ERROR: No description");
160          return;
161      }
162      $tk_popup->withdraw();
163      my $id = $db->new_disk(
164              $reverse_category{$add_category},
165              CATEGORY => $reverse_category{$add_category},
166              DESCRIPTION => $description
167          );
168      $db = undef;
169
170      populate_list();
171
172      if (defined($id)) {
173          info("Added $id");
174      } else {
175          error("Could not add $id");
176      }
177  }
178  ########################################################
179  # do_modify -- Actually modify the information
180  ########################################################
181  sub do_modify($)
182  {
183      my $id = shift;
184      my $db = disks->new($db_file, 0);
```

```
185      if ($description =~ /^\s*$/) {
186          error("No description.");
187          return;
188      }
189      $tk_popup->withdraw();
190
191      my $cat = substr($id, 0, 1);
192      $db->update_disk($id,
193              CATEGORY => $cat,
194              DESCRIPTION => $description
195          );
196      $db = undef;
197
198      populate_list();
199      info("Updated $id");
200  }
201  ########################################################
202  # add_modify($id) -- Do an add or modify
203  #
204  # If $id is defined, modify it.  Otherwise add it
205  ########################################################
206  sub add_modify($) {
207      my $id = shift;     # Id of the disk to modify
208                          # undef if no such disk
209
210      # Remove any old popup window
211      if (Exists($tk_popup)) {
212          $tk_popup->destroy();
213      }
214      # Top level window
215      $tk_popup = $tk_mw->Toplevel();
216
217      # List of categories for the option
218      my @options = (sort values %category_to_name);
219
220      if (defined($id)) {
221          # The database for the information
222          my $db = disks->new($db_file, 1);
223
224          # Data for the disk
225          my $data = $db->get_disk($id);
226
227          $description = $data->{DESCRIPTION};
228          $tk_popup->Label(
229                  -text => $category_to_name{$data->{CATEGORY}}
230              )->pack(
231                  -side => 'top'
232              );
233      } else {
234          $description = "";
235
236          $tk_popup->Optionmenu(
```

continues

Listing 15.6 **Continued**

```
237                      -options => [@options],
238                      -variable => \$add_category
239              )->pack(
240                  -side => 'top'
241              );
242      }
243
244      $tk_popup->LabEntry(
245              -label => "Description",
246              -textvariable => \$description,
247              -labelPack => [ -side => 'left']
248          )->pack(
249              -side => 'top',
250              -expand => 1,
251              -fill => 'x'
252          );
253
254      my $tk_action = $tk_popup->Frame(
255              )->pack(
256                  -side => 'bottom',
257                  -expand => 1,
258                  -fill => 'x'
259              );
260
261      if (defined($id)) {
262          $tk_action->Button(
263                  -text => "Modify",
264                  -command => sub {do_modify($id);}
265              )->pack(
266                  -side => 'left'
267              );
268      } else {
269          $tk_action->Button(
270                  -text => "Add",
271                  -command => \&do_add
272              )->pack(
273                  -side => 'left'
274              );
275      }
276      $tk_action->Button(
277              -text => "Cancel",
278              -command => sub {$tk_popup->destroy();}
279          )->pack(
280              -side => 'right'
281          );
282  }
283
284  #######################################################
285  # add_disk -- Add a disk to the set
286  #######################################################
287  sub add_disk {
288      add_modify(undef);
```

```
289  }
290  ########################################################
291  # modify_disk -- Modify a disk
292  ########################################################
293  sub modify_disk {
294      my $selection = $tk_list->curselection();
295      if (not defined($selection)) {
296          error("No disk selected.");
297          return;
298      }
299      add_modify($id_list[$selection]);
300  }
301  my $tk_find;    # Find dialog
302  my $find_str;   # String to find
303  ########################################################
304  # do_find -- Find the next entry that matches
305  #       the find string
306  ########################################################
307  sub do_find($) {
308      my $start = shift;   # Element to start searching at
309
310      $tk_find_next->configure(-state => 'disabled');
311      if ($find_str ne "") {
312          $tk_find_next->configure(-state => 'normal');
313      }
314      for (my $current = $start;
315           $current < $tk_list->index('end');
316           $current++) {
317
318          # Check the line against what are looking at
319          my $line = $tk_list->get($current);
320          if ($line =~ $find_str) {
321              $tk_list->selectionClear(0, 'end');
322              $tk_list->selectionSet($current);
323              $tk_list->see($current);
324              return;
325          }
326      }
327      error("Not found");
328  }
329
330  ########################################################
331  # find_next -- find the next string in the list
332  ########################################################
333  sub find_next()
334  {
335      do_find($tk_list->curselection()+1);
336  }
337  ########################################################
338  # find -- Find the first element that matches a patter
339  ########################################################
340  sub find()
```

continues

Listing 15.6 **Continued**

```
341  {
342      # Remove any old popup window
343      if (Exists($tk_find)) {
344          $tk_find->destroy();
345      }
346      # Top level window
347      $tk_find = $tk_mw->Toplevel();
348
349      $tk_find->LabEntry(
350              -label => "Find: ",
351              -textvariable => \$find_str,
352              -labelPack => [ -side => 'left']
353          )->pack(
354              -side => 'top',
355              -expand => 1,
356              -fill => 'x'
357          );
358
359      my $tk_action = $tk_find->Frame(
360              )->pack(
361                  -side => 'bottom',
362                  -expand => 1,
363                  -fill => 'x'
364              );
365
366      $tk_action->Button(
367              -text => "Find",
368              -command => sub {$tk_find->withdraw();do_find(0);}
369          )->pack(
370              -side => 'left'
371          );
372      $tk_action->Button(
373              -text => "Cancel",
374              -command => sub {$tk_find->destroy();}
375          )->pack(
376              -side => 'right'
377          );
378  }
379
380  #######################################################
381  # Main program
382  #######################################################
383  $tk_mw = MainWindow->new();
384
385  # The list of the types of disks we can have
386  my @options = ((sort values %category_to_name), "All");
387
388  # Category name to key translation
389  %reverse_category = reverse %category_to_name;
390
391  # Define the type selector at the top of the screen
392  my $tk_option = $tk_mw->Optionmenu(
```

```
393              -options => [@options],
394              -command => \&change_option,
395              -variable => \$cur_category
396        )->pack(
397              -side => 'top'
398        );
399
400   $tk_option->setOption("All");
401
402   $tk_list = $tk_mw->Scrolled(
403          'Listbox',
404          -scrollbars => "ose",
405          -width => 50
406        )->pack(
407              -side => 'top',
408              -expand => 'yes',
409              -fill => 'both'
410        );
411   populate_list();
412
413   # The frame containing the action buttons at the bottom
414   # of the screen
415   my $tk_action_frame = $tk_mw->Frame(
416        )->pack(
417              -side => 'bottom',
418              -fill => "x"
419        );
420
421   $tk_action_frame->Button(
422              -text => "Add",
423              -command => \&add_disk
424        )->pack(
425              -side => 'left'
426        );
427
428   $tk_action_frame->Button(
429              -text => "Remove",
430              -command => \&remove_disk
431        )->pack(
432              -side => 'left'
433        );
434
435   $tk_action_frame->Button(
436              -text => "Modify",
437              -command => \&modify_disk
438        )->pack(
439              -side => 'left'
440        );
441
442   $tk_action_frame->Button(
443              -text => "Find",
444              -command => \&find
```

continues

Listing 15.6 **Continued**

```
445         )->pack(
446             -side => 'left'
447         );
448
449 $tk_find_next = $tk_action_frame->Button(
450             -text => "Find Next",
451             -command => \&find_next,
452             -state => 'disabled'
453         )->pack(
454             -side => 'left'
455         );
456
457
458 $tk_action_frame->Button(
459             -text => "Exit",
460             -command => sub {exit(0);}
461         )->pack(
462             -side => 'right'
463         );
464 MainLoop();
```

The CGI Version

In addition to the command-line and GUI versions, a CGI version of the program is created. Figure 15.3 shows the basic screen.

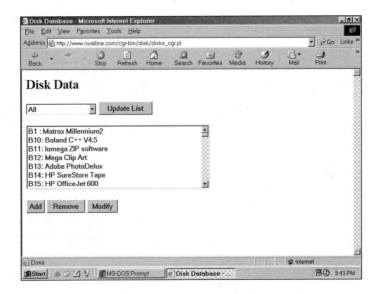

Figure 15.3 Basic CGI screen.

Note that four buttons are on this screen:

- **Update List**—Clicked after the user has changed categories to update the list of disks displayed.
- **Add**—Brings up a new form that lets the user add a disk.
- **Remove**—Removes a disk.
- **Modify**—Modifies a disk.

Each of these buttons is named SUBMIT. The value of the button ("Add", "Remove", "Modify", and "Update List") determines what the program does and which form it displays next.

Thus the program starts off with a large if/else chain that examines the value of this button and then performs the appropriate work:

```
269  if ($cgi_data{SUBMIT} eq "Update List") {
270      # Display the form
271      display_form($category, undef);
272  } elsif ($cgi_data{SUBMIT} eq "Add") {
273      add_modify_form($category, undef);
274  #-------------------------------------------------------
275  } elsif ($cgi_data{SUBMIT} eq "Remove") {
....
288  #-------------------------------------------------------
289  } elsif ($cgi_data{SUBMIT} eq "Modify") {
....
297  #-------------------------------------------------------
298  } elsif ($cgi_data{SUBMIT} eq "Add Disk") {
....
315  #-------------------------------------------------------
316  } elsif ($cgi_data{SUBMIT} eq "Modify Disk") {
....
327  } else {
328      # This should never happen.  But if it does
329      display_form($category, undef);
330  }
```

You may have noticed that the code checks for two additional buttons: Add Disk and Modify Disk.

The Add button causes the system to display the Add screen as shown in Figure 15.4.

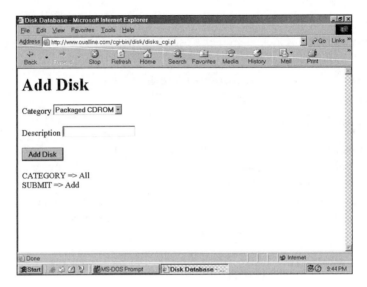

Figure 15.4   The Add screen.

Notice that the button at the bottom of the screen is Add Disk. Make sure that the button is not named Add. The Add button tells the program to display the Add screen. The Add Disk button tells the system to add a disk and return to the main display screen.

Disk modification is handled much the same way. The Modify button displays a Modify screen (see Figure 15.5).

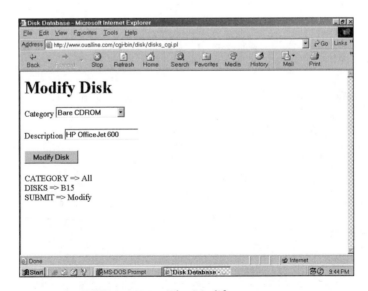

Figure 15.5   The Modify screen.

Again, an action button at the bottom of the screen is named Modify Disk.

By creating unique names for your buttons, you can use the SUBMIT item to control the flow of the program. The flowchart is displayed in Figure 15.6.

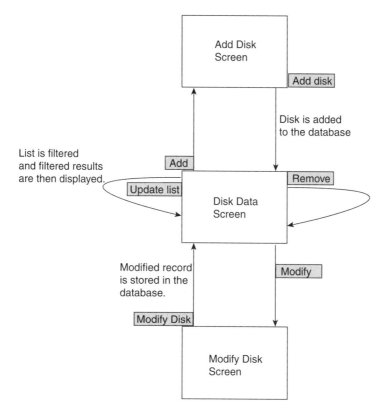

Figure 15.6   `disks_cgi.pl` program flow.

Errors and Messages

One problem with CGI programs is figuring out where to display error and information messages. If this were a GUI-based program, you would use a pop-up window.

Pop-up windows are difficult in CGI programs. You need some Java or JavaScript code to display them. It's bad enough having to deal with HTML and Perl without adding a new language to the mix, so pop-up windows are out.

If you are going to stick with a pure HTML/Perl solution, then the only output mechanism you have is the web page. You can either stick the messages on a page by themselves or add them to an existing page. The second way is the simpler and easier method, so that's what's done in the example. At the top of the `display_form` are a few lines that output any message you want the user to see:

```
115          if (defined($msg)) {
116              print "<H1>$msg</H1><P>\n";
117              print "<HR>\n";
118          }
```

This includes error messages such as "Please select a disk" and information messages such as "Disk B32 created."

Debugging

Debugging CGI programs is always a problem. To help you debug this program, some debug code was installed. This code prints the value of all the items in the `%cgi_data` hash.

The nice thing about this debug output is that it can be turned on and off. If the file `/tmp/debug.disk` exists, debugging is turned on. If it's not there, nothing is output. The full debug function is

```
58   sub debug()
59   {
60       if (-f "/tmp/debug.disk") {
61           foreach my $cur_key (sort keys %cgi_data) {
62               print encode_entities($cur_key), " =&gt; ",
63                   encode_entities($cgi_data{$cur_key}),
64   .               "<BR>\n";
65           }
66       }
67   }
```

Although simple, this function provides a lot of useful debug information.

The Cookie

The example program was embellished with one extra feature. The system uses a cookie to remember the last selected category. The information is recorded by sending the web browser a cookie. To do this, the program uses the function `Set_Cookie` to create the cookie and a `print` statement to send it to the web server:

```
251  # The cookie to send to the user
252  my $cookie;
253  $cookie = Set_Cookie(
254      NAME => "CATEGORY",    # Cookie's name
255      VALUE => $category,    # Value for the cookie
256      EXPIRE => "+2d",       # Keep cookie for 2 days
257  );
258  print "$cookie";
```

In this example, the name of the cookie is `CATEGORY`, and it will expire in two days. The value of the cookie is the current category.

The cookie is printed using a `print` statement. The cookie line is actually part of the header sent back to the browser. The other header line used is the `"Content-type"` line. For a full description of the various elements of a heading, check out the standard at `http://www.w3c.org/Protocols/`.

The first time the program is run, the cookie is set. The next time the browser accesses the program, it sends the cookie back to you. Actually, the browser sends back all the relevant cookies at once (you can set more than one). You can check the cookie using the `Parse_Cookie` function:

```
239  # Cookie information
240  my %cookies = Parse_Cookies();
241
242  # The weight from the cookie
243  my $category = $cookies{CATEGORY};
244  if (not defined ($category)) {
245      $category = "All";
246  }
```

This code gives you the default category.

Debugging Cookies

Debugging with cookies is a little difficult because they are stored by the browser. Fortunately, Netscape has an option that warns you when a cookie is being sent from the web server to the browser. To turn it on, select Edit, Preferences. This brings up the Preferences window (see Figure 15.7).
If you are using Microsoft Internet Explorer 6.0, you can turn off cookies through the Tools, Internet Options, Privacy, Advanced menu.

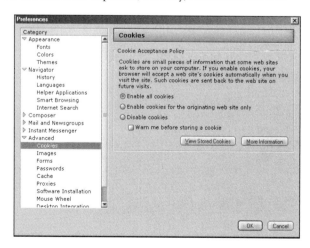

Figure 15.7   Netscape Preferences.

In the Category list on the left, click Advanced. On the bottom right, you see a box you can check titled Warn Me Before Storing a Cookie.

Now when you run the program, you can "see" the cookie being sent. That's because Netscape displays a pop-up window when it accepts a cookie (see Figure 15.8).

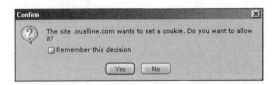

Figure 15.8   Netscape accepting a cookie.

I discovered one problem when debugging the cookie logic. My web server is named www.oualline.com. On my local network, I can refer to it as www. As a security measure, Netscape won't accept cookies that say they are coming from one machine (www.oualline.com) when the web page comes from another (www). As a result, none of my cookie-setting code worked until I started using the server www.oualline.com rather than www.

The CGI Program

Listing 15.7 shows the full version of the CGI program.

Listing 15.7   *disks_cgi.pl*

```
 1  #!/home/oualline/local/bin/perl -T -I.
 2  =pod
 3
 4  =head1 NAME
 5
 6  disks_cgi.pl - Handle all disk related web pages
 7
 8  =head1 SYNOPSIS
 9
10      <FORM ACTION="disks_cgi.pl">
11
12  =head1 DESCRIPTION
13
14  The I<disks_cgi.pl> handles the disk database.  It first displays
15  a report screen.  The user can then select an entry and modify
16  or delete it.
17
18  He can also press another button and create a disk.
19
20  =head1 FILES
21
```

```
22  =over 4
23
24  =item disks.db
25
26  The name of the database file.  The actual path to this file is
27  controlled by the I<disks_config.pm> package.
28
29  =back
30
31  =head1 AUTHOR
32
33  Steve Oualline, E<lt>oualline@www.oualline.comE<gt>.
34
35  =head1 COPYRIGHT
36
37  This program is distributed under the GPL.
38
39  =cut
40  use strict;
41  use warnings;
42
43  use CGI::Thin;
44  use CGI::Thin::Cookies;
45  use CGI::Carp;
46  use POSIX;
47  use HTML::Entities;
48
49  use disks_config;
50  use disks;
51
52  # The data from the form
53  my %cgi_data = Parse_CGI();
54
55  ######################################################
56  # debug -- print debugging information
57  ######################################################
58  sub debug()
59  {
60      if (-f "/tmp/debug.disk") {
61          foreach my $cur_key (sort keys %cgi_data) {
62              print encode_entities($cur_key), " =&gt; ",
63                  encode_entities($cgi_data{$cur_key}),
64                  "<BR>\n";
65          }
66      }
67  }
68  ######################################################
69  # print_category($current, %name_to_cat)
70  #
71  # Print a category option list.
72  ######################################################
73  sub print_category($%)
```

continues

Listing 15.7   **Continued**

```
 74 {
 75     my $selected = shift;      # Currently selected category
 76     my %names = @_;            # The hash of the possibilities
 77
 78     print "    <SELECT NAME=\"CATEGORY\">\n";
 79
 80     # Loop over each and print it.
 81     foreach my $cur_cat (sort keys %names) {
 82         # Check to see if we are selected
 83         if ($cur_cat eq $selected) {
 84             print "        <OPTION VALUE=\"$cur_cat\" SELECTED>",
 85             "$names{$cur_cat}</option>\n";
 86         } else {
 87             print "        <OPTION VALUE=\"$cur_cat\">",
 88             "$names{$cur_cat}</OPTION>\n";
 89         }
 90     }
 91     print "    </SELECT>\n";
 92 }
 93 #####################################################
 94 # display_form($user_cat, $msg) -- Display the
 95 #       report form with the selected category as
 96 #       the default.
 97 #####################################################
 98 sub display_form($$)
 99 {
100     my $user_cat = shift;      # The user selected category
101     my $msg = shift;           # Message for the top of the screen
102
103     # The database for reading the current data
104     my $db = disks->new($db_file, 0);
105     print <<EOF;
106 Content-type: text/html
107
108 <html>
109 <head>
110 <title>Disk Database</title>
111 </head>
112
113 <body bgcolor="#FFFFFF">
114 EOF
115         if (defined($msg)) {
116             print "<H1>$msg</H1><P>\n";
117             print "<HR>\n";
118         }
119     print <<EOF;
120 <h2>Disk Data</h2>
121 <form method="post" action="disks_cgi.pl" name="disk">
122 <p>
123 EOF
124     print_category($user_cat, %category_to_name, "All" => "All");
125     print <<EOF;
```

```
126   <INPUT TYPE="SUBMIT" NAME="SUBMIT" VALUE="Update List">
127   </P>
128   <P ALIGN="LEFT">
129       <SELECT NAME="DISKS" SIZE="7">
130   EOF
131
132       # Loop through each item in the database
133       foreach my $cur_id (sort $db->get_keys()) {
134           # Filter on category
135           my $cur_entry = $db->get_disk($cur_id);
136
137           if (not defined($cur_entry->{CATEGORY})) {
138               $cur_entry->{CATEGORY} = "X";
139           }
140           # Filter on category
141           if (($user_cat ne "All") and
142                   ($user_cat ne $cur_entry->{CATEGORY})) {
143               next;
144           }
145
146           # The description as a nice thing for the CGI screen
147           my $cur_desc = encode_entities(
148                   sprintf "%-3s: %-s", $cur_id,
149                           $cur_entry->{DESCRIPTION});
149
150           print "<option value=\"$cur_id\">$cur_desc</option>\n";
151       }
152
153       print <<EOF;
154       </select>
155   </p>
156   <p align="left">
157   <input type="SUBMIT" name="SUBMIT" value="Add">
158   <input type="SUBMIT" name="SUBMIT" value="Remove">
159   <input type="SUBMIT" name="SUBMIT" value="Modify">
160   </p>
161   EOF
162       debug();
163       print <<EOF;
164   </form>
165   </body>
166   </html>
167   EOF
168       exit (0);
169   }
170
171
172   #########################################################
173   # add_modify_form($$) -- Display a add or modify
174   #       page.
175   #
176   # $category -- The category selected
```

continues

Listing 15.7 **Continued**

```
177  # $modify_id -- True if this is a modification request
178  ######################################################
179  sub add_modify_form($$)
180  {
181      my $category = shift;      # Current category
182      my $modify_id = shift;     # Add or modify
183
184      my $add_mod = "Add";       # Add or modify?
185      my $description = "";      # Description of the disk
186
187      if (defined($modify_id)) {
188          my $db = disks->new($db_file, 0);
189          $add_mod = "Modify";
190
191          # Data for this disk
192          my $data = $db->get_disk($modify_id);
193
194          $description = $data->{DESCRIPTION};
195          if (not defined($description)) {
196              $description = "";
197          }
198      }
199      print <<EOF;
200  Content-type: text/html
201
202  <html>
203  <head>
204  <title>Disk Database</title>
205  </head>
206
207  <body bgcolor="#FFFFFF">
208  <h1>$add_mod Disk</h1>
209  <form method="post" action="disks_cgi.pl" name="disk">
210  <p align="left">Category
211  EOF
212
213      print_category($category, %category_to_name);
214
215      my $enc_description = encode_entities($description);
216
217      if (defined($modify_id)) {
218          print "<INPUT TYPE=\"HIDDEN\" ",
219                  "NAME=\"ID\" VALUE=\"$modify_id\">\n";
220      }
221      print <<EOF;
222      </p>
223      <p align="left"> Description
224        <input type="text" name="DESCRIPTION" VALUE="$enc_description">
225      </p>
226      <p align="left">
227        <input type="submit" name="SUBMIT" value="$add_mod Disk">
228      </p>
```

```
229  EOF
230      debug();
231      print <<EOF;
232    </form>
233  </body>
234  </html>
235  EOF
236      exit (0);
237  }
238
239  # Cookie information
240  my %cookies = Parse_Cookies();
241
242  # The weight from the cookie
243  my $category = $cookies{CATEGORY};
244  if (not defined ($category)) {
245      $category = "All";
246  }
247  if (defined($cgi_data{CATEGORY})) {
248      $category = $cgi_data{CATEGORY};
249  }
250
251  # The cookie to send to the user
252  my $cookie;
253  $cookie = Set_Cookie(
254      NAME => "CATEGORY",    # Cookie's name
255      VALUE => $category,    # Value for the cookie
256      EXPIRE => "+2d",       # Keep cookie for 2 days
257  );
258  print "$cookie";
259
260
261  # Check to see if we should display the form or
262  # record the data
263  if (not defined($cgi_data{SUBMIT})) {
264      # Display the form
265      display_form($category, undef);
266  }
267
268  #----------------------------------------------------------
269  if ($cgi_data{SUBMIT} eq "Update List") {
270      # Display the form
271      display_form($category, undef);
272  } elsif ($cgi_data{SUBMIT} eq "Add") {
273      add_modify_form($category, undef);
274  #----------------------------------------------------------
275  } elsif ($cgi_data{SUBMIT} eq "Remove") {
276      if (not defined($cgi_data{DISKS})) {
277          display_form($category, "ERROR: No disk selected");
278      }
279      # Id of the disk to remove
280      my $id = $cgi_data{DISKS};
```

continues

Listing 15.7   **Continued**

```
281
282     # Open a db to add a disk to
283     my $db = disks->new($db_file, 0);
284     $db->delete_disk($id);
285     $db = undef;        # Close database
286
287     display_form($category, "Disk $id removed");
288   #-------------------------------------------------------
289   } elsif ($cgi_data{SUBMIT} eq "Modify") {
290       if (not defined($cgi_data{DISKS})) {
291           display_form($category, "ERROR: No disk selected");
292       }
293       # Id of the disk to modify
294       my $id = $cgi_data{DISKS};
295
296       add_modify_form($category, $id);
297   #-------------------------------------------------------
298   } elsif ($cgi_data{SUBMIT} eq "Add Disk") {
299       # Open a db to add a disk to
300       my $db = disks->new($db_file, 0);
301
302       # Add the disk
303       my $id = $db->new_disk($category,
304               DESCRIPTION => $cgi_data{DESCRIPTION},
305               CATEGORY => $cgi_data{CATEGORY});
306
307       $db = undef;        # Close database
308
309       # Tell the user the results
310       if (defined($id)) {
311           display_form($category, "Disk $id added");
312       } else {
313           display_form($category, "Error: Could not add disk");
314       }
315   #-------------------------------------------------------
316   } elsif ($cgi_data{SUBMIT} eq "Modify Disk") {
317       my $db = disks->new($db_file, 0);
318       my $id = $cgi_data{"ID"};
319       $id = $db->modify_disk($id,
320               DESCRIPTION => $cgi_data{DESCRIPTION},
321               CATEGORY => $cgi_data{CATEGORY});
322       if (defined($id)) {
323           display_form($category, "Disk $id modified");
324       } else {
325           display_form($category, "Error: Could not modify disk");
326       }
327   } else {
328       # This should never happen.  But if it does
329       display_form($category, undef);
330   }
331
```

You need to do one more thing for the CGI scripts. You need to change the `disks_config.pm` so that the specification for `$db_file` points to the absolute path to the database. If you leave things as they are, the default path (`"disks.db"`) will be used. This puts the `disks.db` file in the CGI directory, which is not good. (A well-configured web server won't let a CGI program create files there.)

Summary

This chapter produced a simple program that touches on most of Perl's advanced features. The main database is a tied hash. There are three user interfaces: a command-line version, the GUI version using Tk, and a web-based interface.

Perl's versatile syntax, string handling, and modules made writing the program straightforward and simple. Hopefully, your future projects will be just as straightforward and simple.

Exercises

1. Create a database in which to organize your audio collection (tapes, records, CDs, and so on).
2. Create a web-based application to keep track of a diet. You should be able to record your weight each day and get reports that include trend lines and moving averages.
3. Write a checkbook program.
4. Write a program for a traveling salesman so he can track the miles he travels for the company. (This is very useful when it comes to tax time.)
5. Write a program to keep track of phone numbers and addresses.

Resources

Online Documentation

- **perldoc -tf tie**—How `tie` is implemented. (Read this only if you are really interested in the internal details of how `tie` works. If you want to use it, read the database documentation for `DB_File`, `MLDBM`, or some other database.)

Modules

- **DB_File**—A simple database.
- **MLDBM**—A wrapper that lets you put complex data in a simple database.
- **Tk**—The TK GUI.
- **Tk::LabEntry**—The label entry widget.
- **CGI::Thin**—CGI parsing routines.
- **CGI::Thin::Cookies**—The cookie-handling module.
- **CGI::Carp**—Module to turn error messages into something the web browser can read.
- **Storable**—Contains function to turn complex data into strings and strings into complex data.
- **Time::ParseDate**—Function to turn a date into UNIX time format.

Web Pages

- **http://www.w3c.org/**—References for all things web-related.
- **http://www.w3c.org/Protocols/**—Reference information on the HTTP protocol.

16

Cookbook

PERL IS DESIGNED TO SOLVE PROBLEMS QUICKLY and efficiently. To demonstrate
the power of this language, this chapter presents a number of common
problems and shows you how to solve them with Perl.

List Differences

The first program checks two lists of words and prints out the difference
between the two. The method used is simple. The words in the first list are
used to populate a hash (%list). The key is the word from the file, and the
value is 1, as shown here:

```
76    while (<IN_FILE>) {
77        chomp($_);
78        $list{$_} = 1;
79    }
```

(Line numbers refer to the listings that follow.)

Now the words in the other file are used to populate the list. This is more
complex because you already have items in the list. The rule used for
population is simple: If the word is already in the list, change the 1 to a B.
If it's not, insert it with a value of 2. For example:

```
85    while (<IN_FILE>) {
86        chomp($_);
87        if (defined($list{$_})) {
88            $list{$_} = 'B';
89        } else {
90            $list{$_} = 2;
91        }
92    }
```

The result is that %list contains all the words in both files. The key is the
word. The value depends on which file the word is in. Words that appear only
in file 1 have a value of 1. If a word appears only in the second file, the value is
2. Common words contained by both files have the value B.

From this point, it's a simple process of printing out each of these categories
of words. For example, to print the words that appear only in the first file, use
the following code:

```
95    print "Words only in $ARGV[0]\n";
96    foreach my $cur_key (sort keys %list) {
97        if ($list{$cur_key} eq 1) {
98            print "\t$cur_key\n";
99        }
100   }
```

The full difference program appears in Listing 16.1.

Listing 16.1   *diff.pl*

```
1     =pod
2
3     =head1 NAME
4
5     diff.pl - Check two word lists for differences
6
7     =head1 SYNOPSIS
8
9         diff.pl <file1> <file2>
10
11    =head1 DESCRIPTION
12
13    The I<diff.pl> checks the two word lists and prints out a list
14    of words that:
15
16    =over 4
17
18    =item 1.
19
20    Appear in the first file, but not the second.
21
22    =item 2.
23
24    Appear in the second file, but not the first.
```

```
25
26    =item 3.
27
28    Appear in both files.
29
30    =back
31
32    =head1 EXAMPLES
33
34    =head2 File: list1.txt
35
36        alpha
37        beta
38        gamma
39        fred
40
41    =head2 File: list2.txt
42
43        joe
44        alpha
45        beta
46        gamma
47
48    =head3 Sample run
49
50        $ perl diff.pl list1.txt list2.txt
51
52        Words only in list1.txt
53                fred
54        Words only in list2.txt
55                joe
56        Words in both list1.txt and list2.txt
57                alpha
58                beta
59                gamma
60
61    =cut
62    use strict;
63    use warnings;
64
65    if ($#ARGV != 1) {
66        print STDERR "Usage is $0 <list1> <list2>\n";
67        exit (8);
68    }
69
70    my %list = ();   # Key = word, value = 1,2,B depending on
71                     # which file the work occurs in
72
73    open IN_FILE, "<$ARGV[0]" or
74        die("Could not open $ARGV[0]");
75
76    while (<IN_FILE>) {
```

continues

Listing 16.1   **Continued**

```
77          chomp($_);
78          $list{$_} = 1;
79      }
80      close (IN_FILE);
81      #---------------------------------------------
82      open IN_FILE, "<$ARGV[1]" or
83          die("Could not open $ARGV[1]");
84
85      while (<IN_FILE>) {
86          chomp($_);
87          if (defined($list{$_})) {
88              $list{$_} = 'B';
89          } else {
90              $list{$_} = 2;
91          }
92      }
93      close (IN_FILE);
94      #---------------------------------------------
95      print "Words only in $ARGV[0]\n";
96      foreach my $cur_key (sort keys %list) {
97          if ($list{$cur_key} eq 1) {
98              print "\t$cur_key\n";
99          }
100     }
101     #---------------------------------------------
102     print "Words only in $ARGV[1]\n";
103     foreach my $cur_key (sort keys %list) {
104         if ($list{$cur_key} eq 2) {
105             print "\t$cur_key\n";
106         }
107     }
108     #---------------------------------------------
109     print "Words in both $ARGV[0] and $ARGV[1]\n";
110     foreach my $cur_key (sort keys %list) {
111         if ($list{$cur_key} eq 'B') {
112             print "\t$cur_key\n";
113         }
114     }
```

Call 1-800-Confuse-Me

If you're like me, you hate people who give out phone numbers containing only letters—for example: 1-800-555-junk. Dialing this is a slow process. It's much easier to dial the numbers: 1-800-555-5865. (Please don't dial this number, I made it up.)

Perl comes to the rescue and lets you convert alphanumeric phone numbers into real ones.

The `phone.pl` program (see Listing 16.2) takes a letter phone number on the command line and outputs a numeric version. The basic algorithm is to split apart the argument into individual letters and then process them through a translation hash.

The only tricky part is turning a string such as "junk" into an array such as ("j","u","n","k"). The natural solution when you need to break up something is to look at the `unpack` function. But after looking at the documentation for `unpack` and experimenting with many different packing specifications, I concluded that `unpack` just wouldn't work. Sometimes the natural solution is not the correct one in Perl.

I remembered the `split` function. Specifically, what happens if someone tries to use the following statement to split a line into a bunch of words is something like the following:

```
# Classic mistake
my @words = split /\s*/, $line;
```

This does not split the words at whitespace (\s) boundaries because the * says 0 or more times, and Perl likes to choose. The result is that this line gets split into single characters. (See Chapter 3, "Arrays," if you've forgotten about this.)

So `split` works if used properly. But what should you use as a field separator? The answer is nothing. You want every character to be a field. So to split the argument into single characters, use this statement:

```
49    my @chars = split //, $string;
```

That being done, all you need are some loops and `print` statements, and you're in business.

Listing 16.2   *phone.pl*

```
 1    =pod
 2
 3    =head1 NAME
 4
 5    phone.pl - Turn alphabetic phone numbers into numbers
 6
 7    =head1 SYNOPSIS
 8
 9        perl phone.pl <number-string>
10
11    =head1 DESCRIPTION
12
13    The I<phone.pl> program turns phone numbers containing letters
14    into something you can dial.  For example:
15
16            1-800-POORNUM
17
```

continues

Listing 16.2 **Continued**

```
18    becomes
19
20              1-800-7667686
21
22    =cut
23    use strict;
24    use warnings;
25
26    # A hash  keys=letters, values=numbers
27    my %xlate = (
28        'a' => 2, 'b' => 2, 'c' => 2,
29        'd' => 3, 'e' => 3, 'f' => 3,
30        'g' => 4, 'h' => 4, 'i' => 4,
31        'j' => 5, 'k' => 5, 'l' => 5,
32        'm' => 6, 'n' => 6, 'o' => 6,
33        'p' => 7, 'q' => 7, 'r' => 7, 's' => 7,
34        't' => 8, 'u' => 8, 'v' => 8,
35        'w' => 9, 'x' => 9, 'y' => 9, 'z' => 9,
36        'A' => 2, 'B' => 2, 'C' => 2,
37        'D' => 3, 'E' => 3, 'F' => 3,
38        'G' => 4, 'H' => 4, 'I' => 4,
39        'J' => 5, 'K' => 5, 'L' => 5,
40        'M' => 6, 'N' => 6, 'O' => 6,
41        'P' => 7, 'Q' => 7, 'R' => 7, 'S' => 7,
42        'T' => 8, 'U' => 8, 'V' => 8,
43        'W' => 9, 'X' => 9, 'Y' => 9, 'Z' => 9);
44
45    # Put together all the arguments as one big string
46    my $string = join ' ', @ARGV;
47
48    # Now split things up into characters
49    my @chars = split //, $string;
50
51    # Go through each character and translate it
52    foreach my $cur_char (@chars)
53    {
54        if (defined($xlate{$cur_char})) {
55            print $xlate{$cur_char};
56        } else {
57            print $cur_char;
58        }
59    }
60    print "\n";
61
62
```

Time Adjustment

Perl is not the first language that comes to mind when you say "number crunching." After all, the math in Perl is slow and inexact. You have much better control over your numbers if you use C or C++.

But it turns out that most number crunching applications don't do all that much math. Instead, they spend a lot of time reading the input and parsing it, and a lot of time formatting the output with a little number work in the middle.

Perl is excellent for the beginning and end of this process. And if the middle (the numbers) is small, it can be an ideal language for the job.

One of my hobbies is horology (*horology* is the study of time measurement and the making of clocks). I have a number of antique clocks around that I am constantly fiddling with. I wind and set them one day, and then check them another. Based on the results, I make some adjustments to see whether I can get them to be more accurate.

To get an idea of how accurate my clocks are, I wrote a little script that computes the daily time error and normalizes it so that I get an error based on a 24-hour period.

As you can see in Listing 16.3, 97 percent of the program is concerned with decoding the input, about 2 percent performing the calculations, and 1 percent doing the output.

Listing 16.3   *time_diff.pl*

```
1    =pod
2
3    =head1 NAME
4
5    time_diff.pl -
     Compute the difference between what the clock says and now.
6
7    =head1 SYNOPSIS
8
9        time_diff.pl <set-time> <clock-time> <actual-time>
10
11   =head1 DESCRIPTION
12
13   The I<time_diff.pl> program is designed to be a tool for use
14   by horologists who need help adjusting their clocks.
15
16   The idea is that you set your clock on day 1.  On day 2 you record
17   the actual time (as given by an accurate clock) and the time
18   reported by the clock you are adjusting.
19
20   You then feed these values into this program which gives you an
```

continues

Listing 16.3   **Continued**

```
21    idea of how far you are off as a percentage.  Hopefully you can
22    use this information to properly adjust your clocks.
23
24    =head1 EXAMPLES
25
26    We set our clock at noon.  The next day at 11:00 we checked
27    on it and it said 11:47.
28
29        $ perl time_diff.pl 12:00 11:47 11:00
30
31        Clock is fast by 47 minutes
32        Error rate:  3.41 percent
33
34    =head1 NOTES
35
36    No matter what you do to a Congreve clock the best you can hope for
37    is an error rate of 20 minutes a day.
38
39    =cut
40    use strict;
41    use warnings;
42
43    sub decode($)
44    {
45        my $time = shift;
46        my @parts = split /:/, $time;
47
48        return ($parts[0] * 60 + $parts[1]);
49    }
50    # The number of minutes in a day
51    my $DAY = (24 * 60);
52
53    if ($#ARGV != 2) {
54        print "Usage is $0 <set-time> <clock-time> <actual-time>\n";
55        exit (8);
56    }
57
58    # Time we set the clock
59    my $set_time = decode($ARGV[0]);
60
61    # Time the clock shows now
62    my $clock_time = decode($ARGV[1]);
63
64    # Real time
65    my $actual_time = decode($ARGV[2]);
66
67    $clock_time += $DAY;
68    $actual_time += $DAY;
69
70    if ($clock_time < $actual_time) {
71        print "Clock is slow by ", $actual_time -
➥$clock_time, " minutes\n";
```

```
72    } elsif ($clock_time > $actual_time) {
73        print "Clock is fast by ", $clock_time -
              $actual_time, " minutes\n";
74    } else {
75        print "Clock is on time!\n";
76    }
77
78    # The difference
79    my $ratio = ($clock_time - $set_time) / ($actual_time - $set_time);
80    $ratio = ($ratio - 1.0) * 100.0;
81    printf "Error rate: %5.2f percent\n", $ratio;
82
```

The Congreve Clock

I collect Congreve clocks (see Figure 16.1). Back in the early days of English clocks, everyone was trying to invent a way of making an accurate clock. William Congreve came up with a brilliant idea. He figured that the less a clock ticked, the less error would be introduced by the spring, gears, and ticking mechanism. Now with pendulum clocks, the way you did that was to make the pendulum longer. But there's a limit on how long you can make a pendulum (usually limited by the height of the building housing the clock).

Figure 16.1   A Congreve clock.

Mr. Congreve's idea was to use a rolling ball rather than a pendulum. The ball rolls down a track in an inclined plane. When it reaches the bottom, it hits a lever, and the clock ticks and in the process reverses the slope of the plane causing the ball to roll in the other direction. Thus you can easily make a clock that ticks only once every 30 seconds.

The inventor calculated that his inclined plane was the equivalent to a pendulum of 30 feet in length. He had a brilliant theory and an inventive concept. The only problem was that it didn't work.

The problem is that whereas a pendulum has a natural frequency, a falling ball doesn't. Every speck of dust, every temperature change, every bump on the track causes inaccuracies in the system. A good Congreve clock is accurate to within 20 minutes a day.

Like most engineering, what sounds good on paper doesn't quite work in the field.

Calendar Programs

Like most people, I need to help keeping tracking of dates. I have trouble with two types of dates: the ones in the future (upcoming events) and the ones in the past.

The `cal.pl` program is designed to help me. It examines a calendar file and decides whether an event is approaching. It then writes out a warning message. The default format of an entry in this file is

```
<date>    <Event>
```

For example:

```
1/27 Wife's Birthday
```

This causes the program to warn me seven days before my wife's birthday.

But for some events, I want more advanced warning. So another optional field is added to tell the program to give me that much extra time. The format of this field is +*<warn-time>*. For example:

```
1/27 +30 Wife's Birthday
```

gives me 30 days warning of the approaching event.

Another function of this program is to keep track of events in the past. For example, it could track the number of days since I sent out my rebate form to Canon. For those types of events, the file format is changed slightly. A minus (–) is used to indicate that this event is in the past and to count the number of days since it occurred.

```
9/25 - Canon rebate
```

Date Formats

This program makes extensive use of date parsing and date calculations. To make things easier, the system keeps track of time as the number of days since Jan 1, 1970.

You may wonder why this date is special. It seems that the people who created the Posix standard decided that it would be a good idea to "start the clock" on this date. The standard time format is the number of seconds since this date.

That standard is used by Posix and Perl. The Perl `time` function returns the current time based on this standard. The date parsing functions use it as well.

If you are interested in days, all you have to do is divide by the number of seconds in a day for your calculations.

The Program

The program starts by reading the file and extracting the date:

```
80       # Decode the line
81       #   <spaces>(date-$1)<spaces>(rest-$2)
82       $line =~ /^\s*(\S+)\s(.*)/;
83       my $date_str = $1;   # Get the date
84       my $rest = $2;       # Get the rest of the line
```

One problem with the format used here is that the second field is optional, so you need to check and see whether it's there. (If it's not, create some defaults.) For example:

```
87       # We might have a line like:
88       #   ([+-]digits-$1)<spaces>($rest-$2)
89       if ($rest =~ /^([+-]\S*)\s*(.*)$/) {
90           $flag = $1;      # Grab the flag
91
92           # Put in a default number of days if needed
93           if ($flag eq "-") {
94               $flag = -9999;
95           }
96
97           $rest = $2;      # Grab the rest
98       } else {
99           $flag = 7;       # Assume the flag is +7
100      }
```

Next, turn the date into something useful:

```
102      my $date = parsedate($date_str);
103      if (not defined($date)) {
104          print STDERR "Unable to parse date: $date_str\n";
105          next;
106      }
```

Finally, you need to decide whether the event warrants printing. This involves simple date calculations and conditionals:

```
111        if ($flag > 0) {
112            if ($diff < 0) {
113                next;
114            }
115            if ($diff < $flag) {
116                print "$date_str ($diff) $rest\n";
117            }
118        } else {
119            # Is the event so old it's in the future
120            if ($diff > 0) {
121                $diff -= 365;
122            }
123            if ($diff > $flag) {
124                print "$date_str ($diff) $rest\n";
125            }
126        }
```

Again, you have a small, simple program designed to solve a problem thanks to the power of Perl (see Listing 16.4).

Listing 16.4 *cal.pl*

```
 1    =pod
 2
 3    =head1 NAME
 4
 5    cal.pl - Check a calendar for things coming up and things past
 6
 7    =head1 SYNOPSIS
 8
 9        cal.pl <calendar-file>
10
11    =head1 DESCRIPTION
12
13    The I<cal.pl> checks the calendar file to see if anything is coming
14    up soon.  It also reminds you of past events and how long they
15    happened.
16
17    The format of the calendar file is:
18
19    I<date> [I<flags>] I<information>
20
21    The <date> is a date in any format so long as there are no spaces in
22    in it.
23
24    The I<flags> are:
25
26    =over 4
27
28    =item +I<days>
```

```
29
30    Remind me of an event that's coming up in I<days> days or less.
31
32    =item -
33
34    Tell me about an event that's passed.  (This is so I can see how
35    long it's been sent I sent out that rebate request.)
36
37    =back
38
39    The I<information> field is the text that describes the event.
40
41    =head1 EXAMPLES
42
43    I sent the rebate out on March 30.  How many days ago was that?
44
45        3/30 - Epson Rebate
46
47    Remind me two weeks before about my dentist visit on June 1.
48
49        1-June-2002 +14 Dentist
50
51    =cut
52    use strict;
53    use warnings;
54    use Time::ParseDate;
55
56    if ($#ARGV != 0) {
57        print "Usage is $0 <calendar file>\n";exit(8);
58    }
59
60    # The number of seconds per day
61    my $SECONDS_PER_DAY = 60 * 60 * 24;
62
63    open CAL_FILE, "<$ARGV[0]" or
64        die("Could not open $ARGV[0]");
65
66    # Today's date (in system format)
67    my $today = time();
68
69    while (1) {
70        # The line from the input file
71        my $line = <CAL_FILE>;
72        if (not defined($line)) {
73            last;
74        }
75        chomp($line);
76        if ($line eq "") {
77            next;
78        }
79
```

continues

Listing 16.4   **Continued**

```
80          # Decode the line
81          #    <spaces>(date-$1)<spaces>(rest-$2)
82          $line =~ /^\s*(\S+)\s(.*)/;
83          my $date_str = $1;   # Get the date
84          my $rest = $2;        # Get the rest of the line
85          my $flag;             # Flag information
86
87          # We might have a line like:
88          #    ([+-]digits-$1)<spaces>($rest-$2)
89          if ($rest =~ /^([+-]\S*)\s*(.*)$/) {
90              $flag = $1;       # Grab the flag
91
92              # Put in a default number of days if needed
93              if ($flag eq "-") {
94                  $flag = -9999;
95              }
96
97              $rest = $2;       # Grab the rest
98          } else {
99              $flag = 7;        # Assume the flag is +7
100         }
101
102         my $date = parsedate($date_str);
103         if (not defined($date)) {
104             print STDERR "Unable to parse date: $date_str\n";
105             next;
106         }
107
108         # Compute difference between today and the date given
109         my $diff = int (($date - $today) / $SECONDS_PER_DAY);
110
111         if ($flag > 0) {
112             if ($diff < 0) {
113                 next;
114             }
115             if ($diff < $flag) {
116                 print "$date_str ($diff) $rest\n";
117             }
118         } else {
119             # Is the event so old it's in the future
120             if ($diff > 0) {
121                 $diff -= 365;
122             }
123             if ($diff > $flag) {
124                 print "$date_str ($diff) $rest\n";
125             }
126         }
127     }
```

Duplicate File Checker

If you're like me, you have many files on your computer—sometimes too many. In my case, one of my favorite tricks is to download pictures from my camera multiple times. These images are big and take up a lot of space. Storing multiple copies is not a good idea.

To help me keep track of things, I wrote a program to scan a directory (or series of directories) for duplicate files.

The basic operations of the program are

1. Find all the files.

2. Check for duplicates.

The first part of the program, find all the files, was largely written by the utility find2perl. It takes the same argument as the UNIX find command, only instead of actually finding the files, the program writes out a Perl script that does the work.

The command to generate the seed used to create this program is

```
find2perl @ARGV -type f -exec do_it \; >dup.pl
```

This writes out a script that makes extensive use of the File::Find module to do the work. The arguments to this script are

- **@ARGV**—A directory (or set of directories) in which to start the search.

- **-type f**—Only worry about the files that are real files. (Skip directories or links.)

- **-exec do_it**—When you find a file, execute the command do_it.

The result of this script is

```
1    #! /home/oualline/local/bin/perl -w
2        eval 'exec /home/sdo/local/bin/perl -S $0 ${1+"$@"}'
3            if 0; #$running_under_some_shell
4
5    use strict;
6    use File::Find ();
7
8    # Set the variable $File::Find::dont_use_nlink if you're using AFS,
9    # since AFS cheats.
10
11   # for the convenience of &wanted calls, including -eval statements:
12   use vars qw/*name *dir *prune/;
13   *name   = *File::Find::name;
14   *dir    = *File::Find::dir;
15   *prune  = *File::Find::prune;
16
17
```

```
18    # Traverse desired filesystems
19    File::Find::find({wanted => \&wanted}, '@ARGV');
20    exit;
21
22
23    sub wanted {
24        my ($dev,$ino,$mode,$nlink,$uid,$gid);
25
26        (($dev,$ino,$mode,$nlink,$uid,$gid) = lstat($_)) &&
27        -f _ &&
28        &doexec(0, 'do_it');
29    }
30
31
32    use Cwd ();
33    my $cwd = Cwd::cwd();
34
35    sub doexec {
36        my $ok = shift;
37        for my $word (@_)
38            { $word =~ s#{}#$name#g }
39        if ($ok) {
40            my $old = select(STDOUT);
41            $| = 1;
42            print "@_";
43            select($old);
44            return 0 unless <STDIN> =~ /^y/;
45        }
46        chdir $cwd; #sigh
47        system @_;
48        chdir $File::Find::dir;
49        return !$?;
50    }
```

Although this works, you need to do some hacking to make things right. First of all, the main program is

```
18    # Traverse desired filesystems
19    File::Find::find({wanted => \&wanted}, '@ARGV');
20    exit;
```

This is moved to the end of the program. Also the quotes are removed from @ARGV. (You don't want to start your search in the directory whose name is literally @ARGV.) The results are

```
79    # Process each directory on the line
80    File::Find::find({wanted => \&wanted}, @ARGV);
```

Next, all the garbage concerning the functions doexec and do_it are chopped out. These would be useful if there was a system command named "do_it" that you want executed. In this case, you are going to write your own function to process the file.

So lines 32–50 are deleted, and the wanted function is edited:

```
71    sub wanted {
72        my ($dev,$ino,$mode,$nlink,$uid,$gid);
73
74        (($dev,$ino,$mode,$nlink,$uid,$gid) = lstat($_)) &&
75        -f _ &&
76        process($name);
77    }
```

The process function checks each file and decides whether it's a duplicate. It does this by computing an md5 checksum using the module Digest::MD5:

```
46        # Checksum object
47        my $digest = Digest::MD5->new();
48
49        # Checksum the file
50        open IN_FILE, "<$file" or
51            die("Could not read $file");
52        $digest->addfile(*IN_FILE);
53        close(IN_FILE);
54
55        # Get the checksum
56        my $checksum = $digest->b64digest();
```

This checksum is used as the key in a hash. If another element with this key already exists, it is a duplicate, and the match is printed:

```
58        # Does a file already exist with this checksum?
59        if (defined($file_hash{$checksum})) {
60            # Yes -- duplicate
61            print "Duplicate:\n";
62            print "\t$file_hash{$checksum}\n";
63            print "\t$file\n";
64        } else {
65            # No, store results
66            $file_hash{$checksum} = $file;
67        }
```

One nice thing about a program like this is that it easily can be adapted to fit different circumstances. For example, it easily can decide whether a file is redundant and eliminate it or perform other cleanup functions.

Listing 16.5 shows the full program.

Listing 16.5 *dup.pl*

```
1    =pod
2
3    =head1 NAME
4
5    dup.pl - Check one or more directories for duplicate files
6
7    =head1 SYNOPSIS
```

continues

Listing 16.5   **Continued**

```
8
9            dup.pl <dir> [<dir> ....]
10
11   =head1 DESCRIPTION
12
13   The I<dup.pl> scans directories and reports any duplicate files.
14
15   =head1 EXAMPLES
16
17   To check to see if any files are
18   duplicated in /home/oualline/work
19   requires the command:
20
21            perl dup.pl /home/oualline/work
22   =cut
23   use strict;
24   use warnings;
25   use File::Find ();
26   use Digest::MD5;
27
28   # A hash keys=checksum values=files
29   my %file_hash = ();
30
31   # Generated by find2html
32   # for the convenience of &wanted calls, including -eval statements:
33   use vars qw/*name *dir *prune/;
34   *name   = *File::Find::name;
35   *dir    = *File::Find::dir;
36   *prune  = *File::Find::prune;
37
38   ####################################################
39   # process($file) -- process a single file and
40   #        report if it's a duplicates
41   ####################################################
42   sub process($)
43   {
44       my $file = shift;    # The file to check
45
46       # Checksum object
47       my $digest = Digest::MD5->new();
48
49       # Checksum the file
50       open IN_FILE, "<$file" or
51           die("Could not read $file");
52       $digest->addfile(*IN_FILE);
53       close(IN_FILE);
54
55       # Get the checksum
56       my $checksum = $digest->b64digest();
57
58       # Does a file already exist with this checksum?
```

```
59        if (defined($file_hash{$checksum})) {
60            # Yes -- duplicate
61            print "Duplicate:\n";
62            print "\t$file_hash{$checksum}\n";
63            print "\t$file\n";
64        } else {
65            # No, store results
66            $file_hash{$checksum} = $file;
67        }
68    }
69
70    # Generated by find2pl
71    sub wanted {
72        my ($dev,$ino,$mode,$nlink,$uid,$gid);
73
74        (($dev,$ino,$mode,$nlink,$uid,$gid) = lstat($_)) &&
75        -f _  &&
76        process($name);
77    }
78
79    # Process each directory on the line
80    File::Find::find({wanted => \&wanted}, @ARGV);
81
```

Note that this program fails with a strange error if you don't specify any
directories. However, the addition of proper error checking code is left as an
exercise for the reader.

Table Formatting

Many text files contain tabular data. Unfortunately, getting the columns to line
up can prove difficult. For example, here is a typical file:

```
/dev/cdrom /mnt/cdrom iso9660 user,unhide,ro 0 0
/dev/scd1 /mnt/cdrom1 iso9660 noauto,unhide,user,ro 0 0
/dev/scd0 /mnt/cdrom2 iso9660 noauto,unhide,user,ro 0 0
/dev/loop0 /mnt/cdrom_l iso9660 noauto,unhide,user,ro 0 0
/dev/sda1 /mnt/optical ext2 defaults,noauto,user 0 0
```

It would be nice to see something like this:

```
/dev/cdrom  /mnt/cdrom   iso9660 user,unhide,ro        0 0
/dev/scd1   /mnt/cdrom1  iso9660 noauto,unhide,user,ro 0 0
/dev/scd0   /mnt/cdrom2  iso9660 noauto,unhide,user,ro 0 0
/dev/loop0  /mnt/cdrom_l iso9660 noauto,unhide,user,ro 0 0
/dev/sda1   /mnt/optical ext2    defaults,noauto,user  0 0
```

You can write a Perl program to process this text and make it look pretty. Start
by reading in the data and dividing it up into words:

```
28   while (<>) {
29       chomp($_);
30       my @words = split /\s+/, $_;
31       push (@lines, [@words]);
32   }
```

This example uses the magic Perl file <>, which goes through all the arguments on the command line. The result is an array called @lines in which each element is a line from the input.

The actual element is not stored as a string but rather as an array of words.

Next, this data structure is processed to determine which line has the most words on it:

```
37   my $n_fields = 0;
38
39   foreach my $cur_line (@lines) {
40       if ($#$cur_line > $n_fields) {
41           $n_fields = $#$cur_line;
42       }
43   }
```

Now you can go through and compute the size of each field:

```
48   my @field_size = ();
49   for (my $cur_field = 0;
50            $cur_field <= $n_fields;
51            $cur_field++) {
52
53       $field_size[$cur_field] = 0;
54       foreach my $cur_line (@lines) {
55           if (not defined($cur_line->[$cur_field])) {
56               next;
57           }
58           if (length($cur_line->[$cur_field]) >
59                   $field_size[$cur_field]) {
60               $field_size[$cur_field] =
61                   length($cur_line->[$cur_field]);
62           }
63       }
64   }
```

You're almost there. You need to create a format string that can be used for printing the table:

```
69   my $format = "";
70   foreach my $cur_field (@field_size) {
71       if ($format ne "") {
72           $format .= " ";
73       }
74       $format .= "%-${cur_field}s";
75   }
76   $format .= "\n";
```

Finally, there's nothing left to do but print it:

```
81    foreach my $cur_line (@lines) {
82        printf $format, @$cur_line;
83    }
```

The result is a beautifully formatted table. The entire program is presented in
Listing 16.6.

Listing 16.6 **table.pl**

```
1    =pod
2
3    =head1 NAME
4
5    table.pl - Print out tables nicely formatted
6
7    =head1 SYNOPSIS
8
9        table.pl <file> [<file> ....]
10
11   =head1 DESCRIPTION
12
13   The I<table.pl> examines the input files which are assumed to contain
14   data in columns and prints them nicely.  In other words, it makes
15   the tables look nice.
16
17   =cut
18   use strict;
19   use warnings;
20
21
22   # The input as lines, then as columns
23   my @lines = ();
24
25   #
26   # Grab input, break apart into fields
27   #
28   while (<>) {
29       chomp($_);
30       my @words = split /\s+/, $_;
31       push (@lines, [@words]);
32   }
33
34   #
35   # Find out how many fields there are
36   #
37   my $n_fields = 0;
38
39   foreach my $cur_line (@lines) {
40       if ($#$cur_line > $n_fields) {
41           $n_fields = $#$cur_line;
42       }
```

continues

314 Chapter 16 Cookbook

Listing 16.6 **Continued**

```
43    }
44
45    #
46    # Find the size of each field.
47    #
48    my @field_size = ();
49    for (my $cur_field = 0;
50            $cur_field <= $n_fields;
51            $cur_field++) {
52
53        $field_size[$cur_field] = 0;
54        foreach my $cur_line (@lines) {
55            if (not defined($cur_line->[$cur_field])) {
56                next;
57            }
58            if (length($cur_line->[$cur_field]) >
59                    $field_size[$cur_field]) {
60                $field_size[$cur_field] =
61                    length($cur_line->[$cur_field]);
62            }
63        }
64    }
65
66    #
67    # Build the printing format
68    #
69    my $format = "";
70    foreach my $cur_field (@field_size) {
71        if ($format ne "") {
72            $format .= " ";
73        }
74        $format .= "%-${cur_field}s";
75    }
76    $format .= "\n";
77
78    #
79    # Print
80    #
81    foreach my $cur_line (@lines) {
82        printf $format, @$cur_line;
83    }
84
```

Log File Viewer

C programming is a simple process. Do a make, take care of the errors, do a make, take care of the errors, and so on. Unless, you've got my job, which is do a make, go to lunch, come back, and see whether three-quarters of a million lines have finished compiling; then look through the huge log file for errors.

To make spotting errors easier, you can create a Perl program that goes through a log file and highlights the errors.

But what constitutes an error? Obviously, a line with the word "Error" on it. But that's not always true. Sometimes someone produces a module with a name like: `STR_Error.c`. Compiling this is not an error.

So your program must be flexible in deciding what is an error and what isn't. You can solve this problem by partly weaseling out of it and letting the user control what is and is not an error through a configuration file.

The file looks like

```
ERROR
regular expression
regular expression
....
IGNORE
regular expression
regular expression
....
```

Anything in the ERROR section will be an error, unless it's in the IGNORE section, in which case it's not an error. This means that you can tell the system that all lines with "Error" in them are errors (they would appear in the ERROR section), unless the line looks like:

```
cc -g -c ErrorMessages.c
```

In this case we'd put the line in the IGNORE section and it would not be counted as an error.

Now you need to design a GUI for the program. The results can be seen in Figure 16.2.

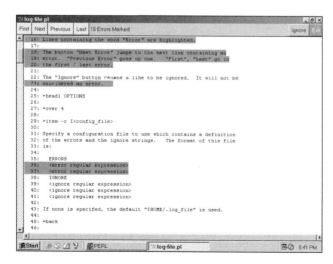

Figure 16.2   GUI for log file viewing.

The first four buttons, First, Next, Previous, and Last, select which error is shown on the screen. The Ignore button causes the system to add the current line to the list of ignored expressions. Finally, the Exit button stops the program.

The program makes extensive use of the Tk widgets for its work. One of the more interesting is the `Text` widget. This is used to hold the log file.

The program is designed to display the error lines in red. It does this through the use of a *text tag*. This is the name given to a group of attributes applied to some of the text in a `Text` widget.

To use a text tag, you first must define it. This is done through the `tagConfigure` method. This changes the attributes of a tag if it exists, or creates one if it does not:

```
196        $text_box->tagConfigure('highlight',
197                -background => 'Red');
```

In this case, a tag called `highlight` is created, which turns the background of the text to red. (The name `highlight` was arbitrarily chosen; you can use any name that makes sense.)

Now you need to apply it to the error text. This is done through the `tagAdd` method. You need to tell this function which characters get the highlight. There are several different ways of specifying a location in a text box. (These locations go by the name of *character index*.)

One way is to use *<line>.<character>*. *<line>* is the line number of the text starting with 1. The *<character>* parameter denotes the character number starting with 0. So the start of the tenth line is "10.0".

A character index can have an adjustment following the initial location specification. For example, `linestart` moves the location to the start of a line, and `lineend` moves it to the end.

To highlight a single line, you highlight from the start of the line (`$text_line.0`) to the end (`$text_line.0 lineend`) as shown in the following code:

```
132                # Text box uses 1 based number/Perl uses 0
133                my $text_line = $line_number + 1;
134                $text_box->tagAdd(
135                    "highlight",
136                    "$text_line.0",
137                    "$text_line.0 lineend"
138                );
```

The only other interesting item in the code is the use of a named block. The program goes through the list of ignore commands, and if one matches, the line is not an error (see lines 120–127). If a line is not ignored, it is checked against the error list and highlighted if it's on the error list (see lines 128–141).

Suppose that you have discovered that a line needs to be ignored, and you do this in the conditional at line 123:

```
123                    if ($line =~ /$cur_ignore/)
```

Now you have a problem. You need to ignore the line. That means starting work on the line list. In other words, starting the loop on line 115 over again.

But if you use the `next` command, the program starts the loop at 121 over again. If you use the `last` command, execution continues with line 128.

You need to tell Perl to do a `next` not on this loop, but on the loop outside this one. To do this, you first must name the loop. In this case, the name is LINE_LOOP. Then use the statement

```
125                    next LINE_LOOP;
```

to tell Perl to break out of the current loop and start the next iteration of LINE_LOOP.

The looping code is shown here:

```
114    LINE_LOOP:
115        for (my $line_number = 0;
116            $line_number <= $#file_lines;
117            $line_number++)
118        {
119            # The line we are reading
120            my $line = $file_lines[$line_number];
121            foreach my $cur_ignore (@ignore_list)
122            {
123                if ($line =~ /$cur_ignore/)
124                {
125                    next LINE_LOOP;
126                }
127            }
128            foreach my $cur_error (@error_check)
129            {
130                if ($line =~ /$cur_error/)
131                {
132                    # Text box uses 1 based number/Perl uses 0
133                    my $text_line = $line_number + 1;
134                    $text_box->tagAdd(
135                        "highlight",
136                        "$text_line.0",
137                        "$text_line.0 lineend"
138                    );
139                    push(@error_loc, $text_line);
140                    last;
141                }
142            }
143        }
```

Most of the rest of the program is devoted to the code used to build the GUI
and handle the bookkeeping. There's a little code to move the selected error
up and down and so forth.

This program does contain a few bugs, however. The biggest one is that the
current error is not highlighted any differently from any of the others. As a
result, if more than one error is on the screen, you can't tell which one is
current. This can easily lead to confusion.

However, this program is much better than going through a log file using
just the more command and has proven itself useful. The full program is shown
in Listing 16.7.

Listing 16.7 *log-file.pl*

```
1   =pod
2
3   =head1 NAME
4
5   log_file - View log files.
6
7   =head1 SYNOPSIS
8
9   B<log_file>
10  [B<-c> I<config_file>]
11  I<log_file>
12
13  =head1 DESCRIPTION
14
15  The I<log_file> reads a log file and displays it in a window.
16  Lines containing the word "Error" are highlighted.
17
18  The button "Next Error" jumps to the next line containing an
19  error.  "Previous Error" goes up one.   "First", "Last" go to
20  the first / last error.
21
22  The "Ignore" button causes a line to be ignored.  It will not be
23  considered an error.
24
25  =head1 OPTIONS
26
27  =over 4
28
29  =item -c I<config_file>
30
31  Specify a configuration file to use which contains a definition
32  of the errors and the ignore strings.   The format of this file
33  is:
34
35          ERRORS
36          <error regular expression>
37          <error regular expression>
```

```
38            IGNORE
39            <ignore regular expression>
40            <ignore regular expression>
41            <ignore regular expression>
42
43   If none is specified, the default "$HOME/.log_file" is used.
44
45   =back
46
47   =cut
48
49   use strict;
50   use warnings;
51   use Getopt::Std;
52   use Tk;
53
54   # The strings that indicate we have an error (default value)
55   my @error_check = ('\bError\b', '\berror\b');
56
57   # Location list (where the errors are)
58   my @error_loc = ();
59
60   my $loc_index = 0;      # Index into the error location list
61
62   my @ignore_list = ();   # List of lines to ignore
63
64   my $main_window;        # Top window
65   my $text_box;           # Widget containing the error information
66   my $count_label;        # label containing the error count
67
68   my @file_lines = ();    # The lines in the file
69
70   my $config_change = 0;  # True if we changed the configuration
71
72   use vars qw($opt_c);
73
74   #######################################################
75   # Tell user what to do
76   #######################################################
77   sub usage()
78   {
79       print STDERR "Usage is: $0 [-c <config>] <log-file>\n";
80       exit (8);
81   }
82   #######################################################
83   # show_loc -- Make sure that the current error location is
84   # visible on the screen.
85   #######################################################
86   sub show_loc()
87   {
88       # Make sure that $loc_index in range
89       if ($loc_index < 0)
```

continues

Listing 16.7 **Continued**

```
 90        {
 91            $loc_index = 0;
 92        }
 93        if ($loc_index > $#error_loc)
 94        {
 95            $loc_index  = $#error_loc;
 96        }
 97        if ($#error_loc < 0)
 98        {
 99            return;
100        }
101        $text_box->yview(-pickplace, "$error_loc[$loc_index].0");
102    }
103    #######################################################
104    # find_errors -- Locate the lines within the text which contain
105    # errors
106    #######################################################
107    sub find_errors()
108    {
109        @error_loc = ();     # Zero the error location list
110
111        my $old_cursor = $main_window->cget(-cursor);
112        $main_window->configure(-cursor => "watch");
113        # The line number of the current line.
114    LINE_LOOP:
115        for (my $line_number = 0;
116             $line_number <= $#file_lines;
117             $line_number++)
118        {
119            # The line we are reading
120            my $line = $file_lines[$line_number];
121            foreach my $cur_ignore (@ignore_list)
122            {
123                if ($line =~ /$cur_ignore/)
124                {
125                    next LINE_LOOP;
126                }
127            }
128            foreach my $cur_error (@error_check)
129            {
130                if ($line =~ /$cur_error/)
131                {
132                    # Text box uses 1 based number/Perl uses 0
133                    my $text_line = $line_number + 1;
134                    $text_box->tagAdd(
135                            "highlight",
136                            "$text_line.0",
137                            "$text_line.0 lineend"
138                        );
139                    push(@error_loc, $text_line);
140                    last;
141                }
```

```
142                 }
143             }
144         show_loc();
145         $main_window->configure(-cursor => $old_cursor);
146         my $error_count = $#error_loc+1;
147         $count_label->configure(-text => "$error_count Errors Marked");
148     }
149     ######################################################
150     # ignore_cb -- Callback for the ignore button
151     #
152     # Add the excluded line to the list of lines we don't check and
153     # re-do the highlighting
154     ######################################################
155     sub ignore_cb
156     {
157         # The line number of the line we are ignoring
158         my $line_number = $error_loc[$loc_index];
159         # The line we are looking at
160         my $line = $text_box->gct(
161                 "$line_number.0", "$line_number.0 lineend");
162         # Quote all special characters
163         $line =~ s/^ *\d+: //;
164         # Escape        . [ ] * + \ ( )
165         $line =~ s/([\.\[\]\*\+\\\(\)])/\\$1/g;
166         push(@ignore_list, $line);
167
168         $text_box->tagRemove('highlight', "0.0", "end");
169         find_errors();
170         $config_change = 1;
171     }
172     ######################################################
173     # do_file($file_name) -- Process a file.
174     ######################################################
175     sub do_file($)
176     {
177         # The current file name
178         my $file_name = shift;
179
180         open IN_FILE, "<$file_name" or
181             die("Could not open input file: $file_name");
182
183         # The main window for our GUI
184         $main_window = MainWindow->new;
185         $main_window->title("$file_name");
186         $text_box = $main_window->Scrolled("Text")->pack(
187                 -side => 'bottom',
188                 -fill => 'both',
189                 -expand => 1
190                 );
191         $text_box->configure(
192                 -wrap => "none",
193                 -background => "white",
```

continues

Listing 16.7 **Continued**

```
194                    -foreground => "black"
195                );
196            $text_box->tagConfigure('highlight',
197                    -background => 'Red');
198
199            $main_window->Button(
200                    -text => 'First',
201                    -command => sub {
202                        $loc_index = 0;
203                        show_loc();
204                    },
205                    -background => "Cyan"
206            )->pack(
207                -side => 'left'
208            );
209            $main_window->Button(
210                    -text => 'Next',
211                    -command => sub {
212                        $loc_index++;
213                        show_loc();
214                    },
215                    -background => "Cyan"
216            )->pack(
217                    -side => 'left'
218                );
219            $main_window->Button(
220                    -text => 'Previous',
221                    -command => sub {
222                        $loc_index--;
223                        show_loc();
224                    },
225                    -background => "Cyan"
226            )->pack(
227                    -side => 'left'
228                );
229            $main_window->Button(
230                    -text => 'Last',
231                    -command => sub {
232                        $loc_index = $#error_loc;
233                        show_loc();
234                    },
235                    -background => "Cyan"
236            )->pack(
237                    -side => 'left'
238                );
239            $count_label = $main_window->Label(
240                    -text => "x Errors Marked"
241            )->pack(
242                    -side => 'left'
243                );
244            $main_window->Button(
245                    -text => 'Exit',
```

```
246                     -command => sub {
247                         write_config();
248                         exit(0);
249                     },
250                     -background => "red",
251                     -foreground => "white"
252                 )->pack(
253                     -side => 'right'
254                 );
255         $main_window->Button(
256                     -text => 'Ignore',
257                     -command => \&ignore_cb,
258                     -background => "grey",
259                     -foreground => "black"
260         )->pack(
261                 -side => 'right'
262         );
263         # Loop through numbering each line
264         for (my $line_number = 1; ;$line_number++)
265         {
266             my $line = <IN_FILE>;
267             if (!defined($line))
268             {
269                 last;
270             }
271             push(@file_lines, $line);
272             # The line with line number
273             my $full_line = sprintf "%4d: %s", $line_number, $line;
274             $text_box->insert("end", $full_line);
275         }
276         close (IN_FILE);
277         $text_box->configure(-state => 'disabled');
278         find_errors();
279
280         MainLoop();
281     }
282     my $config_name;                # name of the configuration file
283     ########################################################
284     # Configuration file format
285     #
286     #       ERRORS
287     #       <error regular expression>
288     #       <error regular expression>
289     #       IGNORE
290     #       <ignore regular expression>
291     #       <ignore regular expression>
292     #       <ignore regular expression>
293     ########################################################
294
295     ########################################################
296     # read_config($config_name, $error_flag)
297     #
```

continues

Listing 16.7 **Continued**

```
298     # Read the configuration file.
299     ########################################################
300     sub read_config($$)
301     {
302         # Set the name of the configuration file
303         $config_name = shift;
304
305         # if true, exit on error
306         my $error_flag = shift;
307
308
309         if (!open(CONFIG_FILE, "<$config_name"))
310         {
311             if ($error_flag)
312             {
313                 die("Could not open $config_name");
314             }
315             return;
316         }
317
318         @error_check = ();
319         @ignore_list = ();
320
321         while (<CONFIG_FILE>)
322         {
323             if (/^ERRORS$/)
324             {
325                 next;
326             }
327             if (/^IGNORE$/)
328             {
329                 last;
330             }
331             chomp($_);
332             push(@error_check, $_);
333         }
334         while (<CONFIG_FILE>)
335         {
336             chomp($_);
337             push(@ignore_list, $_);
338         }
339         close CONFIG_FILE;
340     }
341     ########################################################
342     # write_config() -- Write the configuration file
343     ########################################################
344     sub write_config()
345     {
346         if (!$config_change)
347         {
348             return;
349         }
```

```
350     open CONFIG_FILE, ">$config_name"
351         or die("Unable to open $config_name for writing");
352     print CONFIG_FILE "ERRORS\n";
353     foreach (@error_check)
354     {
355         print CONFIG_FILE "$_\n";
356     }
357     print CONFIG_FILE "IGNORE\n";
358     foreach (@ignore_list)
359     {
360         print CONFIG_FILE "$_\n";
361     }
362     close CONFIG_FILE;
363 }
364
365 ##########################################################
366 ##########################################################
367 if (($#ARGV >= 0) && ($ARGV[0] eq "--help"))
368 {
369     system("perldoc $0");
370     exit;
371 }
372 my $status = getopts("c:");
373 if (!$status)
374 {
375     usage();
376 }
377 if ($opt_c)
378 {
379     read_config($opt_c, 1);
380 }
381 else
382 {
383     read_config("$ENV{HOME}/.log_file", 0);
384 }
385
386 if ($#ARGV == -1)
387 {
388     usage();
309 }
390 do_file($ARGV[0]);
```

Note that this program is UNIX/Linux specific because it uses the environment variable $HOME ($ENV{HOME}). If you want to make it work on Microsoft Windows, you will have to replace this code with something else.

Also if you look at the online documentation for perlvar, you can discover the internal variable that Perl uses to indicate the operating system type. Using that variable, it would be easy to write a system-independent script.

Web Site Checker

I run a small web site (http://www.oualline.com), and I want to make sure that it is consistent. In other words, I want to check for

- Broken links
- Files in the HTML tree that are never referenced (orphans)

This section shows you how to write a program to do this. First, the program needs to go through the web pages and extract the links. A Perl module does most of that: HTML::SimpleLinkExtor.

You also need to go through the file tree and get a list of all the files. A Perl module also does that: File::Find.

You need to check to make sure that all the referenced files (internal links) exist. A Perl operator does that: -f.

Finally, you need to check to see whether the external links are valid. A Perl module does that LWP::Simple.

You also need something to call these modules and handle all the bookkeeping—you'll have to do that for yourself.

Parsing the Files

The program starts by walking down the tree of all the web pages accessed directly or indirectly from the top-level page. The search stops if the file has already been processed or if the file does not exist. For example:

```
 92    sub process_file($)
 93    {
 94        my $file_name = shift;      # The file to process
 95        my $dir_name = dirname($file_name);
 96
 97        # Did we do it already
 98        if ($file_seen{$file_name}) {
 99            return;
100        }
101        $file_seen{$file_name} = 1;
102        if (! -f $file_name) {
103            push(@bad_files, $file_name);
104            return;
105        }
```

The program also makes no attempt to handle files that are not HTML:

```
107        if (($file_name !~ /\.html$/) and ($file_name !~ /\.htm$/)) {
108            return;
109        }
```

The program then uses the HTML::SimpleLinkExtor module to extract the links from the file. This is done in three stages: create an extraction object (line 111), parse the file (line 114), and grab the links (line 117). These steps are shown in the following code:

```
110        # The parser object to extract the list
111        my $extractor = HTML::SimpleLinkExtor->new();
112
113        # Parse the file
114        $extractor->parse_file($file_name);
115
116        # The list of all the links in the file
117        my @all_links = $extractor->links();
```

The links then are processed. External links are stored on the list @external_links. Local links are processed recursively through the process_file function. For example:

```
120        foreach my $cur_link (@all_links) {
121
122            # Is the link external
123            if ($cur_link =~ /^http:\/\//) {
124                # Put it on the list of external links
125                push(@external_links, {
126                    file => $file_name,
127                    link => $cur_link});
128                next;
129            }
130            # Get the name of the file
131            my $next_file = "$dir_name/$cur_link";
132
133            # Remove any funny characters in the name
134            $next_file = File::Spec->canonpath($next_file);
135
136            # Follow the links in this file
137            process_file($next_file);
138        }
```

Orphan Detection

You now have a list of all the files accessible (directly or indirectly) from the top web page. This list is made up of the keys of the %file_seen hash. You need to know the names of all the files on the system to do orphan checking.

This is accomplished with the File::Find module. Actually, the program uses your old friend find2perl to create the code that calls this module and then adapts it to your needs.

The `find` is kicked off using the statement

```
160   # Traverse desired filesystems
161   File::Find::find({wanted => \&wanted}, dirname($ARGV[0]));
```

The wanted function just puts the files on the list:

```
76    sub wanted {
77        if (-f "$name") {
78            push(@full_file_list, $name);
79        }
80        return (1);
81    }
```

Now that you have two lists, one of the files accessible on the web site, and the other containing all the files on the web site, comparing the two lists produces a list of orphans:

```
168   print "Orphan Files\n";
169   foreach my $cur_file (sort @full_file_list)
170   {
171       if (not defined($file_seen{$cur_file})) {
172           print "\t$cur_file\n";
173       }
174   }
```

External Link Checking

During the file processing, you stored away a list of external links
(`@external_links`). To check to see whether these are valid, you must go
through them and use the `LWP::Simple` module to check the links.

Actually, what you try to do is use the head function out of this module to
retrieve the header. If the header exists, then the link is valid:

```
181   print "Broken External Links\n";
182   foreach my $cur_file (sort @external_links) {
183       if (not (head($cur_file->{link}))) {
184           print "\t$cur_file->{file} => $cur_file->{link}\n";
185       }
186   }
```

You could have grabbed the entire web page using the `get` function, but the
header works just as well and uses less bandwidth.

Summary of Web Site Checker

I originally wrote the `link-check.pl` program in C++. It was several thousand
lines long. As you can see in Listing 16.8, the Perl version of this program is
only 186 lines long.

The reason for this vast difference is that Perl supplies modules that do most of the work. Also, the rich set of language features means that you can concentrate on getting the logic right and not have to worry about memory allocations, array bounds, and other such details—and therein lies the true power of Perl.

Listing 16.8 *link-check.pl*

```
1
2    =pod
3
4    =head1 NAME
5
6    link-check.pl - Check the links in a local web site
7
8    =head1 SYNOPSIS
9
10       perl link-check.pl <top-level-file>
11
12   =head1 DESCRIPTION
13
14   The I<link-check.pl> program checks a web site for:
15
16   =over 4
17
18   =item *
19
20   Broken internal links
21
22   =item *
23
24   Orphan files (files that no one links to)
25
26   =item *
27
28   Broken external links
29
30   =back
31
32   The program first makes a catalog of all the links in
33   the I<top-level-file> and all the files linked to by
34   all the files accessible from the I<top-level-file>.
35   (This includes all the directly accessible files as well
36   as all the files that are accessed through multiple links.)
37
38   It then goes through the directory tree in which the
39   I<top-level-file> resides and gets a list of all the
40   available files.   Any file that's in the directory that's
41   not accessible from I<top-level-file> is considered an
42   orphan.
43
```

continues

Listing 16.8   **Continued**

```
44   =cut
45   #
46   # Usage: link_check <top-file>
47   #
48   use strict;
49   use warnings;
50
51   use HTML::SimpleLinkExtor;
52   use LWP::Simple;
53   use File::Basename;
54   use File::Spec::Functions;
55   use File::Find ();
56
57   # Generated by find2pl
58   # for the convenience of &wanted calls, including -eval statements:
59   use vars qw/*name *dir *prune/;
60   *name   = *File::Find::name;
61   *dir    = *File::Find::dir;
62   *prune  = *File::Find::prune;
63
64   my %file_seen = ();      # True if we've seen a file
65   my @external_links = ();# List of external links
66
67   my @bad_files = ();      # Files we did not see
68   my @full_file_list = ();# List of all the files
69
70
71   ######################################################
72   # wanted -- Called by the find routine, this returns
73   #      true if the file is wanted.  As a side effect
74   #      it records any normal file seen in "full_file_list".
75   ######################################################
76   sub wanted {
77       if (-f "$name") {
78           push(@full_file_list, $name);
79       }
80       return (1);
81   }
82
83   ######################################################
84   # process_file($file)
85   #
86   # Read an html file and extract the tags.
87   #
88   # If the file does not exist, put it in the list of
89   # bad files.
90   ######################################################
91   sub process_file($);    # Needed because this is recursive
92   sub process_file($)
93   {
94       my $file_name = shift;      # The file to process
95       my $dir_name = dirname($file_name);
```

```
96
97          # Did we do it already
98          if ($file_seen{$file_name}) {
99              return;
100         }
101         $file_seen{$file_name} = 1;
102         if (! -f $file_name) {
103             push(@bad_files, $file_name);
104             return;
105         }
106
107         if (($file_name !~ /\.html$/) and ($file_name !~ /\.htm$/)) {
108             return;
109         }
110         # The parser object to extract the list
111         my $extractor = HTML::SimpleLinkExtor->new();
112
113         # Parse the file
114         $extractor->parse_file($file_name);
115
116         # The list of all the links in the file
117         my @all_links = $extractor->links();
118
119         # Check each link
120         foreach my $cur_link (@all_links) {
121
122             # Is the link external
123             if ($cur_link =~ /^http:\/\//) {
124                 # Put it on the list of external links
125                 push(@external_links, {
126                     file => $file_name,
127                     link => $cur_link});
128                 next;
129             }
130             # Get the name of the file
131             my $next_file = "$dir_name/$cur_link";
132
133             # Remove any funny characters in the name
134             $next_file - File::Spec->canonpath($next_file);
135
136             # Follow the links in this file
137             process_file($next_file);
138         }
139     }
140
141     if ($#ARGV != 0) {
142         print STDERR "Usage: $0 <top-file>\n";
143         exit (8);
144     }
145
146     # Top level file
147     my $top_file = $ARGV[0];
```

continues

Listing 16.8   **Continued**

```
148    if (-d $top_file) {
149        $top_file .= "/index.html";
150    }
151    if (! -f $top_file) {
152        print STDERR "ERROR: No such file $top_file\n";
153        exit (8);
154    }
155
156
157    # Scan all the links
158    process_file($top_file);
159
160    # Traverse desired filesystems
161    File::Find::find({wanted => \&wanted}, dirname($ARGV[0]));
162
163    print "External links\n";
164    foreach my $link (@external_links) {
165        print "\t$link\n";
166    }
167
168    print "Orphan Files\n";
169    foreach my $cur_file (sort @full_file_list)
170    {
171        if (not defined($file_seen{$cur_file})) {
172            print "\t$cur_file\n";
173        }
174    }
175
176    print "Broken Internal Links\n";
177    foreach my $cur_file (sort @bad_files)
178    {
179        print "\t$cur_file\n";
180    }
181    print "Broken External Links\n";
182    foreach my $cur_file (sort @external_links) {
183        if (not (head($cur_file->{link}))) {
184            print "\t$cur_file->{file} => $cur_file->{link}\n";
185        }
186    }
```

Object File Cross-Reference System

As a professional C programmer, I've had to deal with extremely large programs. Part of this work involved integration of software whose components were made in Finland, the United States, China, and Korea. Needless to say, sometimes the parts don't go together smoothly.

One common problem I have to deal with is symbol conflicts that occur at link time. Frequently, I will get duplicate symbols or undefined symbols.

Using grep to search through several thousand files is prohibitively slow, so I devised the object cross-referencing system. It consists of two parts: the ox-gen.pl program that generates the object cross-reference and the ox.pl program that queries it.

ox-gen.pl

The job of the ox-gen.pl program is to find all the object files, read their symbol tables, and store the information in a hash.

The structure of the data is

```
%object_xref --
        Key => the symbol name
        value => hash reference
            key => defined
            data => array of files where the symbol is defined

            key -> used
            data => array of files where the symbol is used
```

Or to put this in C terms:

```
struct single_object {
    struct object_info {
        char *defined[];
        char *data[];
    }
} object_xref[<indexed by symbol>];
```

The first step in this process is to find all the object files. Anytime the term "find" is used in a sentence, you know that find2perl probably is going to be used to generate some code. Here's the code (slightly modified) that finds all the object files (files ending in .o) and calls the function gen_xref on each one:

```
109 # Generated by find2perl
110 sub wanted {
111     /^.*\.o\z/s &&
112     gen_xref($name);
113 }
114
115 # Traverse desired filesystems
116 File::Find::find({wanted => \&wanted}, '.');
```

The gen_xref subroutine uses the standard UNIX command nm to extract the symbol from the files.

Microsoft Window users can find a Windows version of this command in the Cygwin tool set (http://www.cygwin.org). Microsoft itself provides a utility called dumpbin with its C++ development system, but the output is different, so these programs will need editing before they will work with it:

```
53 sub gen_xref($)
54 {
55      # The name of the file we're examining
56      my $file_name = shift;
57
58      # The symbol information
59      my @lines = `nm $top_dir/$file_name`;
```

The output of the nm command looks something like

```
00000000 T XS_mt_mod_mt_op
         U _GLOBAL_OFFSET_TABLE_
00000360 T boot_mt_mod
         U mt_op
```

In this case, this file defines the symbols XS_mt_mod_mt_op and boot_mt_mod. It uses the symbols GLOBAL_OFFSET_TABLE_ and mt_op.

Your first job is to break apart this line into its three components: the value of the symbol (if any), the symbol code (T or U or whatever), and the name of the symbol.

This calls for a moderately large regular expression:

```
61      # Loop over each line in the symbol data
62      foreach my $cur_line (@lines) {
63          # Decode the line
64          #                  +++++++------------------ Any Hex digit
65          #                  ||||||||*----------------- Zero or more
66          #                  +|||||||||+--------------- Put in $1
67          #                  |||||||||||++------------- Whitespace (\s)
68          #                  |||||||||||||+------------ 1 or more (+)
69          #                  ||||||||||||| +---------- Any char (.)
70          #                  |||||||||||||+|+--------- Put in $2 ($type)
71          #                  ||||||||||||||||||++------- Whitespace (\s)
72          #                  |||||||||||||||||||||+------ 1 or more (+)
73          #                  |||||||||||||||||||||| ++--- Any character (.)
74          #                  |||||||||||||||||||||| ||    repeat 0
75          #                  |||||||||||||||||||||| ||    or more times(*)
76          #                  |||||||||||||||||||||||+||+-- Put in $3
77          $cur_line =~ /^([0-9a-f]*)\s+(.)\s+(.*)$/;
```

Now that you have the information about the symbol, you can see whether you have a record for it. If you don't, a new one is created:

```
82      # If we don't have an entry for this thing, create it
83          if (not defined($object_xref{$name})) {
84              $object_xref{$name} = {
85                  'used' => [],
86                  'defined' => []
87              };
88          }
```

Finally, you must decide whether this is a symbol use or a symbol definition and add the filename to the list of files in the record, as shown here:

```
90      # Check to see if it's used or defined
91          if ($value eq "") {
92              push(@{$object_xref{$name}->{'used'}}, $file_name);
93          } else {
94              push(@{$object_xref{$name}->{'defined'}}, $file_name);
95          }
```

The only thing left is to store the results for later use. That's handled by the `Storable` module, so all you have to do is call it:

```
118 store \%object_xref, "object_xref.dat";
```

This program illustrates the type of work that Perl is really good at. It is good at parsing the output of other programs (in this case, the `nm`) and munching the data. In this case, you use Perl's hashes and arrays to good advantage.

The result is something that is both simple and powerful—and even useful. Listing 16.9 shows the complete code for `ox-gen.pl`.

Listing 16.9   *ox-gen.pl*

```
 1 =pod
 2
 3 =head1 NAME
 4
 5 ox-gen.pl - Generate an object cross reference database
 6
 7 =head1 SYNOPSIS
 8
 9     perl on-gen.pl
10
11 =head1 DESCRIPTION
12
13 The I<ox-gen.pl> command searches the current directory and
14 all sub-directory for I<.o> files and generates a cross reference
15 of all the symbols in each of them.  This database can then be used
16 by the I<ox.pl> program to find symbols and their use.
17
18 =head1 FILES
19
20 =over 4
21
22 =item object_xref.dat
23
24 The database containing the symbol information.
25
26 =back
27
28 =head1 SEE ALSO
29
30 L<ox.pl>, L<nm>
31
```

Listing 16.9   *ox-gen.pl*

```
32  =cut
33  use strict;
34  use warnings;
35  use POSIX (qw(getcwd));
36  use Storable;
37  use File::Find ();
38
39  # Key -- Function name
40  # Value --
41  #       defined => List of files that define this symbol
42  #       used => List of files that use this symbol
43  #
44  my %object_xref;
45
46  # The directory we started for
47  my $top_dir = getcwd();
48
49  ########################################################
50  # gen_xref($file) -- Add cross reference information for
51  #    the given file.
52  ########################################################
53  sub gen_xref($)
54  {
55      # The name of the file we're examining
56      my $file_name = shift;
57
58      # The symbol information
59      my @lines = `nm $top_dir/$file_name`;
60
61      # Loop over each line in the symbol data
62      foreach my $cur_line (@lines) {
63          # Decode the line
64          #                 ++++++++----------------- Any Hex digit
65          #                 |||||||||*--------------- Zero or more
66          #                 +|||||||||+-------------- Put in $1
67          #                 ||||||||||||++----------- Whitespace (\s)
68          #                 |||||||||||||+----------- 1 or more (+)
69          #                 |||||||||||||| +--------- Any char (.)
70          #                 ||||||||||||||||+|+------- Put in $2 ($type)
71          #                 |||||||||||||||||||++----- Whitespace (\s)
72          #                 ||||||||||||||||||||+------ 1 or more (+)
73          #                 |||||||||||||||||||||| ++--- Any character (.)
74          #                 |||||||||||||||||||||| ||   repeat 0
75          #                 |||||||||||||||||||||| ||   or more times(*)
76          #                 ||||||||||||||||||||||||+||+-- Put in $3
77          $cur_line =~ /^([0-9a-f]*)\s+(.)\s+(.*)$/;
78          my $value = $1; # Value of the symbol
79          my $type = $2;     # Type code
80          my $name = $3;     # Name of the symbol
81
82      # If we don't have an entry for this thing, create it
83          if (not defined($object_xref{$name})) {
```

```
84                 $object_xref{$name} = {
85                     'used' => [],
86                     'defined' => []
87                 };
88             }
89
90     # Check to see if it's used or defined
91         if ($value eq "") {
92             push(@{$object_xref{$name}->{'used'}}, $file_name);
93         } else {
94             push(@{$object_xref{$name}->{'defined'}}, $file_name);
95         }
96     }
97 }
98
99 # Set the variable $File::Find::dont_use_nlink if you're using AFS,
100 # since AFS cheats.
101
102 # for the convenience of &wanted calls, including -eval statements:
103 use vars qw/*name *dir *prune/;
104 *name   = *File::Find::name;
105 *dir    = *File::Find::dir;
106 *prune  = *File::Find::prune;
107
108
109 # Generated by find2perl
110 sub wanted {
111     /^.*\.o\z/s &&
112     gen_xref($name);
113 }
114
115 # Traverse desired filesystems
116 File::Find::find({wanted => \&wanted}, '.');
117 # Store the results
118 store \%object_xref, "object_xref.dat";
```

Extracting Information with *ox.pl*

The ox.pl program is the companion to ox-gen.pl. It generates reports based on the information gathered by ox-gen.pl.

The program itself is simple. First you grab the data stored by ox-gen.pl:

```
35 my $object_xref = retrieve("object_xref.dat");
```

Then you print the entry for each symbol entered on the command line:

```
45     my $info = $object_xref->{$sym};
46     if (not defined($info)) {
47         print "$sym:   UNDEFINED\n";
48         next;
49     }
```

```
50        # Print the information
51        print "$sym\n";
52        print "    Defined: @{$info->{'defined'}}\n";
53        print "    Used: @{$info->{'used'}}\n";
```

That's it—database retrieval and report generation in one easy lesson. The program is shown in its entirety in Listing 16.10.

Listing 16.10   *ox.pl*

```
1 =pod
2
3 =head1 NAME
4
5 ox.pl - Print out object cross reference information
6
7 =head1 SYNOPSIS
8
9     ox.pl <symbol> [<symbol> ...]
10
11 =head1 DESCRIPTION
12
13 The I<ox.pl> prints out where a symbol is defined and used.
14
15 =head1 FILES
16
17 =over 4
18
19 =item object_xref.dat
20
21 The database containing the symbol information.
22
23 =back
24
25 =head1 SEE ALSO
26
27 L<ox-gen.pl>, L<nm>
28
29 =cut
30 use strict;
31 use warnings;
32 use Storable;
33
34 # The cross reference data
35 my $object_xref = retrieve("object_xref.dat");
36
37 if (not defined($object_xref)) {
38     print "Could not find data file\n";
39     exit (8);
40 }
41
42 # Look through each symbol on the command line
43 foreach my $sym (@ARGV) {
```

```
44      # Get the information about this symbol
45      my $info = $object_xref->{$sym};
46      if (not defined($info)) {
47          print "$sym:   UNDEFINED\n";
48          next;
49      }
50      # Print the information
51      print "$sym\n";
52      print "    Defined: @{$info->{'defined'}}\n";
53      print "    Used: @{$info->{'used'}}\n";
54 }
```

Additional Work

You can use the object cross-reference database in other ways also. For example, you could use it to check to see what symbols are defined but never used. Or you could count the dependencies between modules.

The point is that you have the data stored in a way that can be conveniently accessed. What you do with it is up to you.

Counting Web Page Hits

I run a web server and get dozens of hits a day. It would be nice to see which pages are the most popular. This easily can be done with a Perl program.

The *web.pm* Module

Start with a general purpose module that reads and parses the web server log files. In this case, the web server is Apache, and a typical log file looks the following:

```
64.246.28.18 - - [14/Apr/2002:04:08:53 -0700] "GET / HTTP/1.1" 200 3329
210.49.177.106 - - [14/Apr/2002:04:15:04 -0700] "GET /not/ HTTP/1.0" 200 1471
210.49.177.106 - - [14/Apr/2002:04:15:16 -0700]
"GET /not/prog_1.html HTTP/1.0" 200 835
210.49.177.106 - - [14/Apr/2002:04:15:25 -0700]
"GET /not/hint_1.html HTTP/1.0" 200 511
210.49.177.106 - - [14/Apr/2002:04:15:40 -0700]
"GET /not/answer_1.html HTTP/1.0" 200 911
210.49.177.106 - - [14/Apr/2002:04:15:58 -0700]
"GET /not/prog_2.html HTTP/1.0" 200 1418
210.49.177.106 - - [14/Apr/2002:04:21:12 -0700] "-" 408 -
210.49.209.115 - - [14/Apr/2002:04:35:19 -0700]
"GET /col/cpm.html HTTP/1.1" 200 7632
217.163.5.253 - - [14/Apr/2002:04:39:32 -0700]
"GET /robots.txt HTTP/1.1" 200 27
68.81.4.54 - - [14/Apr/2002:04:40:47 -0700] "GET /style/index.html HTTP/1.1"
200 1998
```

The first line shows that system 64.246.28.18 grabbed page "/" (the home page) at 14/Apr/2002:04:08:53.

The main function in web.pl, read_info, is designed to go through the log file a line at a time, parse it, and store the results.

The code for opening the file and looping over each line should be familiar to you by now:

```
77    open IN_FILE, "<$file_name" or
78    die("Could not open $file_name");
79
80    while (<IN_FILE>) {
```

Parsing it is done through a simple regular expression. However, because there's a lot to parse, it's a big, simple regular expression. It splits up the line into the accessing system ($1), the access time ($2), the operation code ($3), and the page read ($4):

```
81    #     ++++++------------------------------------------- Digits or dot
82    #     |||||+------------------------------------------- Zero or more
83    #     +|||||||+----------------------------------------- Put in $1
84    #     |||||||||++--------------------------------------- Space
85    #     |||||||||||+--------------------------------------- Zero or more
86    #     |||||||||||+--------------------------------------- Char -
87    #     ||||||||||||||++----------------------------------- Space
88    #     |||||||||||||||||+--------------------------------- Zero or more
89    #     |||||||||||||||||+--------------------------------- Char -
90    #     |||||||||||||||||||++------------------------------- Space
91    #     ||||||||||||||||||||+------------------------------- Zero or more
92    #     |||||||||||||||||||||++----------------------------- Char [
93    #     ||||||||||||||||||||||||| +++++--------------------- Not ]
94    #     ||||||||||||||||||||||||| |||||+------------------- Zero or more
95    #     |||||||||||||||||||||||||+||||||+------------------- Put in $2
96    #     |||||||||||||||||||||||||||||||||||++--------------- ] Char.
97    #     |||||||||||||||||||||||||||||||||||||+------------- Space Char.
98    #     ||||||||||||||||||||||||||||||||||||||+------------- " Char.
99    #     ||||||||||||||||||||||||||||||||||||||| ++--------- Non-space
100   #     ||||||||||||||||||||||||||||||||||||||| ||+--------- One or more
101   #     |||||||||||||||||||||||||||||||||||||||+|||+--------- Put in $3
102   #     |||||||||||||||||||||||||||||||||||||||||||++------- Space
103   #     ||||||||||||||||||||||||||||||||||||||||||||||+----- One or more
104   #     |||||||||||||||||||||||||||||||||||||||||||||| ++---- Non-space
105   #     ||||||||||||||||||||||||||||||||||||||||||||| ||+--- One or more
106   #     |||||||||||||||||||||||||||||||||||||||||||||+|||+-- Put in $4
107   if (/([0-9.]*)\s*-\s*-\s*\[([^\]]*)\] "(\S+)\s+(\S+)/) {
```

Now that things are split up, check the operation code to see whether it's what you want:

```
108       # $3 -- The operation code
109       if ($3 ne "GET") {
110           next;
111       }
```

Finally, store the data in an array named @hit_info. The data itself is a hash with a component for each datum in the record:

```
112        # Entry we are adding
113        my %new_entry = (
114               host => $1,
115               date => $2,
116               page => $4
117                    );
118        push(@hit_info, {%new_entry});
```

After reading the log files, you have the raw data. You can do many things with it, such as see which system looked at the most files; but in this case, you want to compute hit counts.

The function do_count accumulates these statistics. It's designed to go through the @hit_info array and compute how many times each page was hit. The result is an array whose elements are a hash with a key for the page name ("page") and the number of hits ("count").

Listing 16.11 shows the full version of this function.

Listing 16.11 *web.pm*

```
 1 =pod
 2
 3 =head1 NAME
 4
 5 web.pm - Analyze log files.
 6
 7 =head1 SYNOPSIS
 8
 9     use web;
10     my @hit_info;
11     read_info($file_name)
12     $info = do_count()
13
14 =head1 DESCRIPTION
15
16 The I<web.pm> module provides function to read and analyze
17 Apache web logs.
18
19 =head1 Exports
20
21 =over 4
22
23 =item @hit_info
24
25 An array of hashes containing information about each web hit.
26 The fields in each entry is:
27
28 =over 4
```

continues

Listing 16.11　**Continued**

```
29
30 =item B<host>
31
32 The host which read this page
33
34 =item B<date>
35
36 The date/time when it was accessed.
37
38 =item B<page>
39
40 The page.
41
42 =back
43
44 =item read_file($file_name)
45
46 Read a Apache log file and store the results in I<@hit_info>.
47
48 =item $result = do_count()
49
50 Return an array of hashes contains a compilation of the data
51 in I<@hit_info>.  The result is an array of hashes.  The fields
52 in the hash are:  page -- The page name, count -- Number of time it
53 was accessed.
54
55 =back
56
57 =cut
58 package web;
59 use strict;
60 use warnings;
61
62 require Exporter;
63 use vars qw(@EXPORT @ISA @hit_info);
64 @ISA = 'Exporter';
65 @EXPORT = qw(&read_info @hit_info &do_count);
66
67 @hit_info = ();
68
69 #################################################
70 # read_info($file_name) -- Read information about
71 #    hits.
72 #################################################
73 sub read_info($)
74 {
75     my $file_name = shift;  # Get the name of the file
76
77     open IN_FILE, "<$file_name" or
78     die("Could not open $file_name");
79
```

```
80     while (<IN_FILE>) {
81     #      +++++-------------------------------------------- Digits or dot
82     #      ||||| +------------------------------------------ Zero or more
83     #     +||||||| +---------------------------------------- Put in $1
84     #     |||||||||| ++-------------------------------------- Space
85     #     ||||||||||| +-------------------------------------- Zero or more
86     #     |||||||||||| +------------------------------------- Char -
87     #     ||||||||||||| ++------------------------------------ Space
88     #     ||||||||||||||| +---------------------------------- Zero or more
89     #     |||||||||||||||| +--------------------------------- Char -
90     #     |||||||||||||||| ++-------------------------------- Space
91     #     ||||||||||||||||| +-------------------------------- Zero or more
92     #     |||||||||||||||||| ++------------------------------ Char [
93     #     ||||||||||||||||||||  +++++-------------------- Not ]
94     #     ||||||||||||||||||||  ||||| +------------------ Zero or more
95     #     ||||||||||||||||||||||| +||||| +---------------- Put in $2
96     #     ||||||||||||||||||||||||||||||| ++-------------- ] Char.
97     #     |||||||||||||||||||||||||||||||| +------------- Space Char.
98     #     |||||||||||||||||||||||||||||||||| +------------ " Char.
99     #     ||||||||||||||||||||||||||||||||||||  ++---------- Non-space
100    #     |||||||||||||||||||||||||||||||||||||| ||+---------- One or more
101    #     ||||||||||||||||||||||||||||||||||||||| +|||+-------- Put in $3
102    #     ||||||||||||||||||||||||||||||||||||||||| ++-------- Space
103    #     |||||||||||||||||||||||||||||||||||||||||| +------- One or more
104    #     ||||||||||||||||||||||||||||||||||||||||||| ++----- Non-space
105    #     ||||||||||||||||||||||||||||||||||||||||||| ||+--- One or more
106    #     ||||||||||||||||||||||||||||||||||||||||||||+|||+-- Put in $4
107    if (/([0-9.]*)\s*-\s*-\s*\[([^\]]*)\] "(\S+)\s+(\S+)/) {
108        # $3 -- The operation code
109        if ($3 ne "GET") {
110            next;
111        }
112        # Entry we are adding
113        my %new_entry = (
114                host => $1,
115                date => $2,
116                page => $4
117                    );
118        push(@hit_info, {%new_entry});
119    }
120    }
121    close IN_FILE;
122 }
123
124
125 #######################################################
126 # do_count -- Count the number of hits in the data.
127 #
128 # Returns an array reference.  Each element is a hash
129 # with the following keys:
130 #   page -- The page name
131 #   count -- Number of element in the page
```

continues

Listing 16.11 **Continued**

```
132  #######################################################
133  sub do_count()
134  {
135      # Count of the number of hits
136      #       key = page
137      #       value = count
138      my %counts = ();
139      foreach my $cur_hit (@hit_info) {
140          if (not defined($counts{$cur_hit->{page}})) {
141              $counts{$cur_hit->{page}} = 1;
142          } else {
143              $counts{$cur_hit->{page}}++;
144          }
145      }
146
147      my @stat_array = ();     # Array of statistics
148
149      # Loop through the entire count array
150      foreach my $cur_count (sort keys %counts) {
151          push(@stat_array, {
152                  page => $cur_count,
153                  count => $counts{$cur_count}
154                  });
155      }
156      return (\@stat_array);
157  }
158
159  1;
```

Computing Hit Counts

Now you can produce a report that shows how many times each page is hit. A sample report looks like

```
1493     /writing.long/cow.gif
1272     /vim-cook.html
1270     /
1151     /style/index.html
818      /style/styleTOC.pdf
751      /not/index.html
696      /style/c03.pdf
649      /style/c02.pdf
606      /style/c01.pdf
467      /robots.txt
443      /style/c07.pdf
414      /style/styleRULE.pdf
.....
```

Start by parsing the log files:

```
22 foreach my $file (@ARGV) {
23     read_info($file);
24 }
```

Next, compute the hit counts using the do_count function:

```
32 my $stat_array = do_count();
```

This returns

```
A reference to
    An array of
        Hashes containing
            key => page, value => name of the web page
            key => count, value => count of the number of hits
```

However, this array is in random order. You want it in hit order, so you need to sort it by hit count:

```
34 # The array sorted by highest first
35 my @sort_array = sort {$b->{count} <=> $a->{count};}  @$stat_array;
```

Finally, you can print the results:

```
37 foreach my $index (0..$#sort_array) {
38     print "$sort_array[$index]->{count}\t$sort_array[$index]->{page}\n";
39 }
```

The entire program is presented in Listing 16.12.

Listing 16.12 *web.pl*

```
 1 =pod
 2
 3 =head1 NAME
 4
 5 web.pl - Write out a list of the top web sites visited
 6
 7 =head1 SYNOPSIS
 8
 9     perl web.pl <log-file> [<log-file> ...]
10
11 =head1 DESCRIPTION
12
13 The I<web.pl> analyzes the log files and produces a list of
14 how many times each web page has been accessed.  The list
15 is sorted by number of hits.
16
17 =cut
18 use strict;
19 use warnings;
20 use web;
21
22 foreach my $file (@ARGV) {
```

continues

Listing 16.12   **Continued**

```
23      read_info($file);
24 }
25 # An array of the stats on a page
26 #
27 # Array of hashes
28 #    hash contains
29 #            page => <page name>
30 #            value => <number of hits>
31 #
32 my $stat_array = do_count();
33
34 # The array sorted by highest first
35 my @sort_array = sort {$b->{count} <=> $a->{count};}  @$stat_array;
36
37 foreach my $index (0..$#sort_array) {
38     print "$sort_array[$index]->{count}\t$sort_array[$index]->{page}\n";
39 }
```

Graphing the Results

Text is boring. People want pictures. You need some way of displaying your
results graphically. The solution is to use the GD::Graph set of modules from
CPAN. Figure 16.3 shows a typical graph.

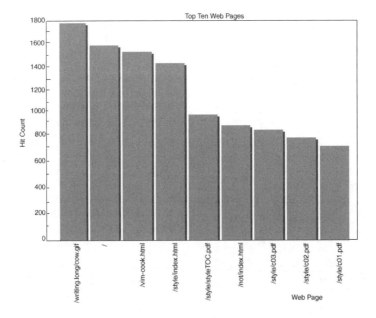

Figure 16.3   Web site hit graph.

The first step in creating a graph is getting the data ready. The `GD::Graph::bars` graph uses a two-dimensional array for its data. The first row of the array is the data for the X axis of the graph; in this case, it's the pages to be used.

The second row is the Y data—in this case, the page count.

You get the raw data using code similar to `web.pl`. In fact, that's where I stole it from:

```
40 # The stats from the logs
41 my $stat_array = do_count();
42
43 # The sorted version of static
44 my @sort_array = sort {$b->{count} <=> $a->{count};}  @$stat_array;
```

But then you need to limit yourself to the first 10 elements:

```
46 # Limit the number of elements in the limit
47 if ($#sort_array > LIMIT) {
48     @sort_array = @sort_array[0..LIMIT];
49 }
```

Now transform the `@sort_array` into a format used by `GD::Chart` (`@raw_data`). At the same time, you need to get the maximum value of the data and put it into `$max`:

```
51 my $max = 0;        # The largest number of hits
52
53 # The data for plotting
54 #    $raw_data[0] -- The page name
55 #    $raw_data[1] -- The counts
56 my @raw_data = ([], []);
57
58 # Build the data and at the same time
59 # compute the maximum
60 foreach my $cur_sort (@sort_array) {
61     push(@{$raw_data[0]}, $cur_sort->{page});
62     push(@{$raw_data[1]}, $cur_sort->{count});
63     if ($cur_sort->{count} > $max) {
64         $max = $cur_sort->{count};
65     }
66 }
```

To make the graph look nice, you need to round up `$max` to the next 100 boundary:

```
67 # Round the max up to the next 100
68 $max = int(($max + 100) / 100) * 100;
```

Now you can start making the graph. The first step is to create a new graph object. In this case, you are using a bar chart, and the resulting image is

800×600 pixels. The new function creates the blank canvas. Because this is a bar chart, you actually use the function `GD::Graph::bars->new()`:

```
70 # Create the graph
71 my $my_graph = GD::Graph::bars->new(800, 600);
```

Next, set the options for the graph. The `set` function sets a whole slew of options for the graph:

```
73 # Set the parameters
74 $my_graph->set(
75     x_label          => 'Web Page',
76     y_label          => 'Hit Count',
77
78     title            => 'Top Ten Web Pages',
79     y_max_value      => $max,
80     y_tick_number    => $max/100,
81     y_label_skip     => 2,
82
83     x_labels_vertical => 1,
84
85     # shadows
86     bar_spacing      => 8,
87     shadow_depth     => 4,
88     shadowclr        => 'dred',
89
90     transparent      => 0,
91 )
92 or warn $my_graph->error;
```

These options are

- **x_label**—The label for the X axis of the graph.
- **y_label**—The label for the Y axis of the graph.
- **title**—Title of the graph.
- **y_max_value**—The maximum value along the Y axis. The example rounds this up to make things look nice.
- **y_tick_number**—The number of ticks for the Y axis. In this case, it's one tick per 100 hits.
- **y_label_skip**—With this, you skip the label every other tick when you create the graph. In other words, although you have ticks at 100, 200, 300, 400, and 500, you only put labels on 200, 400, and so on.
- **x_labels_vertical**—Print the page names vertically. If you printed them horizontally, they would overwrite each other.
- **bar_spacking**—Number of pixels between bars.
- **shadow_depth**—The size of the shadow in pixels.

- **shadowclr**—The color for the shadow—in this case, dark red (dred). (Note: Color is abbreviated clr because the author uses British English and got tired of dealing with the color/colour problem.) For a complete list of colors, see the online document GD::Graph::colour.

- **transparent**—Is the background transparent? In this case, no.

Now that the options are out of the way, you can send the data to the graph. The plot function actually plots the data:

```
94 # Plot the data
95 $my_graph->plot(\@raw_data) or die $my_graph->error;
```

The final step is to write the output file. Use the png format for the graph. The GD package converts the canvas to a png image when you call the $my_graph->gd->png() function. All you have to do is open a file and write things out:

```
 97 # Send the data to the file
 98 open(OUT, ">top_web.png") or
 99     die "Cannot open top-web.png for write: $!";
100 binmode OUT;
101 print OUT $my_graph->gd->png();
102 close OUT;
```

The graphing program is shown in Listing 16.13.

Listing 16.13   *web-graph.pl*

```
 1 =pod
 2
 3 =head1 NAME
 4
 5 web-graph.pl - A program to produce a graph of the top ten web pages
 6 on your server
 7
 8 =head1 SYNOPSIS
 9
10     perl web-graph.pl <log-file> [<log-file> ...]
11
12 =head1 DESCRIPTION
13
14 The I<web-graph.pl> analyzes your web logs (from the Apache
15 web server) and create a graph (in the file I<top_web.png>).
16
17 =head1 FILES
18
19 =over 4
20
21 =item top_web.png
22
23 The file in which the graph is written.
```

continues

Listing 16.13   **Continued**

```
24
25 =back
26
27 =cut
28 use strict;
29 use warnings;
30 use GD::Graph::bars;
31 use web;
32
33 # Max number of items in the graph
34 use constant LIMIT => 9;
35
36 # Read each file in the list
37 foreach my $file (@ARGV) {
38     read_info($file);
39 }
40 # The stats from the logs
41 my $stat_array = do_count();
42
43 # The sorted version of static
44 my @sort_array = sort {$b->{count} <=> $a->{count};}  @$stat_array;
45
46 # Limit the number of elements in the limit
47 if ($#sort_array > LIMIT) {
48     @sort_array = @sort_array[0..LIMIT];
49 }
50
51 my $max = 0;        # The largest number of hits
52
53 # The data for plotting
54 #   $raw_data[0] -- The page name
55 #   $raw_data[1] -- The counts
56 my @raw_data = ([], []);
57
58 # Build the data and at the same time
59 # compute the maximum
60 foreach my $cur_sort (@sort_array) {
61     push(@{$raw_data[0]}, $cur_sort->{page});
62     push(@{$raw_data[1]}, $cur_sort->{count});
63     if ($cur_sort->{count} > $max) {
64         $max = $cur_sort->{count};
65     }
66 }
67 # Round the max up to the next 100
68 $max = int(($max + 100) / 100) * 100;
69
70 # Create the graph
71 my $my_graph = GD::Graph::bars->new(800, 600);
72
73 # Set the parameters
74 $my_graph->set(
```

```
75      x_label         => 'Web Page',
76      y_label         => 'Hit Count',
77
78      title           => 'Top Ten Web Pages',
79      y_max_value     => $max,
80      y_tick_number   => $max/100,
81      y_label_skip    => 2,
82
83      x_labels_vertical => 1,
84
85      # shadows
86      bar_spacing     => 8,
87      shadow_depth    => 4,
88      shadowclr       => 'dred',
89
90      transparent     => 0,
91  )
92  or warn $my_graph->error;
93
94  # Plot the data
95  $my_graph->plot(\@raw_data) or die $my_graph->error;
96
97  # Send the data to the file
98  open(OUT, ">top_web.png") or
99      die "Cannot open top-web.png for write: $!";
100 binmode OUT;
101 print OUT $my_graph->gd->png();
102 close OUT;
```

Dynamic Web Page Graphs

It would be nice to be able to access this graph from the web. Better still, it
would be nice to have the system produce to-the-second results. This can be
done using a simple CGI program that runs the graph routine and then displays the results:

```
1  #!/usr/local/bin/perl
2  use strict;
3  use warnings;
4
5  system("cd /home/httpd/html/web;/usr/local/bin/perl
       /home/httpd/cgi-bin/web-graph.pl /var/log/httpd/access*");
6
7  print <<EOF
8  Content-type: text/html
9
10 <HEAD><TITLE>Web Hits</TITLE></HEAD>
11 <BODY BGCOLOR="#FFFFFF">
12 <IMG SRC="/web/top_web.png">
13 EOF
```

One thing to remember about CGI scripts: you can't put data and programs in the same directory. In fact, with Apache, the default installation has one directory tree for web pages and another for CGI programs.

This is due to security. Anything in a CGI directory may be executed. If an outside user can write into this directory, he or she could easily break into the system.

Also remember that permissions are a significant problem when dealing with CGI scripts. Normally, CGI scripts are run as a special, limited access user. For this script to work, the following permissions must be in place:

- The "CGI user" must be able to read all the web server log files.
- The "CGI user" must be able to read and execute the script.
- The "CGI users" must have the ability to write to the file in the directory web-top/web/top_web.png (where web-top is the root directory for the web pages).

Notes on Web Page Counting

It takes about five seconds for the Perl script to go through all my web logs and produce a plot. This is a little long to wait for a web page. Also, I run a miniscule web site, so for any larger site, the wait would be unacceptable.

If you wanted to run this for a large site, performance would be an issue. There are many ways of doing this. One is to only update the graph periodically. Another is to cache the computed data and store it for later use. Subsequent runs of the program would need only to parse entries that were added since the cache was updated.

Or you could use the author's cop-out and say that this exercise is left to the reader.

Summary

Perl is a flexible and compact language. The examples in this chapter show how Perl can be used to quickly write useful and powerful programs with a small amount of code.

Now that you've seen how to slay a few dragons in this chapter, you're ready to go out into the real world and slay a few dragons of your own.
Ch. 16 Perl for C Programmers 1228x

Exercises

1. Create a web-based to-do list which allows the user to insert, delete, and check off items to do. (You can do a Tk version instead if you want to.)

2. Write a Perl script that creates a report listing the top 10 disk space users. (Parsing the output of the Linux/UNIX du command is the easiest way of doing this.)

   Add an exclude list to the program so you can exclude special users.

3. Create a program that reads the output of compilations and prints not only the error message, but also the line of the source file containing the error.

4. Write a Perl script to find all backup files that have not been modified in the last three days and move them to a recycle bin. (Linux/UNIX users can make up your own directory for this bin.)

   Have the script remove any files that have been in the recycle bin for more than 30 days.

5. You know enough Perl to solve some of your own problems. So solve some of them.

Resources

Modules

- **Digest::MD5**—Creates an MD5 checksum for a file (or other data).
- **File::Basename**—Parses filenames into their components.
- **File::Find**—Finds files in a directory tree.
- **File::Spec::Functions**—Filename manipulation functions.
- **GD::Graph**—Produces a variety of graphs. (This single CPAN module installs a number of modules in your Perl library.)
- **GD::Graph3d**—Produces 3D graphs. (Again, this installs a set of modules.)
- **HTML::SimpleLinkExtor**—Extracts links from web pages.
- **LWP::Simple**—Package to grab web pages from the net.

- **POSIX**—Posix functions such as getcwd (gets current directory).
- **Storable**—Loads and stores complex data.
- **Tk**—The interface to the Tk GUI package.

Programs

- **find2perl**—Turns find commands into Perl programs.

17

Creating Modules

As you have seen, a main feature of Perl is its extensive module library. Modules are available for just about everything. But there are some things you just can't find a module for. In that case, Perl provides you the tools to write your own.

Note that the examples used in this chapter have been generated and tested on a Linux system. They should work the same way on any UNIX system. Microsoft Window, users will notice minor differences in the generation process. Also note that the module described here is Linux/UNIX operating system dependent.

The Module Creation Process

Perl provides the module creator a set of tools to make his life easier. The main one is called h2xs. This is a program that translates C header files (h files) into Perl external subroutine specifications (xs files).

In C, you use a header file to define an interface to the module. A Perl module is no different; it starts with a C header file.

This example defines a function that manipulates a magnetic tape drive. In other words, it allows the user to rewind the tape, forward space files, and so on.

The header appears in Listing 17.1.

Listing 17.1 *mt_op.h*

```
/* Magnetic Tape operations [Not all operations supported by all drivers]: */
#define MTRESET   0    /* +reset drive in case of problems */
#define MTFSF     1    /* forward space over FileMark,
                        * position at first record of next file
                        */
#define MTBSF     2    /* backward space FileMark (position before FM) */
#define MTFSR     3    /* forward space record */
#define MTBSR     4    /* backward space record */
#define MTWEOF    5    /* write an end-of-file record (mark) */
#define MTREW     6    /* rewind */
#define MTOFFL    7    /* rewind and put the drive offline (eject?) */
#define MTRETEN   9    /* retension tape */
#define MTBSFM    10   /* +backward space FileMark, position at FM */
#define MTFSFM    11   /* +forward space FileMark, position at FM */
#define MTEOM     12   /* goto end of recorded media (for appending files).
                        * MTEOM positions after the last FM, ready for
                        * appending another file.
                        */
#define MTERASE 13     /* erase tape -- be careful! */

/*
 * Perform an operation on the file who's descriptor
 * is fd.  The operation is one of the constants listed
 * above (i.e. MTFSF) and the count is the number of items
 * to space.  (Count is not used on all operations)
 */
int mt_op(const int fd, const int op, const int count);
```

With this file, you can start to create the module. The first step is to create the prototype files using the command

```
$ h2xs -An mt_op
Writing mt_op/mt_op.pm
Writing mt_op/mt_op.xs
Writing mt_op/Makefile.PL
Writing mt_op/README
Writing mt_op/test.pl
Writing mt_op/Changes
Writing mt_op/MANIFEST
```

(Be careful with the order of the flags. -An works; -nA does not.)

The program h2xs is the Perl utility used to create modules from header files. The -n flag tells the program that this program is called mt_op. The -A flag tells Perl to omit the autoloader flag. (This makes things simpler, and simple is good for now.)

The program creates a directory called `mt_op` (the name of the module) and a number of files in it. These are

- **`mt_op.pm`**—The Perl interface to the module. This file contains the code that actually loads the C functions.

- **`mt_op.xs`**—The external subroutine specification. This code is a special sort of half Perl, half C language used to create the interface between the Perl and C code.

- **`Makefile.PL`**—The Perl version of the `Makefile`. Actually, the Perl script that generates the `Makefile`.

- **`README`**—A prototype `README` file. (For you to edit and fill in.)

- **`test.pl`**—A test script. (You are encouraged to add your own tests to this script.)

- **`Changes`**—A change history.

- **`MANIFEST`**—A list of files included in this module.

If you're interested, you can examine these files now, but the real fun is about to begin. You need to copy the header file into the `mt_op` directory and run `h2xs` again. But before you start, first install the module `C::Scan` if you have not already done so. Then you can copy the header file and run `h2xs` again (from the same directory as the previous `h2xs` command). For example:

```
$ cp mt_op.h mt_op
$ h2xs -OAxn mt_op mt_op.h
Overwriting existing mt_op!!!
Scanning typemaps...
Scanning mt_op.h for functions...
Scanning mt_op.h for typedefs...
Writing mt_op/mt_op.pm
Writing mt_op/mt_op.xs
Writing mt_op/typemap
Writing mt_op/Makefile.PL
Writing mt_op/README
Writing mt_op/test.pl
Writing mt_op/Changes
Writing mt_op/MANIFEST
```

The preceding code uses a few new flags. The `-O` flag tells `h2xs` to overwrite existing files. The `-x` indicator tells the program to scan the header files listed on the command line (`mt_op.h`) for function prototype and constants and to generate code based on what it finds there.

You may wonder why you couldn't run the program like this in the first place. Why run it twice?

The reason is that h2xs scans the header files only if they are in the module's directory. The first run creates the directory; the second does the work. (I don't know why things are this way, but they are.)

Filling Out the Files

The key file that's been generated is called mt_op.xs. It will be translated by the xsubpp program into a C module. The current version is somewhat incomplete, but you can see it in Listing 17.2.

Listing 17.2 *mt_op.xs* **(Unmodified)**

```
#include "EXTERN.h"
#include "perl.h"
#include "XSUB.h"

#include <mt_op.h>


MODULE = mt_op        PACKAGE = mt_op


int
mt_op(fd, op, count)
    int     fd
    int     op
    int     count
```

The file starts with a number of include directives. These are actually C statements. In fact, everything up to the MODULE line is C code and will be copied verbatim into the C file. Edit this section and remove the line

```
#include <mt_op.h>
```

You can't use this header file because it contains symbols that conflict with the official system header file.

You also need to add this line:

```
#include <sys/mtio.h>
```

This brings in the official system file.

The MODULE and PACKAGE definitions identify the name of the module. In this case, it's mt_op. (Normally, the module and package names are the same.)

Tell Perl that you want to generate prototypes for this module. To do that, you need to add the following line after the MODULE directive:

```
PROTOTYPES: ENABLE
```

This is followed by the definitions of the functions in the module. In this case, the mt_op function definition.

Spacing and line breaks are important in this file. The return type must begin in column 1 and be on a line by itself. The rest of the prototype follows.

Now you need to fill in the rest of the function. The C version of the function looks like this:

```
int mt_op(int fd, int op, int count)
{
    struct mt_op cmd;
    cmd.mt_op = op;
    cmd.mt_count = count;
    return (ioctl(fd, MTIOCTOP, &cmd));
}
```

The Perl XS version looks like the following:

```
int
mt_op(fd, op, count)
    int     fd
    int     op
    int     count

    PREINIT:
        struct mtop arg;

    CODE:
    cmd.mt_op = op;
    cmd.mt_count = count;
    RETVAL = ioctl(fd, MTIOCTOP, &cmd));
    OUTPUT:
        RETVAL
```

Variables are declared in the PREINIT section. (They have to be put in their own section because of what goes on during the translation process.)

The code goes in a CODE section. (That's simple enough.) The only funny thing about this is the special variable RETVAL. This is used to indicate the value returned from the function.

At the end is the OUTPUT section, which tells Perl what's actually output from the function. Listing 17.3 shows the modified mod_mt.xs file.

Listing 17.3   *mod_mt.xs* (**Modified**)

```
#include "EXTERN.h"
#include "perl.h"
#include "XSUB.h"

#include <sys/mtio.h>
```

continues

Listing 17.3 **Continued**

```
MODULE = mt_op          PACKAGE = mt_op

PROTOTYPES: ENABLE


int
mt_op(fd, op, count)
    int     fd
    int     op
    int     count

    PREINIT:
        struct mtop arg;

    CODE:
    arg.mt_op = op;
    arg.mt_count = count;
        RETVAL = ioctl(fd, op, count);
    OUTPUT:
        RETVAL
```

You also need to modify the POD section of the `mt_op.pm` file. Perl's `h2xs` program puts in a template for the documentation, but you'll need to make it real. You'll also need to modify the `README` file as well.

The `Makefile.PL` file needs to be edited to include any special compilation flags or libraries needed to build the module. In this case, you are including any of them, so there's no need to edit the file.

Finally, the `typemap` file is used by Perl to do automatic type conversions. This feature is not used in this example program, so delete the entries in the `typemap` file.

Now that everything is ready, you can install and test the file.

Building the Module

In Chapter 1, "Exploring Perl," you learned how to build, test, and install modules. This module is no different. It starts with the command

```
$ perl Makefile.PL
Checking if your kit is complete...
Looks good
Writing Makefile for mt_op
```

Note that if you are installing private modules on UNIX/Linux, make sure that you include the `"PREFIX="` option. (See Chapter 1 for more details.)

This is followed by the `make` command, which generates the code. (If you are using Microsoft's Visual C++, the command is `nmake`.) For example:

```
$ make
cp mt_op.pm blib/lib/mt_op.pm
/usr/bin/perl -I/usr/lib/perl5/5.6.1/i586-linux -I/usr/lib/perl5/5.6.1
/usr/lib/perl5/5.6.1/ExtUtils/xsubpp  -typemap
/usr/lib/perl5/5.6.1/ExtUtils/typemap -typemap typemap mt_op.xs >
mt_op.xsc && mv mt_op.xsc mt_op.c
cc -c -I. -DDEBUGGING -fno-strict-aliasing -I/usr/local/include
-D_LARGEFILE_SOURCE -D_FILE_OFFSET_BITS=64 -g   -DVERSION=\"0.01\"
-DXS_VERSION=\"0.01\" -fpic -I/usr/lib/perl5/5.6.1/i586-linux/CORE
mt_op.c
Running Mkbootstrap for mt_op ()
chmod 644 mt_op.bs
rm -f blib/arch/auto/mt_op/mt_op.so
LD_RUN_PATH="" cc  -shared -L/usr/local/lib mt_op.o  -o
blib/arch/auto/mt_op/mt_op.so
chmod 755 blib/arch/auto/mt_op/mt_op.so
cp mt_op.bs blib/arch/auto/mt_op/mt_op.bs
chmod 644 blib/arch/auto/mt_op/mt_op.bs
Manifying blib/man3/mt_op.3
```

Now that the module is created, you should test it. The `test.pl` script contains the test for this module. By default, the `h2xs` program generates a single test that checks to see whether the module compiles and the library loads. You can add additional tests to this, but for now go with the default.

The command to run the tests is `make test`:

```
$ make test
PERL_DL_NONLAZY=1 /usr/bin/perl -Iblib/arch -Iblib/lib
-I/usr/lib/perl5/5.6.1/i586-linux -I/usr/lib/perl5/5.6.1 test.pl
1..1
ok 1
```

The text executed correctly. You can now install the module for real using the command

```
$ make install
Installing /usr/lib/perl5/site_perl/5.6.1/i586-linux/auto/mt_op/mt_op.so
Installing /usr/lib/perl5/site_perl/5.6.1/i586-linux/auto/mt_op/mt_op.bs
Files found in blib/arch: installing files in blib/lib into architecture
dependent library tree
Installing /usr/lib/perl5/site_perl/5.6.1/i586-linux/mt_op.pm
Installing /usr/man/man3/mt_op.3
Writing /usr/lib/perl5/site_perl/5.6.1/i586-linux/auto/mt_op/.packlist
Appending installation info to /usr/lib/perl5/5.6.1/i586-linux/perllocal.pod
```

The module is now officially installed and ready for use.

Using the Autoloader

It is possible to generate code with the autoload feature turned on by omitting the -A flag when running h2xs.

By default, the module contains just the function mt_op. If you turn on the autoload feature, it will contain not only the function but all the constant definitions as well (MTREW, MTFSF, and so on).

The code generated also will be more complex.

Module Creation Cookbook

The steps to create a simple module can be summarized as follows:

1. Run h2xs to create the module directory:

```
h2xs -n mt_op
```

2. Copy the header files into the directory you just created:

```
cp mt_op.h mt_op
```

3. Run h2xs again, to create the prototype module files:

```
h2xs -Oxn mt_op mt_op.h
```

4. If you require anything special in your build environment, edit the file Makefile.PL.

5. Edit the README file and put in proper documentation on how to build and install the module.

6. Edit the module file (.pm file) so that the POD section documents your module.

7. Edit the module file (.pm file) and put the names of the functions you want to export by default in the @EXPORT list.

8. Edit the external subroutine (.xs file) and put in your code.

9. Edit the typemap file. (For most programs, this means removing all the entries in this file.)

10. Create the Makefile with the command

```
perl Makefile.PL
```

11. Compile the program with the command

```
make
```

12. Run the basic self-test with the command

```
make test
```

13. Edit the `test.pl` file and add any additional tests you can.

14. Run the tests again

```
make test
```

15. Install the module:

```
make install
```

As part of this example, the files README, mt_mod.pm, and typemap were modified. The modified versions of the files appear in Listings 17.4, 17.5, 17.6, and 17.7.

Listing 17.4 ***README***

```
mt_mod version 0.01
===================

This program allows the caller to manipulate a magnetic tape
similar to what the "mt" command does.

INSTALLATION

To install this module type the following:

   perl Makefile.PL
   make
   make test
   make install

DEPENDENCIES

This module requires the standard include file <sys/mtio.h>


COPYRIGHT AND LICENCE

Copyrighted under the GPL.

Copyright (C) 2002 Steve Oualline
```

Listing 17.5 ***mt_mod.xs***

```
#include "EXTERN.h"
#include "perl.h"
#include "XSUB.h"

#include <sys/mtio.h>
```

continues

Listing 17.5 **Continued**

```
MODULE = mt_mod          PACKAGE = mt_mod

PROTOTYPES: ENABLE


int
mt_op(fd, op, count)
    int     fd
    int     op
    int     count

    PREINIT:
        struct mtop arg;

    CODE:
    arg.mt_op = op;
    arg.mt_count = count;
        RETVAL = ioctl(fd, op, count);
    OUTPUT:
        RETVAL
```

Listing 17.6 *mt_op.pm*

```
package mt_op;

use 5.006;
use strict;
use warnings;

require Exporter;
require DynaLoader;

our @ISA = qw(Exporter DynaLoader);

# Items to export into callers namespace by default. Note: do not export
# names by default without a very good reason. Use EXPORT_OK instead.
# Do not simply export all your public functions/methods/constants.

# This allows declaration    use mt_op ':all';
# If you do not need this, moving things directly into @EXPORT or @EXPORT_OK
# will save memory.
our %EXPORT_TAGS = ( 'all' => [ qw(
    mt_op
) ] );

our @EXPORT_OK = ( @{ $EXPORT_TAGS{'all'} } );

our @EXPORT = qw(
mt_op
```

```
);
our $VERSION = '0.01';

bootstrap mt_op $VERSION;

# Preloaded methods go here.

1;
__END__
# Below is stub documentation for your module. You better edit it!

=head1 NAME

mt_mod - Perl extension for handling magnetic tapes

=head1 SYNOPSIS

  use mt_mod;
  my $status = mt_op($fd, $op, $count);

=head1 DESCRIPTION

The mt_op function allows you to perform operations such as rewind,
forward space file, and others on a magnetic tape.  This is the Perl
version of the I<mt> command.   (See I<E<lt>sys/mtio.hE<gt>> for a
list of operation codes.)

=head2 EXPORT

  mt_op

=head2 Exportable functions

  int mt_op(const int fd, const int op, const int count)

=head1 AUTHOR

Steve Oualline

=head1 SEE ALSO

mt(1)

=cut
```

Listing 17.7 *typemap*

```
# Next line removed
#int                         T_PTROBJ
```

Debugging a Module

Because of the way they are constructed, modules are difficult to debug. The problem is that you have to debug Perl, but the module is not part of the Perl program proper. Instead, it's loaded during the program run.

The first step to debugging a module is to create a debuggable version of Perl. By default, when you build and install Perl, the system builds an optimized version with no debugging information.

To build a debug version of the program, you'll have to rebuild it.

This is done at configuration time. The first step in building the Perl program from source is to run the Configure command. It asks you for the compiler optimizing/debugger flag to be used to create the program. The default (-O2) is good for a production version of the program. For a debug version, you'll need to answer this question flag -g (enable debug).

By default, perl5 compiles with the -O flag to use the optimizer. Alternatively, you might want to use the symbolic debugger, which uses the -g flag (on traditional UNIX systems). To use neither flag, specify the word "none". Either flag can be specified here:

```
What optimizer/debugger flag should be used? [-O2] -g
```

The next question the configuration tool asks is for any additional compilation flags. Because you answered -g in the previous step, the flag -DDEBUGGING will be added to the compiler flags. (Leave this option alone.) The configuration tool continues to run:

```
Checking if your compiler accepts -fno-strict-aliasing
Yes, it does.

Your C compiler may want other flags.  For this question you should include
-I/whatever and -DWHATEVER flags and any other flags used by the C compiler,
but you should NOT include libraries or ld flags like -lwhatever.  If you
want perl5 to honor its debug switch, you should include -DDEBUGGING here.
Your C compiler might also need additional flags, such as -D_POSIX_SOURCE.

To use no flags, specify the word "none".

Any additional cc flags?
[-DDEBUGGING -fno-strict-aliasing -I/usr/local/include]
```

After you've compiled and built the Perl program, you can use it for debugging your modules.

Running the Debugger

To debug the module, you must first run the debugger on Perl. The example in this chapter uses the gdb debugger on Linux. This section shows you how to use this debugger to debug the function.

The first step is to figure out the name of the function. Although it is called mt_op, the Perl-to-C translation program (xsubpp) mangles the name.

Inspect the C code to see what xsubpp generates. In this case, the function declaration is

```
#line 18 "mt_op.c"
XS(XS_mt_op_mt_op)
{
    dXSARGS;
```

From this, you can see that the name of the function generated is XS_mt_op_mt_op. Now that you know what you are debugging, you can start the debugging.

The first thing to do is to start the debugger on the Perl program:

```
$ gdb /home/oualline/local/bin/perl

GNU gdb 5.0
Copyright 2000 Free Software Foundation, Inc.
GDB is free software, covered by the GNU General Public License, and you are
welcome to change it and/or distribute copies of it under certain conditions.
Type "show copying" to see the conditions.
There is absolutely no warranty for GDB.  Type "show warranty" for details.
This GDB was configured as "i586-pc-linux-gnu"...
```

At this point, the module is not loaded, so putting in the breakpoint takes several steps. First, set a breakpoint in the library function that loads the dynamic library (dlopen):

```
(gdb) break dlopen
Breakpoint 1 at 0x805a098
```

Next, run the program. The argument is the name of the script you are running (in this case mk-test.pl):

```
(gdb) run mt-test.pl
Starting program: /home/oualline/local/bin/perl mt-test.pl

Breakpoint 1, 0x805a098 in dlopen ()
```

You've hit the breakpoint. Go up one level (to the function in the Perl program that called the dlopen function) and see what module is being loaded:

```
(gdb) up
#1  0x805a746 in XS_DynaLoader_dl_load_file (cv=0x8168d5c) at
DynaLoader.xs:187
warning: Source file is more recent than executable.
```

```
187        RETVAL = dlopen(filename, mode) ;
(gdb) print filename
$1 = 0x8155288 "/home/oualline/local/lib/perl5/5.6.1/
i586-linux/auto/IO/IO.so"
```

This is not the module you want, so continue as follows:

```
(gdb) cont
Continuing.

Breakpoint 1, 0x805a098 in dlopen ()
```

You've hit the dlopen again, so go up a level and check the filename:

```
(gdb) up
#1  0x805a746 in XS_DynaLoader_dl_load_file (cv=0x8168d5c) at
DynaLoader.xs:187
187        RETVAL = dlopen(filename, mode) ;
(gdb) print filename
$2 = 0x8155248 "/home/oualline/local/lib/perl5/5.6.1/
i586-linux/auto/Fcntl/Fcntl.so"
```

This is still not the module you want, so go on:

```
(gdb) cont
Continuing.

Breakpoint 1, 0x805a098 in dlopen ()
(gdb) up
#1  0x805a746 in XS_DynaLoader_dl_load_file (cv=0x8168d5c) at
DynaLoader.xs:187
187        RETVAL = dlopen(filename, mode) ;
(gdb) print filename
$3 = 0x8155248 "/home/oualline/local/lib/perl5/5.6.1/i586-
linux/auto/Socket/Socket.so"
```

Still not your module. Continue as follows:

```
(gdb) cont
Continuing.

Breakpoint 1, 0x805a098 in dlopen ()
(gdb) up
#1  0x805a746 in XS_DynaLoader_dl_load_file (cv=0x8168d5c) at
DynaLoader.xs:187
187        RETVAL = dlopen(filename, mode) ;
(gdb) print filename
$4 = 0x82c8f88 "/home/oualline/local/lib/perl5/site_perl/5.6.1/
i586-linux/auto/mt_op/mt_op.so"
```

You've finally found the dlopen call that loads the module. You need to set a breakpoint just after the library is loaded. First, use the list command to display the code around the dlopen call:

```
(gdb) list
182         mode |= RTLD_GLOBAL;
183     #else
184         Perl_warn(aTHX_ "Can't make loaded symbols global on
this platform while loading %s",filename);
185     #endif
186         DLDEBUG(1,PerlIO_printf(Perl_debug_log,
"dl_load_file(%s,%x):\n", filename,flags));
187         RETVAL = dlopen(filename, mode) ;
188         DLDEBUG(2,PerlIO_printf(Perl_debug_log, " libref=%lx\n",
(unsigned long) RETVAL));
189         ST(0) = sv_newmortal() ;
190         if (RETVAL == NULL)
191         SaveError(aTHX_ "%s",dlerror()) ;
```

The dlopen call occurs on line 187, so put a breakpoint on the next line, which is line 188:

```
(gdb) break 188
Breakpoint 2 at 0x805a74e: file DynaLoader.xs, line 188.
```

Continue on to the next breakpoint:

```
(gdb) cont
Continuing.

Breakpoint 2, XS_DynaLoader_dl_load_file (cv=0x8168d5c) at DynaLoader.xs:188
188         DLDEBUG(2,PerlIO_printf(Perl_debug_log, " libref=%lx\n",
(unsigned long) RETVAL));
```

At this point, the module is loaded. Finally, you are at a point that allows you to set a breakpoint in the module. Put a breakpoint in the main function and continue, as shown here:

```
(gdb) break XS_mt_op_mt_op
Breakpoint 3 at 0x4017a9a5: file mt_op.c, line 20.
(gdb) cont
Continuing.

Breakpoint 3, XS_mt_op_mt_op (cv=0x82935bc) at mt_op.c:20
20          dXSARGS;
```

You've now stopped at the first line of the module. This means that you can use the normal debugging commands to examine the program. This includes listing the source, single-stepping, and examining variables:

```
(gdb) list
15
16
17      #line 18 "mt_op.c"
18      XS(XS_mt_op_mt_op)
19      {
```

```
20          dXSARGS;
21          if (items != 3)
22          Perl_croak(aTHX_ "Usage: mt_op::mt_op(fd, op, count)");
23          {
24          int    fd = (int)SvIV(ST(0));
(gdb) n
21          if (items != 3)
(gdb) print items
$6 = 3
```

Although you took the long way round, you finally found the way to your module. From here, it's a simple matter of debugging.

Summary

As I noted in the beginning, one of the great things about Perl is its extensive module library. You have now seen why the library is so extensive. It is not that difficult to create your own modules. As we saw, Perl provides all the tools you need to create them. You should be able do so now without any great difficulty.

Exercises

1. Write a module that generates a frequency count of the letters in a string (number of A's, B's, C's, and so on). The function should return a 256-element array whose index is the character number and whose elements are the number of times that character appears in the string.

2. Write a module that computes a frequency count of the pairs of letters in a string. Because returning a 256×256 element array is difficult in Perl, you'll have to create some access functions so that the application can query the counts after you compute them.

3. Create a module to extract any number of bits from a scalar starting at any offset. For example, the function may be asked to return 5 bits in the string starting at bit index 27.

4. Write a module that gives a Perl program direct access to the I/O operations (in and out on the PC class machines).

5. Create a module that allows reading and writing of random bytes in a file. In other words, you can tell this module, "change byte 56 of the file to the letter 'Q'."

Resources

Online Documentation

- **perldoc perlxs**—Reference work for the external subroutine (xs) file specification.
- **perldoc perlxstut**—Tutorial on creating modules.

Programs

- **h2xs**—The program that translates C header files into Perl external subroutine (xs) files.

Modules

- **Extutils::MakeMaker**—Module used by Makefile.PL to generate the real Makefile.
- **C::Scan**—Module used by h2xs to parse the C header file.
- **DynaLoader**—Module to automatically load dynamic libraries.
- **Autoloader**—Module that automatically loads functions. In particular, it handles the calling of dynaloader to load functions in shared libraries.

II

Appendixes

A

Installing Perl

This appendix describes how to install Perl on your system. Before you install it, however, you may need to get a copy. The main Perl repository (http://cpan.perl.org) contains links to the source code for Linux and UNIX systems. For Microsoft Windows binaries, check out http://www.activestate.com.

Installing Perl on Linux

Almost all Linux distributions come with Perl. If it's not already installed, you can use your package manager or whatever installation program your system comes with to install Perl and all its related packages.

Because each distribution is different, a complete discussion of package installation is beyond the scope of this book.

Installing Perl on UNIX or Linux from Source Code

If your system does not have Perl or if your Perl is out-of-date, you can install it from the source code. You can get a copy of the source code from `http://cpan.perl.org`.

This example shows how to download version 5.6.1 of Perl.

During the install process, you will be asked many questions. The default answers work for almost all of them. The questions you have to worry about are

- The location where you want Perl installed
- Whether you want to perform `setuid` emulation

Installation Directory

The installation directory is the name of the directory in which Perl installs the Perl program and related files. Say that you selected `/home/oualline/local` as your installation directory. The following directories are created during the installation process:

`/home/oualline/local/bin`—The programs such as "perl"

`/home/oualline/local/lib`—The modules

`/home/oualline/local/man`—Man format documentation files

setuid Emulation

A `setuid` program is one that runs under the user ID of the owner of the file rather than the user ID of the person running the program.

Many UNIX systems do not allow you to have `setuid` scripts such as Perl programs because they are not secure. Perl has a way around this problem, however. The solution, called *setuid emulation*, is to create a program that makes it look like you have secure `setuid` scripts.

The method Perl uses is to create a helper program called `suidperl`. However, to install this program, you'll need to be root.

> **Note**
>
> If you're doing CGI programming (for web forms), you'll probably want to install a setuid version of Perl. The web server normally runs CGI programs using a special username (such as "nobody"). If you want your CGI programs to run as if they were started by you, you'll need to make them setuid programs.

Step-by-Step Installation

This section goes through the installation process step-by-step.

The first step is to unpack the binary. To do this, use the `zcat` and `tar` commands (you must have the GNU version of `zcat` to unpack the `tar` ball; if this program has not been installed yet, you can get one from `http://www.gzip.org`). For example:

```
$ zcat perl-5.6.1.tar.gz ¦ tar xf -
```

Next, jump into the directory you just created and run the `Configure` command:

```
$ cd perl-5.6.1
$ ./Configure
```

The `Configure` command asks several questions concerning the operating system and environment you are using. Unless you are an expert doing an installation on an unusual system, you'll want to just accept the defaults. After running the command you would see something similar to the output shown below:

```
$ ./Configure

Beginning of configuration questions for perl5.

Checking echo to see how to suppress newlines...
...using -n.
The star should be here-->*

First let's make sure your kit is complete.  Checking...
Looks good...

........

First time through, eh?  I have some defaults handy for some systems
that need some extra help getting the Configure answers right:

3b1          dynix         isc          nonstopux     stellar
aix          dynixptx      isc_2        openbsd       sunos_4_0
altos486     epix          linux        opus          sunos_4_1
amigaos      esix4         lynxos       os2           svr4
apollo       fps           machten      os390         svr5
aux_3        freebsd       machten_2    posix-bc      ti1500
beos         genix         mint         powerux       titanos
bsdos        gnu           mips         qnx           ultrix_4
convexos     greenhills    mpc          rhapsody      umips
cxux         hpux          mpeix        sco           unicos
cygwin       i386          ncr_tower    sco_2_3_0     unicosmk
darwin       irix_4        netbsd       sco_2_3_1     unisysdynix
dcosx        irix_5        newsos4      sco_2_3_2     utekv
dec_osf      irix_6        next_3       sco_2_3_3     uts
```

```
dgux          irix_6_0        next_3_0       sco_2_3_4      uwin
dos_djgpp     irix_6_1        next_4         solaris_2      vmesa

You may give one or more space-separated answers,
➥or "none" if appropriate.
A well-behaved OS will have no hints,
➥so answering "none" or just "Policy"
is a good thing.  DO NOT give a wrong version or a wrong OS.

Which of these apply, if any? [linux]

...
```

Now you have reached the first significant question, the installation prefix. This is the top directory in which Perl installs all its files. This example installs them in ~oualline/local. That means that the `perl` command itself will be installed in /home/oualline/local/bin. For example:

```
By default, perl5 will be installed in /usr/local/bin, manual pages
under /usr/local/man, etc..., i.e. with /usr/local as prefix for all
installation directories. Typically
➥this is something like /usr/local.
If you wish to have binaries under /usr/bin but other parts of the
installation under /usr/local, that's ok: you will be prompted
separately for each of the installation directories, the prefix being
only used to set the defaults.

Installation prefix to use? (~name ok) [/usr/local] ~oualline/local
(That expands to /home/oualline/local on this system.)

...
```

Next the configuration command asks about secure `setuid` scripts. The system should know which systems are secure and which are not, but you are allowed to override the setting.

In this example, the configuration program tells you that it thinks that operating system is not secure (it is not) and then asks whether you want to do secure emulation. In this case, you don't, so accept the default answer (no).

If you answered yes, you will have to change to the root user before doing the last command:

```
make install
```

The following code shows what happens when the Perl installation process performs its `setuid` test (on an insecure Linux system).

```
First let's decide if your kernel supports secure setuid #! scripts.
(If setuid #! scripts would be secure but have been disabled anyway,
don't say that they are secure if asked.)
```

```
If you are not sure if they are secure, I can check but I'll need a
username and password different from the one you are using right now.
If you don't have such a username or don't want me to test, simply
enter 'none'.

Other username to test security of setuid scripts with? [none]
Well, the recommended value is *not* secure.
Does your kernel have *secure* setuid scripts? [n]

Some systems have disabled setuid scripts, especially systems where
setuid scripts cannot be secure.
On systems where setuid scripts have
been disabled, the setuid/setgid bits on scripts are currently
useless.  It is possible for perl5 to detect those bits and emulate
setuid/setgid in a secure fashion.  This emulation will only work if
setuid scripts have been disabled in your kernel.

Do you want to do setuid/setgid emulation? [n]

...
```

The system then does a *dependency check*. This is a precompilation step needed to make sure that the program compiles correctly. The dependency check looks like this:

```
Finding dependencies for util.o.
Finding dependencies for walk.o.
make[2]: Entering directory
`/mnt/sabina/sdo/tools/perl/perl-5.6.1/x2p'
echo Makefile.SH cflags.SH | tr ' ' '\n' >.shlist
make[2]: Leaving directory
`/mnt/sabina/sdo/tools/perl/perl-5.6.1/x2p'
Updating makefile...
make[1]: Leaving directory
`/mnt/sabina/sdo/tools/perl/perl-5.6.1/x2p'
Now you must run 'make'.

If you compile perl5 on a different
machine or from a different object
directory, copy the Policy.sh file from this object directory to the
new one before you run Configure -- this will help you with most of
the policy defaults.
```

After the configuration step is complete, run the make command to create the software. (And take a long break.)

```
$ make

`sh  cflags libperl.a miniperlmain.o`  miniperlmain.c
        CCCMD =  cc -DPERL_CORE -c -fno-strict-aliasing
```

```
→-I/usr/local/include -D_LARGEFILE_SOURCE
→-D_FILE_OFFSET_BITS=64 -O2
`sh  cflags libperl.a perl.o`  perl.c
    CCCMD =  cc -DPERL_CORE -c -fno-strict-aliasing
→-I/usr/local/include -D_LARGEFILE_SOURCE
→-D_FILE_OFFSET_BITS=64 -O2

...

    Everything is up to date. 'make test' to run test suite.
```

At this point, the system suggests that you do a make test to test the system. It doesn't hurt to do this, but if you trust things, you can go directly to the final step and do a make install.

Note that if you are doing setuid emulation, you will need to become root before doing a make install:

```
$ make install

make install.perl install.man STRIPFLAGS=
make[1]: Entering directory `/mnt/sabina/sdo/tools/perl/perl-5.6.1'
    AutoSplitting perl library
./miniperl -Ilib -e 'use AutoSplit; \
autosplit_lib_modules(@ARGV)' lib/*.pm lib/*/*.pm

...

Warning: perl appears in your path in the
→following locations beyond where
we just installed it:
    /usr/bin/perl

...

./perl installman
WARNING: You've never run 'make test'!!!  (Installing anyway.)
  /home/sdo/local/man/man1/perl.1
  /home/sdo/local/man/man1/perl5004delta.1
  /home/sdo/local/man/man1/perl5005delta.1
  /home/sdo/local/man/man1/pstruct.1
  /home/sdo/local/man/man1/xsubpp.1
make[1]: Leaving directory `/mnt/sabina/sdo/tools/perl/perl-5.6.1'
```

At this point, the installation is complete.

UNIX/Linux Installation Quick Reference

Here are the steps you need to perform to do a Perl compilation and installation:

```
$ zcat perl-5.6.1.tar.gz ¦ tar xf -
$ cd perl-5.6.1
$ ./Configure
$ make
$ make tests
$ make install
```

Installing Perl on Microsoft Windows

The people at ActiveState have a precompiled Perl binary that they make available for free. You can get it at `http://www.activestate.com`. (Select Downloads and then select ActivePerl to get to the download screen.)

You may need to download some tools or service packages before you can install ActivePerl. Check the initial download screen for information.

To install the program, download the file and save it to disk. Then from the file browser, double-click on the file, and the installation process begins.

The system asks you a number of questions. The default answer works on most systems.

Note that the system modifies your default path. To get this new path, you'll have to close down any MS-DOS Prompt windows that were open during the installation and start them up again.

B

Turning Perl Scripts into Commands

T HIS APPENDIX TELLS YOU HOW TO turn a Perl script that you execute with the command

```
$ perl script.pl
```

into a command that you can execute directly:

```
$ script
```

There are several methods for doing this depending on what computer you are using and how Perl is installed on it.

The UNIX/Linux Magic String

One way of changing a Perl script into a UNIX or Linux command is to make the first line of the script a "*magic string*," which tells the operating system that this is a Perl script.

For example, if your `perl` executable is located in `/usr/local/bin`, you turn your script into a program by putting the line

```
#!/usr/local/bin/perl
```

at the top of your program. (It must be the first line and must not be preceded by any comments.)

You then need to tell the system that this is an executable program by setting the execute bit for the owner, owner's group, and all other people:

```
$ chmod a+x script.pl
```

Now you can execute the script directly:

```
$ script.pl
```

You might want to rename your file from `script.pl` to `script` to be consistent with the standard UNIX naming convention as well. For example:

```
$ mv script.pl script
```

Note that if your Perl interpreter requires any flags, such as `-I` (specify module directory) or `-T` (turn on security checks), they can be included on the top line as well:

```
#!/usr/local/bin/perl -T -I/home/oualline/local/lib
```

The advantages to doing things this way include

- Simple
- Works for `setuid` scripts

The disadvantage is:

- Nonportable

It is nonportable because the exact path to the `perl` command must be specified, and this can vary from system to system.

Using the *env* Program

The magic string method is nonportable. If the `perl` command is moved to another location or the script is used on another machine, the script will not work.

A solution to this problem is to use the helper program env. This involves putting a new magic string at the top of the script:

```
#!/usr/bin/env perl
```

When the script is run, the env program starts up. Its job is to look at the rest of the command line and run the command specified. So in this case, the first `perl` in your path will be executed.

Advantages of the env approach include

- Simple
- Portable

The disadvantages are

- Won't work for setuid scripts
- Won't work if the perl command is not in your path

The Shell Script Method

The shell script method uses a shell script to start off Perl. You do this by putting the following lines at the beginning of your program:

```
#!/bin/sh
    eval 'exec perl -x -S $0 ${1+"$@"}'
        if 0;
#!/usr/local/bin/perl
```

This code takes a little explaining. The code is bilingual in that it is a perfectly valid shell script and perl program.

Start by looking at the thing as a shell script. The first line tells the system that this is a shell (/bin/sh) script:

```
#!/bin/sh
```

The next line tells the shell to execute the perl command with the -x and -S options. The $0 variable is the name of the program, and ${1+"$@"} is a magic string that passes the command-line arguments from the shell to the perl command. (See your shell documentation if you are really interested in the details.) The line looks like this:

```
    eval 'exec perl -x -S $0 ${1+"$@"}'
```

The exec command causes the shell to execute the specified command (perl) and never return. Because it never returns, the stuff that follows is never read by the shell.

Two options are passed to the perl program. The -S $0 tells perl to search for a script named $0 (the shell variable for the program name) along your path and to begin executing that script. The other option, -x, tells Perl that the perl program is embedded in another script (such as a shell script). The -x flag tells Perl to skip all the garbage at the beginning and look for a magic string to start the program. In this case the magic string is

```
#!/usr/local/bin/perl
```

Note that this line works even if perl is not installed in /usr/local/bin.

Running the Script Directly

Now take a look at what happens if you run the program using the command

```
$ perl script.pl
```

The first line is

```
#!/bin/sh
```

This line starts with a # so that Perl thinks it's a comment.

The next statement is

```
eval 'exec perl -x -S $0 ${1+"$@"}'
    if 0;
```

This is a valid Perl statement that tells Perl to execute a program, but only if the `if` condition is true. The `if` condition is 0, so it's never true. This is a long-winded way of doing a nop.

The following line also starts with a #, so it too is treated as a comment:

```
#!/usr/local/bin/perl
```

The result of all this magic is that if you run the script directly, all the shell stuff is inert and does not affect the program.

Microsoft Windows *.bat* File

To turn a script into a program under Microsoft Windows, use the PL2BAT command. For example:

```
C:\SCRIPTS> pl2bat script.pl
```

The result is a `script.bat` file containing your Perl program. PL2BAT adds a few commands to the beginning of your script that run Perl and tell it to use the body of the batch file as the Perl script.

Listing B.1 contains the result of running PL2BAT on a simple Perl program.

Listing B.1   *hello.bat*

```
@rem = '--*-Perl-*--
@echo off
if "%OS%" == "Windows_NT" goto WinNT
perl -x -S "%0" %1 %2 %3 %4 %5 %6 %7 %8 %9
goto endofperl
:WinNT
perl -x -S %0 %*
if NOT "%COMSPEC%" == "%SystemRoot%\system32\cmd.exe" goto endofperl
if %errorlevel% == 9009 echo You do not have Perl in your PATH.
if errorlevel 1 goto script_failed_so_exit_with_non_zero_val 2>nul
goto endofperl
```

```
@rem ';
#!perl
#line 15
use strict;
use warnings;
print "Hello world\n";

__END__
:endofperl
```

The first line of the program is a comment (rem in Microsoft Windows terms). The next line turns off echo.

Microsoft Windows NT and the other Microsoft operating systems have slightly different batch languages. For most operating systems, the system executes the command

```
perl -x -S "%0" %1 %2 %3 %4 %5 %6 %7 %8 %9
```

This command runs the perl program with the argument -x, which tells Perl to look through the file until it sees the line

```
#!perl
```

Next comes the -S switch, which tell Perl to search along the PATH variable for the script. This is followed by the name of the script ("%0") and up to nine additional arguments (%1 through %9).

This is followed by a goto that causes the Windows command process to skip to the end of the text:

```
goto endofperl
```

On Windows NT, the command executed is

```
perl -x -S %0 %*
```

The -x and -S flag are exactly the same as before. The other arguments pass in the name of the script (%0) and the arguments (%*).

This is followed by some error checking:

```
if NOT "%COMSPEC%" == "%SystemRoot%\system32\cmd.exe" goto endofperl
if %errorlevel% == 9009 echo You do not have Perl in your PATH.
if errorlevel 1 goto script_failed_so_exit_with_non_zero_val 2>nul
```

Next comes goto that gets you out of the program:

```
goto endofperl
```

Resources

Commands

- **pl2bat**—Turns Perl scripts into Microsoft .BAT files.
- **find2perl**—Outputs a script that contains a magic header that makes it possible to run as a standalone script or a Perl program.

Online Documentation

- **perldoc perlrun**—Describes the command-line switches to Perl including the -S and -x switches, which are useful in creating standalone scripts.
- **perl --help**—Gives a quick list of the runtime options for perl.

C

Beyond Perl

PERL IS AN EXCELLENT LANGUAGE FOR WRITING many applications. This appendix discusses some of the more useful ones that you can download from the net. These include programs to do web searching, code browsing, and E-Commerce.

Many helper programs also are available that can work with Perl to create a powerful programming environment. These include databases and text indexing tools.

This combination of Perl and helper programs can produce a system that makes it possible to write programs quickly, with flexibility, and yet create something that also is powerful and useful.

Databases

Perl comes with some database modules. These are limited and wimpy. If you're going to handle only a couple thousand records of limited size, they're okay, but what if you have to deal with millions of records and complex data?

You need a high-quality, fast database. The two major open source ones that are available are MySQL and PostgreSQL. Both are free.

Now, as to the question of which one is better: Because both provide the same basic set of features, it's more a matter of taste than technology. In general, most people make their choice based on two factors:

- They choose the database required for the other programs they install. In other words, if they install an E-Commerce application that was tested on MySQL, that's what they install.

- They install the program they know. (You always can write a program in a language you know much faster than in a language you don't, even if the new language is technically superior.)

You may notice that both these factors do not depend on the technical merits of the database itself. Sometimes the real world trumps technology.

MySQL is available from `http://www.mysql.com/`.

PostgreSQL can be obtained from `http://www.postgresql.org/`.

Tools for C/C++ Programmers

Perl is an ideal language for writing tools for handling large-scale C or C++ programs. It easily lets you analyze large amounts of text and create reports. This section presents two of the more popular tools that are useful for large programming projects. These are LXR, the Linux cross-referencer, and Bugzilla, a bug-tracking system.

Linux Cross-Reference (C Source Cross Reference)

The Linux cross-reference project is a web site that produces a cross-reference of the Linux kernel source. This tool lets you browse through the kernel source (see Figure C.1).

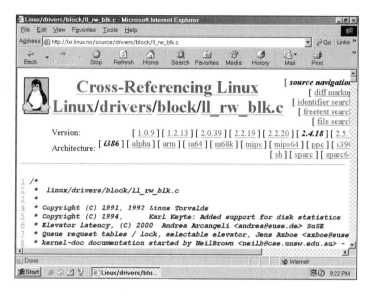

Figure C.1 Linux cross-reference.

Click on an identifier, and you'll be taken to a screen that shows you every place that identifier is defined or used (see Figure C.2).

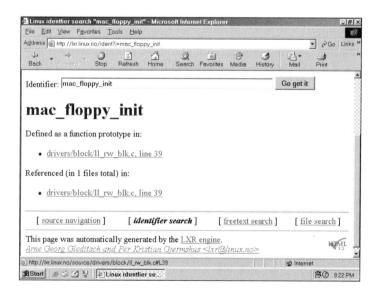

Figure C.2 Linux cross-reference indenture search results.

But the best thing about this is that the source to the utility is available. That means that you can download it and with a little tweaking make it work for any large source project you have.

Be warned, however. The tool is in love with the Linux source tree, and you'll learn a lot about configuration files, HTML, and regular expressions when you adapt it to your software project.

The system requires an external database (glimpse, or MySQL depending on version). It can be found at `http://lxr.linux.no/`.

Bug Tracking with Mozilla

The Mozilla project has a bug-tracking system called Bugzilla. This program consists of a bunch of Perl CGI scripts and tools that are used as a front end to a MySQL database. Because it is used by the Mozilla project, you know that it is able to robustly handle many errors. If your software project is growing beyond about 5 or 10 engineers, you need some sort of bug-tracking system.

This one not only has a track record, but also it's free from `http://www.mozilla.org/` (see Figure C.3).

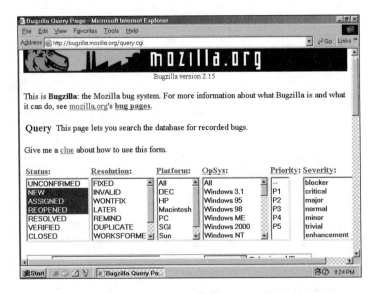

Figure C.3   Main Bugzilla screen.

Web Search Engine

A variety of programs are available that will index a web site and then allow users to search the site. MiniSearch is simple, easy to install, and works fairly well for small sites.

To use this program, all you need to do is install the scripts in your CGI directory. Next, run the script `searchindex` to generate an index of your site.

Next, check the configuration file (`searchdata/config`) and update it as needed. You can now access the admin page for this script through the URL `http://<your-server>/<cgi-install-dir>/searchindex`.

Where:

`<your-server>` is the name of your server.

`<cgi-install-dir>` is the name of the CGI directory in which you installed MiniSearch.

After you log in, you arrive at the administration screen shown in Figure C.4. This screen allows you to adjust the configuration parameters and to reindex the site.

The searches can be made using the URL `http//:<your-server>/<cgi-install-dir>/search`.

MiniSearch can be obtained from `http://www.dansteinman.com/minisearch/`.

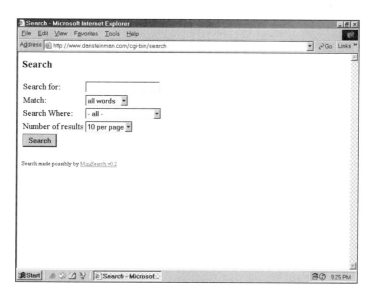

Figure C.4   MiniSearch screen.

Text Search GUI

A nice little search tool called Critter can be found at http://www.mainmatter.com/perltk/. It searches a series of files for a given string. Figure C.5 shows the GUI. Although a high-powered tool, Critter does provide you with a number of bells and whistles. Besides, you get the source, so if you want to add anything, you can.

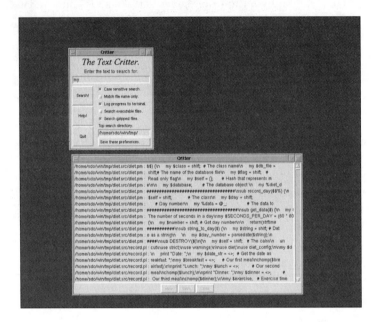

Figure C.5   Critter Search.

Although the basic functions of Critter Search work, I found many minor, annoying flaws in the program, such as the use of uninitialized variables and a directory selection system that could use some improvement. However, you've got the program, and a knowledge of Perl, so it's possible to come up with a solution.

Photo Album

If you have a digital camera, you may want to put your photos on the web. You can write the code to do this yourself, or you can use one of the many different photo album scripts out there.

One of the more complete ones is IDS (Image Display System) available from `http://ids.sourceforge.net/`. This script installs in your CGI directory and lets you and other users on your system generate your own photo albums. Figure C.6 shows one example.

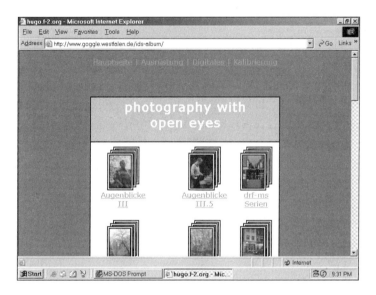

Figure C.6 Sample IDS album.

The program is complex to install, but it contains many features and gets the job done.

E-Commerce

A number of useful E-Commerce solutions are available. I've listed a few of the more interesting ones here. Note that my one foray into E-Commerce was a disaster (not one order), so I really don't know what makes up a good E-Commerce tool or web store.

Here are three that are widely available and provide most of the features you'd expect in a robust E-Commerce site:

- PerlShop `http://www.perlshop.org/`
- ClosedShop `http://closedshop.sourceforge.net/`
- Yams `http://yams.sourceforge.net/`

Resources

Programs

- `http://www.mysql.com/`—MySQL—General-purpose database.
- `http://www.postgresql.org/`—PostgreSQL—General-purpose database.
- `http://lxr.linux.no/`—Linux Cross Reference—Cross-reference utility for the Linux source that can be adapted to any large source project with a minimum of screaming.
- `http://www.mozilla.org/`—Bugzilla—The Mozilla bug-tracking system. (Also the home of the Mozilla web browser.)
- `http://www.dansteinman.com/minisearch/`—Minisearch—Web index and search engine.
- `http://www.mainmatter.com/perltk/`—Critter—File search tool with GUI.
- `http://ids.sourceforge.net/`—Image Display System—Photo Album.
- `http://www.perlshop.org/`—PerlShop—E-Commerce solution.
- `http://closedshop.sourceforge.net/`—ClosedShop—An open source E-Commerce solution.
- `http://yams.sourceforge.net/`—Yet Another Merchant System—E-Commerce system.

Index

Symbols

A

directories
build, 237
installation directory, 376
levels, 7
module directories, locating, 14
troubleshooting, 192
disk.pm module, 254–260
disks_cgi.pl, 281, 284–290
disks_config.pm, 260–261
disk_gui.pl, 269–278
distributable modules, Inline module, 245
dividing programs, 47–48
division (/), 39
do count function, 345
documentation, 180. *See also* **online documentation**
documenting
programs, POD, 171–172
Tk module widgets, 216
dollar signs ($), 54
double quotes (""), 156
dup.pl, 309–311
duplicate files, checking for, 307–311
dynamic web page graphs, 351–352

E

E-Commerce, 395
elements
deleting from hashes, 120
of regular expressions, 92–93, 99
elsif statements, 43
empty strings, 37
End blocks, packages, 143
English module, 68
env program, turning Perl scripts into commands, 384–385
eq (equality operators), 44
equality operators
== (Perl), 44
eq (C programming), 44
error messages, bit handling, C, 236–237
errors, 28
CGIs, 281–282
log files, viewing, 314–325
escape characters, POD, 174
escaped double quotes (\"), 80
events, Tk module, 222

exponentiation (**), 39
Exporter module, 184
Exporter package, 186
exporting methods, 153
EXPR, 6
expressions
/ +/, 65
/,/, 66
/,\s*/, 66
/\n/, 66
/\s*/, 66
/\s+/, 66
/\t/, 65
array expressions, 56
numeric constants, 41
quoting rules, 40
regular expressions. *See* regular expressions
split expressions, 65–66
external links, 327
checking, 328

F

features, write-to-pipe, 162
field points, sv any, 238
file handles
opening, sysopen function, 163
passing to subroutines, 167–168
references to, 168
file handling packages, 167
file test operators, 107
File::Find module, 327
files
.bat files, turning Perl scripts into commands, 386–387
binary files, reading, 164–167
checking for duplicates, 307–311
copying, 51
filling out for modules, 358–360
opening, 161
parsing, checking web sites, 326–327
reading, 49–50
writing, 51
Find buttons, 269–278
find command, 162
Find Next buttons, 269–278
find2perl, 388
finding
modules, UNIX/Linux, 6–7
number of rows in arrays, 126
fixing Makefiles, 94–95

T

HOW TO CONTACT US

VISIT OUR WEB SITE

WWW.NEWRIDERS.COM

On our web site, you'll find information about our other books, authors, tables of contents, and book errata. You will also find information about book registration and how to purchase our books, both domestically and internationally.

EMAIL US

Contact us at: **nrfeedback@newriders.com**

- If you have comments or questions about this book
- To report errors that you have found in this book
- If you have a book proposal to submit or are interested in writing for New Riders
- If you are an expert in a computer topic or technology and are interested in being a technical editor who reviews manuscripts for technical accuracy

Contact us at: **nreducation@newriders.com**

- If you are an instructor from an educational institution who wants to preview New Riders books for classroom use. Email should include your name, title, school, department, address, phone number, office days/hours, text in use, and enrollment, along with your request for desk/examination copies and/or additional information.

Contact us at: **nrmedia@newriders.com**

- If you are a member of the media who is interested in reviewing copies of New Riders books. Send your name, mailing address, and email address, along with the name of the publication or web site you work for.

BULK PURCHASES/CORPORATE SALES

The publisher offers discounts on this book when ordered in quantity for bulk purchases and special sales. For sales within the U.S., please contact: Corporate and Government Sales (800) 382-3419 or **corpsales@pearsontechgroup.com**. Outside of the U.S., please contact: International Sales (317) 581-3793 or **international@pearsontechgroup.com**.

WRITE TO US

New Riders Publishing
201 W. 103rd St.
Indianapolis, IN 46290-1097

CALL/FAX US

Toll-free (800) 571-5840
If outside U.S. (317) 581-3500
Ask for New Riders
FAX: (317) 581-4663

VOICES THAT MATTER

New Riders

Solutions from experts you know and trust.

www.informit.com

ERATING SYSTEMS

EB DEVELOPMENT

OGRAMMING

TWORKING

RTIFICATION

D MORE...

xpert Access.
ee Content.

New Riders has partnered with **InformIT.com** to bring technical information to your desktop. Drawing on New Riders authors and reviewers to provide additional information on topics you're interested in, **InformIT.com** has free, in-depth information you won't find anywhere else.

- **Master the skills you need, when you need them**

- **Call on resources from some of the best minds in the industry**

- **Get answers when you need them, using InformIT's comprehensive library or live experts online**

- **Go above and beyond what you find in New Riders books, extending your knowledge**

As an **InformIT** partner, **New Riders** has shared the wisdom and knowledge of our authors with you online. Visit **InformIT.com** to see what you're missing.

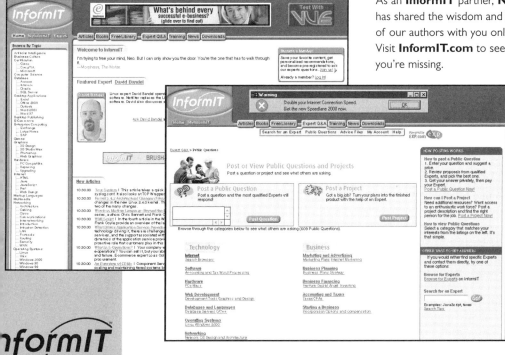

www.informit.com ■ **www.newriders.com**

VIEW CART

search ▷

▸ Registration already a member? Log in. ▸ Book Registration

Publishing
the Voices
that Matter

OUR AUTHORS

PRESS ROOM

| web development | design | photoshop | new media | 3-D | server technologie |

EDUCATORS

ABOUT US

CONTACT US

You already know that New Riders brings you the **Voices that Matter**.

But what does that mean? It means that New Riders brings you the

Voices that challenge your assumptions, take your talents to the next

level, or simply help you better understand the complex technical world

we're all navigating.

Visit **www.newriders.com** to find:

▸ **10% discount** and **free shipping** on all purchases

▸ Never before published chapters

▸ Sample chapters and excerpts

▸ Author bios and interviews

▸ Contests and enter-to-wins

▸ Up-to-date industry event information

▸ Book reviews

▸ Special offers from our friends and partners

▸ Info on how to join our User Group program

▸ Ways to have your Voice heard

New
Riders

WWW.NEWRIDERS.COM

RELATED NEW RIDERS TITLES

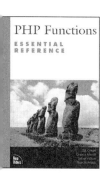

073570970X
US$49.99

PHP Functions Essential Reference

Torben Wilson,
Zak Greant,
Graeme Merrall, and
Brett Michlitsch

Co-authored by some of the leading developers in the PHP community, the *PHP Functions Essential Reference* is guaranteed to help you write effective code that makes full use of the rich variety of functions available in PHP 4.

0735710902
US$49.99

Python Web Programming

Steve Holden
with David Beazley

If you want to skip the introductory details and dive right into using Python within web-enabled applications, this is the perfect book for you! From page one, you'll begin learning how to harness the power of the Python libraries to build systems with less programming effort.

0735711143
US$44.99

Perl for the Web

Chris Radcliff

Build quick-loading high-performance next-generation websites with the help of this book, which provides all the tools and techniques you need to work in Perl on the web.

ISBN: 0735709211
US$49.99

MySQL

Paul DuBois

MySQL teaches you how to use the tools provided by the MySQL distribution, by covering installation, setup, daily use, security, optimization, maintenance, and trouble-shooting. It also discusses important third-party tools, such as the Perl DBI and Apache/PHP interfaces that provide access to MySQL.

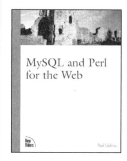

ISBN: 0735710546
US$44.99

MySQL and Perl for the Web

Paul Dubois

Paul DuBois does it again with *MySQL and Perl for the Web*. This time, he tells you how to bring your website to life by using the powerful combination of Perl and MySQL.

ISBN: 0735710015
US$49.99

Vi IMproved (VIM)

Steve Oualline

Real Linux users don't use GUI's. No matter how popular, slick, and sophisticated the interfaces become for Linux and UNIX, you'll always need to be able to navigate in a text editor. The vim editor contains many more feature than the old vi editor including help, multiple windows, syntax highlighting, programmer support, and HTML support. *Vi IMproved* is a concise reference for the vim editor.

Colophon

Pictured on the front cover of this book is the Pyramid of Mycerinus. It was built for Chephren's son, Mycerinus, and is the smallest of the three pyramids of Giza. Many consider this pyramid to be indicative of the start of the decline in the workmanship of Egyptian pyramid building. The pyramid stands 218 feet tall and has an incline of 51 degrees. One striking thing about this pyramid is the front façade which has an enormous hole above the passage. In 1215 the Turks decided to demolish the pyramids and, the Pyramid of Mycerinus being the smallest of the lot, they started with this one. After months of hard work they gave up.

This book was written and edited in Microsoft Word, and laid out in QuarkXPress. The font used for the body text are Bembo and MCPdigital. It was printed on 50# Husky Offset Smooth paper at VonHoffman in Owensville, MO. Prepress consisted of PostScript computer-to-plate technology (filmless process). The cover was printed at Moore Langen Printing in Terre Haute, Indiana, on 12 pt., coated on one side.